Planning for Conservation
An International Perspective

# Planning
# for
# Conservation

edited by

## ROGER KAIN

*The third volume of the trilogy*
*'Planning and the Environment in the Modern World'*

MANSELL, London 1981

ISBN 0 7201 0904 3

Mansell Publishing, a part of Bemrose UK Limited,
3 Bloomsbury Place, London WC1A 2QA

First published 1981

This book was commissioned, edited and designed by
Alexandrine Press, Oxford.

British Library Cataloguing in Publication Data

Planning and the environment in the modern world.
(Studies in history, planning and the environment).
    Vol. 3: Planning for conservation
    1. City planning – History
    2. Regional planning – History
    I. Title        II. Series 711'.09'034        HT166

ISBN 0–7201–0904–3

Text set in 11/12 pt Ehrhardt and printed in Great Britain by Henry Ling
Limited, Dorchester; bound by Mansell (Bookbinders) Ltd., Witham, Essex.

# Foreword

While today there is considerable questioning about the future directions of planning, there is a parallel and growing interest in the origins and history of the planning process and its effects on our environment. In this series, *Studies in History, Planning and the Environment,* we intend to provide in-depth studies of some of the many aspects of that history, to reflect the increasing international interest, and to stimulate ideas for areas of further research.

We shall focus on developments during the last one hundred to one hundred and fifty years and attempt to examine some of the questions relating to the forces which have shaped and guided our contemporary environment—urban, rural and metropolitan—and which demand answers not just for critical analysis in the advance of scholarship, but also for the insights they can provide for the future. Planning policy is constructed from knowledge of the *origins* of problems, as well as the *consequences* of decisions. Planning history therefore looks at processes over time; how and why our contemporary environment is shaped as it is. The broad outlines may be known; exercising an interpretative judgement on the details provides a fascinating field of study in which there are not a few surprises and many lessons for academics and practitioners alike.

In shedding light on the recent past we hope to understand the present; in fusing insights from different subject fields we hope to strengthen the synoptic traditions of both history and planning; in being avowedly inter-national we will reflect the different cultural attitudes to planning and the environment over time.

It is right that the first three volumes, which make up the trilogy *Planning and the Environment in the Modern World,* should derive from the papers presented at the first International Conference of the Planning History Group, held in London in September, 1977. Other conferences and meetings of the Group can be expected to provide material for the series, while indivi-dual initiatives will release the fruits of personal labour.

*Gordon E. Cherry*
*Anthony Sutcliffe*
July 1980

# Acknowledgments

Most of the studies in this volume were first presented at the First International Conference on the History of Urban and Regional Planning, which was organized by the Planning History Group at Bedford College, University of London 14–18th September, 1977. The Group wishes to extend its gratitude to the bodies whose generous grants allowed the conference to take place: the Anglo-German Foundation for the Study of Industrial Society, the British Academy, the Nuffield Foundation, and the Social Science Research Council.

I wish to extend my thanks to those contributors to the conference whose papers are in this volume for their careful re-editing of their work for publication, and to those who have written papers especially for this volume thanks are obviously due.

I am grateful, too, to the many friends and associates who have helped me in various ways: Rodney Fry and Andrew Teed of the Geography Department, University of Exeter, for the line drawings and photographs respectively, and Joan Fry, Nancy Scattergood and Margaret Shaw for typing much of the final text. To Gordon Cherry and Anthony Sutcliffe for all their helpful advice and encouragement as series editors, I am especially grateful.

Finally acknowledgment is made to the Institute of British Geographers for permission to reprint Francis Sandbach's paper first published in the Institute's *Transactions;* to the Board of Regents of the University of Wisconsin for permission to include some material from my own paper which was first published in *Urbanism Past and Present;* to the Secretary of the Eastbourne Borough Council, Mr J. Dartnell, for allowing John Sheail to consult documents in the Council's care, and to Dr Soni of the East Suffolk Record Office and to the staff of the Lincolnshire Record Office for their assistance to him in the preparation of his paper; to Aerofilms Ltd for permission to use the photograph shown in figure 9.1.

*Roger Kain*

# Contents

# Preface

Anthony Sutcliffe has explained the background to the publication of the trilogy *Planning and the Environment in the Modern World* in his Introduction to the first volume, *The Rise of Modern Urban Planning, 1800–1914.* Not all the papers in this, the third volume, originate from the First International Conference on the History of Urban and Regional Planning, held in London in 1977; some have been specially commissioned to deepen the historical dimension and to widen the international perspective, thus demonstrating the development of different aspects of conservation theory and practice both over time and in different geographical contexts.

In order to give structure and coherence to the volume, the papers are divided into three sections:
- (a)  the origins and development of conservation (papers 2 to 6)
- (b)  natural resource and landscape conservation (papers 7 to 10)
- (c)  building preservation and urban conservation (papers 11 to 14).

All five papers in the first section have as their primary focus an examination of contributions to the advance of theory in the early twentieth century. Alan Artibise and Gilbert Stelter discuss the work of the important, but short-lived Canadian Commission of Conservation and assess its influence on the wider fields of urban and regional planning. The three papers by Stefan Muthesius, Peter Breitling, and George and Christiane Collins are all concerned with the influence of developments in the German-speaking countries around the turn of the century. And, lastly, Teresa Zarebska shows how competition entries to find a plan to guide the restoration of the war-ravaged city of Kalisz contributed to the theory and practice of historic monument protection in Poland.

In the first paper of the second section, Andrew Gilg presents a wide-ranging analysis of the various arguments and motives marshalled by supporters of nature conservation over the past one hundred years. Both Francis Sandbach and John Sheail are concerned with developments in interwar England. Francis Sandbach examines the influence of amenity pressure groups and assesses the contribution of political and economic factors in the national parks debate, while John Sheail discusses the way in which some local authorities were obliged, during this period, to take on responsibilities previously borne by public-spirited individuals. Finally, J. B. Smallwood traces the history of river basin development in the United States from the 1900s to the setting up of the Tennessee Valley Authority in 1933.

The final section is concerned, for the most part, with explorations of current policies and practices of conservation. In a legal sense, the historic quarters of French cities, and Paris in particular, are well cared for. Certainly when compared with other West European capitals, the intrusion of the twentieth century's distinctive and often visually disruptive style of building is notably absent from the centre of Paris. Norma Evenson argues, in her paper, that the high degree of unity and harmony within Paris is the result of regulations governing building height, roof profiles and façade projections. The 1962 'Malraux Act' has been held up as one of the most influential pieces of European conservation legislation. My own paper looks at the way it has been implemented in Paris. In the less industrialized countries of Europe, historic monuments and settlements are threatened not so much by economic development as by tourism. The great wealth of Greek architectural heritage is justly famous and protective legislation is highly developed, but Alexander Papageorgiou-Venetas identifies some problems of finance and weaknesses in both the law and its administration. The final paper by Colin Morris raises the question 'Why conserve?'. He reviews some psychological literature on man's need for a time dimension in the visual environment, and presents an analysis of people's attitudes to buildings of different ages.

*Roger Kain*
October 1980

# The Contributors

ALAN F. J. ARTIBISE is Associate Professor in the Department of History at the University of Victoria, British Columbia. He has published studies in Canadian urban history and collaborated on a number of projects with Gilbert A. Stelter, notably a special issue of *Plan Canada* on resource towns and books on the Canadian city both in past and present planning contexts. He is editor of the *Urban History Review* and the series *History of Canadian Cities*.

PETER BREITLING is Dean of the Town Planning Institute at the Technical University of Graz. He is a planning historian and practising conservation planner, serving as rapporteur for Austria to the Council of Europe.

GEORGE R. and CHRISTIANE C. COLLINS are art historians largely concerned with the history of modern architecture and planning. They have collaborated frequently, for example in the translation of Camillo Sitte's *City Planning according to Artistic Principles* discussed in their contribution to this volume. Christiane Collins directs the Library of the Parsons School of Design in New York City and George Collins is Professor of Art History at Columbia University.

NORMA EVENSON is Professor of Architectural History at the University of California, Berkeley. She specializes in the history of modern architectural and urban design. Her major publications include books on Le Corbusier, the design of Chandigarh, Rio de Janerio and Brasilia, and urban renewal in Paris.

ANDREW GILG is a Lecturer in the Department of Geography at the University of Exeter, where he works in the field of environmental planning. He is the author of a book on rural planning and is editor of the *Countryside Planning Yearbook*.

ROGER KAIN is a Lecturer in the Department of Geography at the University of Exeter, and has published studies on the history of classical urban design in France.

COLIN MORRIS works in urban conservation on a freelance basis. His interest in the nature of people's attitudes to buildings and townscapes began at the University of Exeter, where he received his Ph.D. in 1978.

STEFAN MUTHESIUS is a Lecturer in the School of Fine Arts at the University of East Anglia. He was educated in Marburg, Munich and London and has published studies of nineteenth-century German architecture and town planning.

ALEXANDER PAPAGEORGIOU-VENETAS is a professional architect and planner and is at present Professor at the College of Europe. He was educated in Athens, Paris and West Berlin, holds a number of international consultancies, and his wide ranging publications include a seminal study of conservation entitled *Continuity* and *Change.*

FRANCIS SANDBACH is a Lecturer in Interdisciplinary Studies at the University of Kent, and author of a book on environmental problems and policy.

JOHN SHEAIL is a Principal Scientific Officer at the Institute of Terrestrial Ecology, Monks Wood Experimental Station, Huntingdon. He is the author of a book on the development of rural conservation in Britain and has also studied the impact of past land use and management on contemporary wildlife communities.

J. B. SMALLWOOD JR. is Associate Professor of History at North Texas State University. His main research interest is the development of the concept of river basin planning in the United States.

GILBERT A. STELTER is Professor of History at the University of Guelph. He has published studies in Canadian urban history, a number of them in collaboration with Alan Artibise.

TERESA ZAREBSKA is Head of the Architectural History Section of the Faculty of Architecture at Warsaw Technical University. She has worked on conservation plans for a number of towns; her principal publications are studies of renaissance town planning in Italy and Poland.

# 1

# Introduction: definitions, attitudes and debates

## ROGER KAIN

Conservation planning no longer counts only enlightened individuals or altruistic groups as it champions. Nor is it a concern solely of the often small, specialized government departments which nurtured it, but rather it is today a *sine qua non* of environmental management. After considering some matters of definition and attitude, this introductory paper briefly traces the history of the conservation movement from its origins in eighteenth-century romantic and historicist philosophies through the growth of legalized protection in the nineteenth century, to the present day when conservation is a truly popular movement. It ends by suggesting some answers to the question: why conserve?

CONSERVATION DEFINITIONS AND ATTITUDES

'Conservation' as a word is open to a number of interpretations and can describe a variety of philosophical stances in relation to the natural and built environments. Its ethic can be invoked from motives as hard-headed and materialistic as cost minimization by those concerned, for example, with energy conservation and the efficient use of scarce resources. Its umbrella is also wide enough to shelter those who subscribe to the tenet that the rich collage of time expressed in the fabric of historic cities on the one hand, and the rudeness of nature in the wilderness on the other, are essential to man's psychological well-being and can add to the quality of life. The amount of change that can be accepted also varies; the spectrum ranges from out-and-out preservation, associated particularly with those concerned with caring for

FIGURE 1.1. The 'Massacre of Medieval France' by the Second Empire, a satirical engraving by Gustave Doré for the title page of E. de Labédollière, *Nouvelle Paris,* 1860.

the more fragile niches of the natural environment, to an acceptance, particularly in the management of historic city centres, that policies of preservation and restoration must be accompanied by selective demolition to create open space and to allow the introduction of some new buildings and appropriate economic activities.

By attempting to regulate the rate and direction of environmental change, conservationists far from being 'conservative' should perhaps be regarded as 'radicals' [1]. Environmental change is the norm. Natural systems try to maximize entropy and move towards, but only rarely attain, states of equilibrium. The man-made environment is continually rebuilt to reflect changing motives, attitudes and tastes as societies evolve politically, economically and technically. Many of the beauties which we cherish so dearly today only exist because of the demolition of what once stood in their place. For example, much of the beauty of Paris stems from the continued existence of the streets, parks and monumental vistas created during the Second Empire. But nineteenth-century Gothic revivalists were adamantly

FIGURE 1.2. Place de l'Etoile, Paris. View of the Avenue Foch (on the left) leading to the Bois de Boulogne. On the right is the Avenue de la Grande Armée leading today to the tower blocks of the new office centre of La Defénse in the background.

opposed to the speed of change imposed by Napoleon III and Georges-Eugène Haussmann in Paris of the 1850s and 1860s. It was a partnership that was responsible in the view of Prosper Mérimée, first Inspector-General of Historic Monuments, for 'the massacre of medieval France'. Second Empire aesthetics of the straight line, symmetry and perspective were all that the new romantics and medievalists reviled.

Conservation is then radical; it is also recent. As David Eversley notes, 'the whole idea that remnants of the past are worth preserving is not an important strand in Western thinking' [2]. Concern for the past was not effectively institutionalized by law in European countries until the middle years of the nineteenth century, while it is only in very recent times that environmental matters have become of truly international concern [3]. In 1970 the ecological crisis was highlighted by European Conservation Year and in 1975 the problems of historic buildings by European Architectural Heritage Year [4]. But these focus points merely acted as a spur to conservation forces which had arisen far, far earlier. If there ever was a 'beginning', it lies with the new aesthetic constructs, attitudes to nature, and historicist philosophies which emerged in post-Renaissance Europe.

## The Romantic Revival and a Growing Appreciation of Nature

The changing sense of beauty in eighteenth-century Europe was of fundamental importance in fertilizing the seed-bed of the nascent conservation movement [5]. The recognition that nature's own forms were beautiful and the growing appreciation of nature which this engendered were to produce in the nineteenth century a complete *volte face* in man's attitude to the remaining areas of truly natural landscape in the world. There is probably no better example of this developing appreciation of scenery than that which occurred during the colonization of the American West [6].

Today in North America, 'wilderness' enjoys widespread popularity; indeed the success of wilderness preservation is now threatened as much from a plethora of visitors as from economic development. Yet for most of their history, Americans regarded the wilderness as a wasteland fit only for conquest in the name of progress, civilization and Christianity. The European pioneers' attitudes are clearly reflected in their use of military metaphors to discuss the coming of civilization. Wilderness was an enemy to be conquered, subdued and vanquished by a pioneer army.

The pioneer associated wilderness with hardship and danger; the rural, controlled state of nature was the object of his affection and the goal of his labour. 'The pastoral condition seemed closest to paradise and the life of ease and contentment. Americans hardly needed reminding that Eden had been a garden. The rural was also the fruitful and as such satisfied the frontiersman's utilitarian instincts. On both the idyllic and practical counts wilderness landscape was anathema' [7].

Appreciation of the wilderness occurred first among literary élites in the eastern seaboard cities who were coming under the spell of the romantic movement in Europe. The aesthetic category of the 'sublime' dispelled the notion that beauty was to be found only in fruitful, well-ordered 'nature'. It admitted that vast, chaotic scenery could also please. Uvedale Price's and William Gilpin's evangelizing on behalf of the 'picturesque' also bore fruit in the New World and greatly broadened the classical concept of ordered, proportioned beauty. The picturesque admitted the pleasing quality of nature's roughness, irregularity and intricacy as it was expressed in landscape and scenery. Furthermore, deist religious thinking identified wild places as those where spiritual truths emerged most forcibly.

By about 1840, the romantic mood was quite widespread in North America. 'It was commonplace for the literati of the major eastern cities to make periodic excursions into the wilds, collect "impressions" and return to their desks to write descriptive essays which dripped love of scenery and solitude in the grand Romantic manner' [8]. Add to this the transcendentalism invoked by Thoreau, a growing awareness of the link between American national identity and the pioneer past, and there are the seeds of an appreciation of the wilderness and of sadness at its disappearance.

The principle of the preservation of natural, wilderness landscape was put to the test, around the turn of the century, over what has since become known as the Hetch Hetchy valley controversy [9]. A proposal was made to build a reservoir in this valley in Yosemite National Park to supply San Francisco with water. Preservationists lost the fight but as Roderick Nash stresses, the most significant thing about the controversy was that it occurred at all [10]. Only fifty or so years earlier, a proposal to build a dam across a river in the American West would have occasioned hardly a ripple of protest. J. B. Smallwood's paper examines the concept of Federal River Basin Planning which developed from conflicts such as this.

## Historicism and the Path to the 'Institutionalization' of the Past

Besides nurturing the romantic revival which was to so influence man's appreciation of nature, eighteenth-century European society was imbued with a strong sense of historical change. In the field of architecture, for example, this encouraged scholars to study, measure and even replicate the relics of past periods. Relics were touchstones to the past and they were cherished; if there were none to hand, sham ruins were erected, country houses castellated and follies and grottos contrived. The catalytic influence of nineteenth-century men like Augustus Pugin and John Ruskin turned England's back on classicism and replaced it with 'true English architecture'. The richness and splendour of England's Gothic past were recalled; it was an historicist appeal to sentiment and national pride and it was an appeal which largely succeeded.

In 1877, William Morris founded the Society for the Protection of Ancient Buildings (SPAB) in realization of the fact that if each generation continued to 'restore' old buildings to conform to their own ideas of the beauty or 'piety' of antiquity, there would eventually be nothing left. His manifesto may be said to mark the beginning of the movement towards the legalized protection of historic buildings in England. He wrote,

> It is for all buildings, therefore, of all times and styles, that we plead, and call upon those who have to do with them to put Protection in the place of Restoration . . . to resist all tampering with either the fabric or the ornament of the building as it stands . . . in fine to treat our ancient buildings as monuments of a bygone age, created by bygone manners, that modern art cannot meddle with without destroying. . . . Thus, and thus only can we protect our ancient buildings and hand them down instructive, and venerable to those that come after us. [11]

In academic debate scrape and anti-scrape were pushed back and forth, but in 1882 Parliament passed the Historic Monuments Protection Act and the English past was at last institutionalized [12].

In some other European countries, like France for example, all this occurred much earlier. The systematic protection of individual buildings in French towns dates from 1830 when government instituted a Department of Historic Monuments. In 1837 this body set out to draw up a massive inventory of buildings which its first Inspector-General estimated would require some 900 volumes and 200 years to complete! Mérimée quickly reduced the scope of this rather romantic ideal and in 1840 published one of the first 'lists' of buildings in Europe. In keeping with mid-nineteenth-century attitudes to the past all fifty-nine monuments on the list dated from the Middle Ages or earlier. Restoration of great medieval monuments like the cathedral of Notre Dame and the *cité* of Carcassonne was a characteristic nineteenth-century occupation. The protection of classical Renaissance buildings came much later. The *place royale* at Nancy was not listed until 1889 and the Arc de Triomphe de l'Etoile in Paris was one of the few nineteenth-century monuments to be classified before 1900 [13].

## THE TWENTIETH CENTURY: CONSERVATION BECOMES A POPULAR MOVEMENT

Technical, social and economic changes in the present century have had important repercussions for the development of the conservation movement. First, technical innovations have resulted from architectural experimentation; secondly, increasing public awareness of the fragility of natural and historic environments has produced a proliferation of pressure groups with burgeoning membership; while thirdly, increasing land and restoration costs have highlighted the frequent association of 'social injustice' with conservation, especially in city contexts.

### INNOVATION AND TECHNICAL EXPERIMENTATION BEFORE WORLD WAR II

Around the turn of the present century, new philosophies of space under discussion in the German-speaking countries provided some much needed theoretical underpinnings for the growing urban conservation movement and are discussed in papers by Peter Breitling and Stefan Muthesius.

Camillo Sitte in his *City Planning According to Artistic Principles* upheld the idea of vernacular architecture and small-scale spaces not from motives of overt, romantic historicism but as a reaction to large-scale, geometric planning à la Haussmann or Cerda. George and Christianne Collins in their paper view Sitte as an important influence on the 'birth' of modern city planning; his book certainly flourished in German, English and French editions during the years 1889–1921 'which were precisely the decades of the formation of the international profession of city planning' [14]. In the New World, the influential if short-lived Canadian Commission of Conservation (1909–21) signalled a new beginning by integrating both resource conservation and urban planning. Alan Artibise and Gilbert Stelter examine how it accommodated 'increasing concern in the country about the wasteful and destructive use of resources and the growing "evils" of urbanization' [15].

If the turn of the twentieth century was a critical period in the development of conservation philosophy, then the interwar years saw much experimentation and innovation within a movement which had yet to win widespread popular appeal [16]. In her contribution to this volume, Teresa Zarebska identifies some of the lessons learnt by restoration architects during repair of war-devastated cities in Poland. John Sheail examines the way in which in England much responsibility for environmental matters moved from the hands of private land owners to the public arena as local authority powers were elaborated.

ENVIRONMENTAL PRESSURE GROUPS

The last fifty years have seen the proliferation of pressure groups taking on specific concerns or particular areas. Francis Sandbach examines the contribution of the campaigns of local groups to persuade government to designate a national park in the English Lake District. Morris' SPAB was probably the first national group to advocate the care of old buildings; in 1937 its work was augmented by its own daughter Georgian Group, a response to the fact that up to then 'Georgian' buildings had not been considered worth safeguarding. Now there are the Victorian Society (founded 1958), academic bodies like the Council for British Archaeology and more than a thousand local amenity societies affiliated to the Civic Trust and its four Associate Trusts. All these have as one of their aims the alerting of public opinion to the dangers threatening Britain's irreplaceable ancient buildings.

Part of the reason for the growing number of environmental groups lies in the increasing pressures which the twentieth century has brought on all fragile environments. The historic cores of cities in industrialized European countries are paying now for the neglect of the physical fabric of buildings in the nineteenth century and the twin assaults of the motor car and the property speculator. Parisian responses to these sorts of problems are discussed in my own study of the Marais, the showpiece of French conservation and by Norma Evenson in her paper on building controls in modern Paris.

In the less industrialized countries of Europe, pressures on the past are of a different character. As Alexander Papageorgiou-Venetas points out in his paper, the danger to the survival of the traditional architectural and social structure of historic urban centres in Greece comes not from congestion and the proliferation of tertiary functions in what were old residential districts but rather from depopulation and deformation by the tourist trade.

The last twenty years or so have certainly seen a rapid growth in tourism throughout the world and it has become a major element in man's demand upon the land.

FIGURE 1.3. Petrified Forest National Park, Arizona is one of the most fragile of ecosystems. In the last century prospectors blasted the fossilized trees with dynamite to win valuable amethysts. Today the 'logs' are protected but the plethora of visitors makes it necessary to prohibit the collection of even the tiniest souvenir. Rangers are given powers of search to ensure the future of the park.

Wilderness values, for example, are so fragile that when subjected to heavy recreational pressure they disappear. Earlier this century U.S. preservation societies reckoned that to preserve wilderness areas depended 'on getting Americans into them without saws and bulldozers' [17]. In their success they may find their greatest challenge.

If ill-planned or unplanned, recreation use can cause severe damage to our environmental heritage but if well-managed, it can support and encourage the efforts of conservation. Such was in fact the theme of a conference organized by the European Travel Commission in collaboration with Europa Nostra in Copenhagen in November 1973. It was convened in support of the campaign for European Architectural Heritage Year and emphasized the common interest which exists between tourist boards and the tourist industry on the one hand, and organizations concerned with conservation on the other [18]. The interests of tourism demand the protection of the scenic and historic heritage; the offer in the travel brochure must be genuine. The other side of the coin is that entry fees can be used to maintain historic structures and scenic areas. Despite these positive links, many conservationists feel that tourism does present a major threat to the environment. The key is to find a way of working together.

In the U.S. national parks, tourists and nature do coexist fairly happily. In each park a strategy is carefully worked out to provide discrete accommodation and parking, plentiful information, views of the scenic splendours, and glimpses of the wildlife without overtly threatening delicate ecological balances. Of course parks in the New World have the advantage of vast size compared with European parks [19]. They are also part of the public domain but provide, nevertheless, some useful lessons for planners dealing with the larger European recreation areas in say southern Spain or Aquitaine.

THE COST OF CONSERVATION: SOCIAL JUSTICE IMPLICATIONS

To say that the cost of cherishing monuments and natural and historic areas is escalating rapidly sounds just a little trite today; most sectors have experienced run-away cost inflation in recent years. In the last analysis, however, the success or failure of any conservation scheme will depend on the availability of finance to carry it through.

The owners of historic buildings, gardens and parks are trying ever more novel ways of raising money to cover the spiralling costs of maintenance. Marketing the past has become an industry in its own right, again nowhere more so than in the United States, although the 'theme park' is now becoming more familiar in Europe [20]. In England, great houses in the first rank like Blenheim in Oxfordshire or Castle Howard in Yorkshire, receive substantial support from the State while the small listed town house or country cottage is a readily marketable commodity on which the cost of restoration can be recouped in the sale price. It is the 'manor house', the medium-sized country house in its own grounds, now often too large for easy occupation and not grand enough to attract adequate State support, which is at greatest risk [21].

In a city context, one problem is that wherever free market forces prevail, then social change in historic areas is almost inevitable as prestige and prices rise with conservation. In the words of one inhabitant of a flat in Charonne, an 'historic' village swallowed up in the tide of the suburban expansion of eastern Paris, 'whether they come in the name of renewal or restoration, the effect is the same. We are shown the door'.

THE LEGISLATIVE RESPONSE

As a response to the changing theoretical, technical and economic bases of conservation and the galvanizing of public opinion, more and more sophisticated systems of legislation have been enacted. Each State's suite of measures is unique in form and content and has its own particular chronology reflecting individual political systems. There are now a number of easily available comparative studies of legislation to which reference may be made [22]. There are also a number of excellent bibliographies of conservation literature on a world basis. The most recent and comprehensive is by J. F. Smith (1978) *A Critical Bibliography of Building Conservation,* London: Mansell [23].

FIGURE 1.4. In Paris protection by listing has been extended to street furniture like Hector Guimard's Art Nouveau *Métro* station signs.

At the risk of oversimplifying, it is possible to identify a number of general trends. First, there has been an extension of preservation legislation from individual buildings to whole areas in cities and from buildings to the lesser elements of the environment like street furniture. This is a response to the realization that no matter how beautiful an individual structure is, it loses much of its 'meaning' if isolated from its organic environment. Secondly, emphasis has shifted from negative preservation to positive conservation as theoretical and technical advances have been made. However, what conservationists have singularly failed to do explicitly is to address themselves squarely to the fundamental question of precisely what it is that the heritage of the past, the countryside, and natural scenery contribute to the spiritual and physical well-being of man. The final section of this introduction reviews some partial answers to this question which is explored, later in this volume, in greater analytical depth by Colin Morris and greater comparative breadth by Andrew Gilg.

## WHY CONSERVE?

Probably only another committed conservationist would sympathize completely with Wayland Young's rather 'smug' justification of why we seek to preserve an historic building:

> An ancient building is evidence of the way our ancestors lived ... an example of a class of beautiful things ... an emblem of our attachment to values more pleasant or joyful than money ... it is the gentler side of us bodied forth in old stone or brick. We smile at each other when we see it, thinking how much nicer it is than what would have replaced it, and how much nicer we are than the people who wanted to knock it down. [24]

He wrote these words in 1972 and it is perhaps a little unfair to quote them out of context of the full argument of his excellent history of the preservation movement. It is nevertheless an example of the genre, and at a recent conference which addressed itself to the theme, 'Our past before us: why do we save it?', some similar sentiments were echoed [25].

Conservationists concerned with the countryside also tend to call up over-coloured images. Though it is again perhaps a little invidious to single out just one magazine for mention, one might cite the nostalgic, sentimental view of the British countryside put out between the green covers of *The Countryman*. One wonders to what extent a working countryman would sympathize with its urban emigré's image of bucolic nature and a pastoral countryside peopled with rustics exchanging 'tail corn' in unintelligible dialects!

The membership of conservation groups has been condemned as an élite which is losing the right to be heard because of an unrealistic credo that change is of necessity harmful. On the other hand it can also and has been defended as a minority whose divinely appointed duty it is to act for the benefit of an apathetic majority [26]. Instead of exhorting the public to agree that old buildings are to be preferred to new and that nature is somehow invigorating to the spirit, there should be more attempt to explain to the general public why this might be so [27]. A number of architects and planners have, however, recently addressed themselves to these more fundamental philosophical points [28].

Some ten years ago, Roy Worskett, doyen among practising conservation planners wrote that, 'Society needs both cultural and physical roots and a town's visual and historic qualities can satisfy at least part of this need. ... There is plenty of room for research here; we know very little about our conscious or subconscious reactions to the quality of our visual surroundings' [29]. Kevin Lynch, seeking to conceptualize just this problem posed a question in the title of a recent book: *What Time is This Place?* [30]. It deserves to be more widely read than it probably is by those concerned with planning and managing the environment. He argues that man's effective action and inner well-being depend on his possession of a strong image of time in which a vivid sense of the present is connected to both future and past. It follows that the 'best' environment for human development is one which represents 'a collage of time'. Both massive change and rigid, inflexible preservation tend to result in 'one-dimensional areas' which are lacking in depth and continuity. Thus the city, for example, should be so managed that it is layered in 'time-deep areas' of varying intensity which contain both new stimuli and familiar reassurances. 'It is clear that space and time are the great framework within which we order our experience. We live in time-places' [31].

More recent research and theorizing in environmental psychology is showing that man prefers complex visual environments to simple ones [32]. A. Rapoport and R. Kantor describe man's need for complexity in terms of a 'concept of ambiguity'. They argue that contemporary urban design has been 'simplified and cleaned up to such an extent that all it has to say is revealed at a glance. A range of meanings and possibilities has been eliminated. This loss leads to a loss of interest—there is nothing to divert or to hold one as a result of lowered rates of perceptual inputs' [33].

From a different standpoint, Eduardo Lozano argues a case for combining a variety of inputs at the lower hierarchies of a town such as the details of individual house fronts and the maze of secondary streets and alleys, with what he calls orientation inputs at higher levels—prominent buildings, city walls, and the street plan itself. 'Most contemporary urban designs, he says, 'are not based on a combination of visual inputs at different complexity levels, but tend to be influenced by a kind of pendulum law, stressing either an exclusive low-order organization (modern movement purism) or a pseudo-complex organization (superimposed picturesquism)' [34].

Peter Smith in his book, *The Syntax of Cities* focuses not only on the bricks and mortar of urban fabric but also approaches the problem by analysing man's value system in terms of the structure of the mind [35]. His thesis is that aesthetic awareness depends on interaction between the different parts of the brain and that ultimate beauty occurs only when intellect and emotion come together in the harmony of opposites. Modern architecture fails to satisfy because it appeals only to the intellect and denies stimulation once richly provided by towns and cities and found today only in traditional urban ensembles. 'With more and more of our towns becoming transposed into this "higher key", people are being starved of a gut reaction to the built ensemble' [36].

In conclusion, and in Kevin Lynch's terminology, a satisfying environment should represent a collage of time. Without a dialectic rhythm between the intellect and the emotions, 'environment drops psychologically stone dead' [37]. The following papers illustrate the way that concern for maintaining the richness of the collage has grown vigorously from seeds sown in the eighteenth century [38].

NOTES

1. See also the argument developed by Stewart, J. (1974) Conservation a plea for a radical approach. *Planning Outlook,* 15, pp. 35–48.
2. Eversley, D. (1974) Conservation for the minority. *Built Environment,* 3, p. 14.
3. Fawcett, Jane (ed.) (1976) *The Future of the Past, Attitudes to Conservation 1174–1974.* London: Thames and Hudson.
4. Dobby, A. (1978) *Conservation and Planning.* London: Hutchinson; Reynolds, Josephine (ed.) (1976) *Conservation Planning in Town and Country.* Liverpool: Liverpool University Press, being papers first published in *Town Planning Review,* 46 (4), 1975. See also the reviews by Hobhouse, Hermione (1975) European Architectural Heritage Year. *Architectural Design,* 45, pp. 593–97; Albert, S. A. R. le Prince *et al.* (1975) L'année européene du patrimoine architectural. *Habiter,* 64–5, pp. 1–42; Civic Trust/U.K. Secretariat (1976) Report on Heritage Year. *Architects' Journal,* 163 (8), pp. 353–91.
5. Prince, H. C. (1967) *Parks in England.* Shalfleet Manor, Isle of Wight: Pinhorn; Rees, R. (1975) The scenery cult, changing landscape tastes over three centuries. *Landscape,* 19 (3), pp. 39–46; Hunt, J. D. and Willis, P. (eds.) (1975) *The Genius of the Place. The English Landscape Garden, 1620–1820.* London: Paul Elek.
6. Nash, R. (1963) The American wilderness in historical perspective. *Forest History,* 6, pp. 1–13; Nash, R. (1966) The American cult of the primitive. *American Quarterly,* 18, pp. 517–37; Nash, R. (1967) *Wilderness and the American Mind.* New Haven: Yale University Press; Nicolson, Marjorie H. (1959) *Mountain Gloom and Mountain Glory: the Development of the Aesthetics of the Infinite.* New York: Norton (1963 edition); Lewis, G. M. (1965) Three centuries of desert concepts in the Cis-Rocky Mountain West. *Journal of the West,* 4 (3), pp. 457–68; Lewis, G. M. (1966) Regional ideas and reality in the Cis-Rocky Mountain West. *Transactions of the Institute of British Geographers,* 38, pp. 135–50; Watson, J. W. (1967) *Mental Images and Geographical Reality in the Settlement of North America.* Nottingham: University of Nottingham.
7. Nash, R. (1967) *Wilderness and the American Mind.* New Haven: Yale University Press, pp. 30–1.
8. *Ibid.,* p. 60.
9. Richardson, E. R. (1959) The struggle for the valley: California's Hetch Hetchy controversy, 1905–1913. *California Historical Society Quarterly,* 38, pp. 249–58; Ise, J. (1961) *Our National Park Policy,* Baltimore: Johns Hopkins.
10. Nash, R. (1967) *Wilderness and the American Mind.* New Haven: Yale University Press, p. 181.
11. Morris, W. (1877) *Manifesto for the Society for the Protection of Ancient Buildings.* Reprinted in the current pamphlet, *The Activities and Services of the Society.* London: Society for the Protection of Ancient Buildings.
12. The history of nineteenth-century legislation and the institutionalization of conservation are to be found in: Harvey, J. (1972) *Conservation of Buildings.* London: John Baker; Young, W. (Lord Kennett) (1972) *Preservation.* London: Temple Smith; Cherry, G. E. (1974) *The Evolution of British Town Planning.* Leighton Buzzard: Leonard Hill; Grodecki, L. (1974) La protection et l'étude des monuments d'architecture du XIXᵉ siècle. *Les Monuments Historiques de la France,* 20 (1), pp. 2–9; Smith, D. L. (1974) *Amenity and Urban Planning.*

London: Crosby Lockwood Staples; Cherry, G. E. (1975) The conservation movement. *The Planner,* **61** (1), pp. 3–5; Bailly, G. H. (1975) *The Architectural Heritage.* Cheltenham: Stanley Thornes (for Editions Delta, Vevey).

13. Grodecki, L. (1974) La protection et l'étude des monuments d'architecture du XIXᵉ siècle. *Les Monuments Historique de la France,* **20** (1), pp. 2–9.

14. Collins, G. R. and Collins, Christiane, *infra.*

15. Artibise, A. F. J. and Stelter, G. F., *infra.*

16. Papageorgiou, A. (1971) *Continuity and Change.* London: Pall Mall Press; Fitch, J. M. (1973) Environmental aspects of the preservation of historic areas. *Monumentum,* **9,** pp. 39–59; Breitling, P. (1975) *Technical and Practical Means for Conservation and Restoration Operations.* Amsterdam: Council of Europe; *Building Trades Journal and Consulting Engineer* (1978) *Building Conservation,* **176** (5257), a special supplement to the journal.

17. Nash, R. (1967) *Wilderness and the American Mind.* New Haven: Yale University Press, p. 236.

18. Dower, M. (1974) Tourism and conservation working together. *Architects' Journal,* **159** (18), pp. 939–64.

19. Gilg, A. W. (1978) *Countryside Planning.* Newton Abbot: David and Charles.

20. Newcomb, R. M. (1979) *Planning the Past: Historical Landscape Resources and Recreation.* Folkestone: Dawson, and Hamden, Connecticut: Archon Books.

21. Teggin, H. *et al.* (1979) Domus Britannicus—what future for the country house? *Architects' Journal,* **169** (4), pp. 165–200; Cantacuzino, S. (1975) *New Uses for Old Buildings.* London: Architectural Press. For a discussion of the cost problem in an American city, Chicago, see Costonis, J. J. (1974) The costs of preservation: The Chicago Plan and the economics of keeping landmarks in the marketplace. *Architectural Forum,* **140** (1), pp. 61–7.

22. See for example, Haines, G. H. (1974) Conservation in Europe. *Housing and Planning Review,* **30** (1), pp. 2–5; Rodwell, D. (1975) Conservation legislation: a European survey. *European Heritage,* **5,** pp. 32–7; Rodwell, D. (1975) Conservation legislation, in Cantacuzino, S. (ed.) *Architectural Conservation in Europe.* London: Architectural Press, pp. 131–8. There are comparative studies in Ward, Pamela (ed.) (1968) *Conservation and Development in Historic Towns and Cities.* Newcastle upon Tyne: Oriel Press; Matthew, Sir Robert *et al.* (eds.) (1972) *The Conservation of Georgian Edinburgh.* Edinburgh: Edinburgh University Press; and UNESCO (1975) *The Conservation of Cities.* Paris: UNESCO, and London: Croom Helm. The following two general surveys are also very useful: Whittick, A. (ed.) (1974) *Encyclopaedia of Urban Planning.* New York: McGraw-Hill, and Garner, J. F. (ed.) (1975) *Planning Law in Western Europe.* Amsterdam: North-Holland.

23. See also, Jakle, J. A. (1974) *Past Landscapes: A Bibliography for Historic Preservationists Selected from the Literature of Historical Geography.* Council of Planning Librarians Exchange Bibliography No. 651; and Walsh, Joan V. (1975) *Historic Buildings: Preservation Policy,* DoE Bibliography No. 189. London: Department of the Environment.

24. Young, W. (Lord Kennett) (1972) *Preservation.* London: Temple Smith, pp. 13–15.

25. The conference was convened by I.C.O.MO.S. in April 1979. Pending publication of the papers there is a short report by Lowenthal, D. (1979) Reasons for saving

the past. *Geographical Magazine,* 51 (9), pp. 650–2.

26. Eversley, D. (1974) Conservation for the minority. *Built Environment,* 3, pp. 14–15; Cherry, G. E. (1974) *The Evolution of British Town Planning.* Leighton Buzzard: Leonard Hill, pp. 3–5.

27. Morris, C. J. (1978) Townscape Images: A Study in Meaning and Classification. Unpublished Ph.D. thesis, University of Exeter, pp. 38–45.

28. Anstis, D. (1969) Building conservation: the need for a philosphy. *Architectural Association Quarterly,* 1 (4), pp. 14–21; Rock, D. (1974) Conservation a confusion of ideas. *Built Environment,* 3, pp. 363–5; Cantell, T. (1975) Why conserve? *The Planner,* 61 (1), pp. 6–10; Owen, S. (1976) Change and conservation in settlements. *Planning Outlook,* 18, pp. 35–41. See also the printed lecture by Briggs, A. (1975) The philosophy of conservation. *Royal Society of Arts Journal,* 123, pp. 685–95.

29. Worskett, R. (1969) *The Character of Towns. An Approach to Conservation.* London: Architectural Press, p. 12.

30. Lynch, K. (1972) *What Time is This Place?* Cambridge, Mass.: MIT Press.

31. *Ibid.,* p. 241.

32. Morris, C. J. (1978) Townscape Images: A Study in Meaning and Classification. Unpublished Ph.D. thesis, University of Exeter, pp. 48–52.

33. Rapoport, A. and Kantor, R. E. (1967) Complexity and ambiguity in environmental design. *Journal of the American Institute of Planners,* 33 (4), pp. 210–21. See also Tuan, Yi-Fu (1974) *Topophilia. A Study of Environmental Perception, Attitudes, and Values.* Englewood Cliffs: Prentice-Hall.

34. Lozano, E. E. (1974) Visual needs in the urban environment. *Town Planning Review,* 45 (4), p. 354.

35. Smith, P. F. (1977) *The Syntax of Cities.* London: Hutchinson.

36. *Ibid.,* p. 54.

37. Lynch, K. (1972) *What Time is This Place?* Cambridge, Mass.: MIT Press, p. 96.

38. Readers who attended the International Conference in London will note the omission of the paper given by Christopher Tunnard, a doyen of conservation planning. Professor Tunnard fell ill soon after the conference and was not able to prepare his contribution for publication. It was with great sadness that I heard of his death in February 1979. He published a brief account of his work in the Kathmandu Valley of Nepal, the subject of his talk at Bedford College, in his wide-ranging last book, *A World with a View, an Inquiry into the Nature of Scenic Values.* New Haven: Yale University Press, 1978.

# 2

# Conservation planning and urban planning: the Canadian Commission of Conservation in historical perspective

ALAN F. J. ARTIBISE and GILBERT A. STELTER

Conservation planning in Canada began on an organized basis shortly before World War I when a Commission of Conservation was established. Prior to this time, the predominant attitude in Canada in regard to resources was 'the doctrine of usefulness'; an attitude that had at its centre the rapid exploitation of the country's resources in the interests of creating a national economy in the recently confederated nation [1]. The establishment of the Commission of Conservation signalled the beginning of the end of unchecked and unplanned development. Between its establishment in 1909 and its dissolution in 1921, the Commission of Conservation was the main focus of Canadian planning activity. The termination of the Commission marked the onset of a long period of inactivity in both the conservation and urban planning fields; with only a few exceptions, major new initiatives were not taken in either area until near the end of World War II.

Significantly, during its existence, the Commission of Conservation took as its mandate the widest possible view of planning. Rather than limiting its purview to natural resources, the Commission broadened it in such a way that its work entered all areas of the human environment, including, most notably, the urban environment. The reason for this close interrelationship between urban and conservation planning was the particular pattern of

17

Canadian development. The closing years of the nineteenth century had witnessed the rapid physical expansion of the country and the massive exploitation of natural resources. This expansion was aided by and reflected in the growth of Canadian urban centres. By the early 1900s, there was increasing concern in the country about the wasteful and destructive use of resources and the growing 'evils' of urbanization. Both required attention and both received it from the Commission of Conservation, which combined conservation and urban planning in a way never again duplicated by any government or private agency.

## PLANNING IN CANADA TO CIRCA 1900

Conservation planning and urban planning both passed through distinct phases prior to the establishment of the Conservation Commission in 1909. In terms of conservation planning, the period leading up to the early 1900s was characterized by development and exploitation based upon the concept of a relatively inexhaustible supply of resources. Whether the resource was fur, fish, timber, or land, the object of both government and private enterprise was unchecked use. There was, in short, no policy of conservation planning. Resources were to be utilized to promote rapid and sustained growth and to bolster the development of the country. That such growth and development would be prodigal and even wasteful of resources, if perceived at all, was to be regretted as an unfortunate byproduct of an essentially desirable process [2]. In contrast, urban planning passed through two phases prior to 1900. In an initial phase, imperial officials determined the form of colonial towns. Central direction was evident in the planning of early Louisbourg, Halifax, and Toronto. Even some commercial enterprises were planned communities, as in the case of the Canada Company towns of Guelph and Goderich [3]. A second phase was represented by the Victorian era, when *laissez-faire* thinking dominated the question of who should make the decisions which would shape urban communities. It would be a mistake, however, to assume that planning did not take place during this period. Rather, planning was carried out at a private level without regulation by municipal or provincial government. Many new towns founded by corporations in the late nineteenth century were built on the basis of plans drawn up by company officials, including Sudbury, Ontario, by the Canadian Pacific Railway Company, and Nanaimo, British Columbia, by coal barons in London [4]. In the larger cities, however, the results of the private decisions of thousands of individuals and corporations usually led to fragmented patterns of development [5].

By 1900, then, both conservation and urban planning were poorly developed. The policies and programmes of various governments and of private individuals or corporations were unrelated and resource and urban development were largely unchecked. In the first decade of the twentieth century, however, both areas of planning underwent a dramatic transformation.

## URBAN GROWTH AND CITY PLANNING

The surge of interest in both conservation and urban planning that occurred in the decades of the 1890s and the 1900s was a response to the innumerable problems that accompanied the unregulated development of the Victorian period. These problems became more acute and apparent because of rapid urban growth. Between 1881 and 1921, the proportion of Canadians living in urban places doubled from about twenty-five per cent to almost fifty per cent of the total population. The largest cities were the main recipients of this growth. In the forty years after 1881, Montreal grew by four and a half times to a total of 618,506, and Toronto by six times to 521,893. Even more dramatic was the sudden emergence of Winnipeg and Vancouver in the first decade of the twentieth century during which Winnipeg's size increased by more than three times and Vancouver's by almost four [6]. Several factors contributed to this rapid population growth. One was the enlargement of boundaries. In Toronto, a series of annexations took place in the 1880s, which added Yorkville, Rosedale, the Annex, and several other outlying areas to the city. Montreal also annexed several suburbs, including Hochelaga in the 1880s, and incorporated nine more municipalities before 1919. An orgy of suburban subdivision in every major city placed enormous financial and physical strain on the central city's ability to supply services. A second factor was migration to the cities from other Canadian urban centres, from rural areas, and particularly from abroad. Foreign immigration significantly altered the racial composition of every major city, but especially of places such as Winnipeg where the foreign-born constituted 55.9 per cent of the population by 1911. In the eyes of many contemporary observers, rapid urban growth was creating problems of the kind usually found in European cities, for big cities seemed to breed disease, poverty, and crime. Slums had become more visible, and much of the working class was not properly housed [7].

By 1900, 'it was widely accepted that urban growth posed a serious menace to the future of the nation' [8]. A host of reformers including newspapermen, politicians, businessmen, and academics cast about for solutions to the city's ills. Virtually no Canadian institution escaped the impact of these changes. Churches, mourning the passing of rural Canada, responded to the problems of urbanization with the formation of such organizations as the Social Service Council. Businessmen like Herbert Ames and Morley Wickett formed groups dedicated to putting the 'machine' in honest hands [9].

In terms of city planning, several concepts were developed, based on American and British experience. The most sweeping approach was the City Beautiful movement, which was exemplified in the Chicago Exposition in

1893, but whose roots went back at least to baroque planning. Supporters of this approach visualized a civic landscape of monumental public buildings, great diagonal boulevards, squares, and parks, and, especially a magnificently designed civic centre. It was felt that these measures would lead to a miraculous disappearance of the pressing urban problems of slums, poverty and poor health. Another approach to urban planning was the Garden City or New Town movement, which originated about the same time. It was led by a British planner, Ebenezer Howard, who advocated a retreat from big-city life to self-sufficient small towns surrounded by a green belt, with planned preserves for residential, cultural, commercial, and industrial uses. These planned communities were originally proposed by Howard for reasons of health and social advantage; he reacted against the overcrowded conditions of the industrial towns in Britain and advocated the growth of new self-contained settlements in the countryside where housing, jobs, and all the other necessities would be provided.

The Garden City approach to urban planning differed from the City Beautiful approach on the important question of the purpose of planning. While the City Beautiful advocates tended to emphasize urban aesthetics, Garden City planners stressed the health and housing of the residents. In several important respects, however, these two approaches had much in common. In both, planners would have a great deal of power (presumably with the support of government officials) in changing the existing urban structure or planning completely new towns. They both also stressed the segregation and sorting out of various urban functions—residential, commercial, industrial, and institutional. These common features emerged, as Jane Jacobs has pointed out, and became the planning orthodoxy in North America [10].

During the first thirty years of the twentieth century, Canadians experimented with a variety of these planning approaches. The emphasis shifted successively from aesthetics and the large-scale plan to the regulation of suburban expansion, to providing housing for workers, to zoning in order to segregate functions and protect property values. Some of these approaches were advocated or practised at the same time as others, but a rough periodization based on the dominating theme in a particular time period is possible. From the 1890s to the beginning of World War I, the vision of the City Beautiful was in force. The professionals in town planning—architects, engineers, and surveyors—dreamed of coherent, unified streetscapes, of variations in street patterns, and of the grandeur of a city centre. Grandiose plans were drawn up for several cities, including Toronto in 1905 and 1909, Montreal in 1906, Winnipeg in 1913, Calgary in 1914, and Ottawa and Hull in 1915. Little came of these plans, usually because the public was horrified by the enormous costs involved in putting them into practice. By 1914, planners generally were denouncing the entire approach, arguing that beauty and aesthetics were not the top priority in solving urban problems [11].

The City Beautiful idea was far from dead, however. The 1929 Bartholomew Plan for Vancouver incorporated some of its basic principles and several other examples can be cited [12]. Perhaps the most spectacular adoption of the concept in a Canadian city took place late in the 1930s in Prime Minister W. L. Mackenzie King's supervision of the redevelopment of Ottawa as federal capital. King personally hired a French planner, Jacques Gréber, whose views coincided with his own on introducing a sense of grandeur into Ottawa. Whether the Gréber Plan succeeded in this respect is debatable, but it certainly met Mackenzie King's needs. For example, after getting general agreement on the location of the War Memorial monument, King recorded in his diary: 'I at once saw that I had my Champs Elysées, Arc de Triomphe and Place de la Concorde all at a single stroke' [13].

While the City Beautiful approach remained in existence, Garden City planning dominated the thinking of the professional planners and the public from 1914 to the mid-1920s [14]. The impact of the British New Towns movement in Canada was considerable. The diffusion of New Town planning principles and ideology into the Canadian setting involved a variety of channels, including the official influences of the Governors-General of Canada, notably Sir A. H. G. Grey, the Duke of Connaught and the Duke of Devonshire, and the writings of W. L. Mackenzie King [15]. But it was the Commission of Conservation and the work of its town planning adviser, Thomas Adams, that were the most important influences. Indeed, largely as a result of the work of the Commission, the concepts of resource conservation and urban planning were locked firmly together.

## THE ESTABLISHMENT OF THE COMMISSION OF CONSERVATION

The Commission of Conservation was established as an advisory body to the Government of Canada in 1909, but its origins went back several years. The conservation movement in Canada, like its counterparts in the United States, had its birth in the 1890s. Early achievements of the movement included the new profession of forestry and the establishment of a few areas as parks for recreational uses [16]. But if there is a single event and date when the concern for conservation planning can be said to have been born in Canada, it was at the first Canadian Forestry Convention in 1906. This conference, called by Prime Minister Wilfrid Laurier, had as its guest speaker Gifford Pinchot, the apostle of conservation and scientific management in the United States [17]. The main concern of the delegates was with forestry, but the area of forest practices and management was sufficiently broad to lead to frequent discussion of general natural resource issues. The convention also led to regular annual meetings of the Canadian Forestry Association and these meetings were influential in focusing the attention of the Canadian government upon conservation issues at a time when the conservation movement was well underway in the United States. Most important, however, was the fact that the events of 1906 led directly to the sending of a Canadian delegation to the North American Conservation Conference, assembled at the call of President T. Roosevelt in February 1909. Delegates to the conference drew up a Declaration of Principles covering a wide range of natural resources, including forests, waters, land, minerals, and wildlife. Also included among the points in the Declaration was a call for each participating country to establish a commission of conservation [18].

The Canadian government accepted this idea and in the spring of 1909 Prime Minister Laurier introduced in Parliament an Act to Establish a Commission for the Conservation of Natural Resources. The Act provided for the creation of a body on which would sit *ex officio* the federal ministers of the agriculture, interior and mines departments and the members of each provincial government responsible for natural resources. There was also a third group of members that was to include at least one university professor from each province. The Commission was to meet once a year and report to the Governor-General-in-Council. The scope of the Commission was to be all questions related to the conservation and better utilization of the natural resources of Canada [19].

From the outset, the Commission of Conservation was a unique body. It was not a part of the normal governmental administration of the federal government but was intended to be a completely non-partisan body with advisory and consultative powers; it had no administrative or executive powers [20]. In order to facilitate the immense task of gathering information on the natural resources of Canada and of advancing a sound policy for their development, the Commission's first chairman, Clifford Sifton, suggested that the thirty-two members be divided into a number of working committees [21]. Committees were established for each of the major resource areas— lands, forestry, fisheries, game and fur-bearing animals, public health, waters and water powers, and minerals. Another committee, publicity and cooperating organizations, was responsible for publicizing the Commission's activities and organizing public support for the conservation movement. Each year, the committees convened to present a summary of the year's work and to determine the topics of research for the coming year.

The work of the Commission in the twelve years of its existence was considerable and ranged over a wide field of subject matter. Valuable research work was done in each of the main committees and the Commission soon became a major research organization. It published almost 200 papers and studies [22]. Many of these studies were highly technical documents useful only to those closely associated with the subject area, such as *The Canadian Oyster, Animal Sanctuaries in Labrador, Fur Farming in Canada, Altitudes in Canada, Conservation of Coal in Canada, The Prevention of the Pollution of Canadian Surface Waters*, and *Forest Protection in Canada*. Other publications were much less technical and were designed to promote public interest. An example of these less technical works was the regularly published journal, *Conservation of Life,* issued under the Commission's direction from August 1914. It contained articles of interest to those concerned with public health under such titles as 'Disinfection of Shaving Brushes', 'National Committee for Combatting Venereal Disease', and 'Maternal Nursing of Children'. As well, the Commission published annual reports from 1910 to 1919 [23].

In so wide a range of activities, the Commission was able to record a number of accomplishments. It was responsible for water power inventories; a more consolidated federal health service; the fostering of national parks and game preserves; the encouragement of agricultural and technical education; the development of safer practices in mining and the utilization of western coal; the production of studies of mineral and energy resources; the reduction of patronage in the granting of forest licences; and many other related activities [24]. Of special importance, however, was the Commission's committee on public health for it was this committee which forged a link between conservation and urban planning.

### The Committee of Health and the Influence of Thomas Adams

The Committee of Health had been established by the Conservation Commission to undertake an investigation of all matters of public health and its very existence indicated that the body was concerned with the conservation of both the physical and social resources of Canada. Indeed, the health committee soon expanded its role to include broad issues such as town planning. This wide-ranging concern for environmental health grew out of the interests of one of the first specialists appointed by the Commission, Charles Hodgetts. Hodgetts, a former Medical Health Officer in Ontario, joined the Commission in 1909 and until he left in 1915 was able to arouse support and recognition for the need to improve the urban environment. His view was that town planning was an inevitable part of the concern for better health standards. In 1911, for example, Hodgetts stated:

> I would say no government can justify its existence unless it carefully considers this important question [of town planning] and places upon the statute book a law with ample and adequate regulation for dealing with unsanitary houses of all classes in the community and for conferring power on the city, town, or village municipality whereby they may not only control, but in a measure direct, town and suburban planning. [25]

The concern of the Standing Committee on Public Health with urban planning was strengthened considerably when Thomas Adams was invited to join the Commission as Advisor on Town Planning in 1914. The invitation was apparently fostered by Adams' impressive performance at a National Planning Conference held in Philadelphia in 1911. Adams was a noted British planner who had early become acquainted with Patrick Geddes, Ebenezer Howard, and the Garden City movement. In 1900 he had become Secretary of the First Garden City Company at Letchworth and, in 1906, a town planning consultant. He was one of the founders of the British Town Planning Institute and had a solid reputation as a speaker and facilitator. At the time Adams joined the Canadian Commission of Conservation he was serving as an Inspector of the Local Government Board which was responsible for the administration of the British planning act passed in 1909 [26].

Together, the influence of Hodgetts and Adams was such that the Commission of Conservation became a major force in the development of Canadian urban planning.

> Conservation and urban improvement came to be seen as opposite sides of the same coin. Industrialization and rapid urban growth had reduced the city to an obscene and unhealthy excrescence, whereas nature was clean and pure, the resort of fundamental virtues and non-materialistic values. The strength of the country had therefore to be made accessible to the urban workers, through parks and wilderness reserves, industrial villages, and garden cities. Population and industry had also to be decentralized, to clear the way for the task of rebuilding the existing cities. It all added up to an image of powerful emotional appeal imbued with Arcadian romanticism, and strongly influenced by British experiments in town-building and by Ebenezer Howard's Garden City concept. At the same time, of course, nature had to be protected from the continual overspilling of deprived urban humanity. Urban decentralization was therefore to proceed in an orderly and controlled manner and, for all its romanticism and utopian idealism, the Garden City concept was firmly rooted in a belief in efficiently planned urban systems. [27]

As a symbol of the Garden City idea and as Town Planning Advisor to the Commission of Conservation, Adams was influential in promoting the development of urban planning in several respects. The first was provincial legislation regulating suburban expansion. Although planning was a local matter, Adams tactfully and persistently pressed for provincial legislation. Most of the provinces eventually adopted acts closely modelled on the British Housing, Town and Country Planning Act of 1909, or that part of it that dealt with municipal control over land-use planning [28]. The necessity of controlling land likely to be developed was apparent to many observers, for the era was one of incredible suburban subdivision, far in excess of actual population increase [29]. The second area of influence concerned the 'new town' aspect of the British movement. Adams was directly or indirectly involved in planning satellite towns, like Ojibway, an industrial suburb of Windsor, Ontario, and resource towns like Temiscaming, Quebec [30]. A number of other small resource towns planned during this period also reflected these general principles, including Kapaskasing, Iroquis Falls, and Arvida [31].

A third area where the influence of Adams and the Commission of Conservation was felt was in education. One of the first steps taken by Adams following his arrival in Canada was the initiation of the journal *Conservation of Life,* published between 1914 and 1921. It was used by the Commission to encourage town planning along the lines of the British model. Adams was also a tireless lecturer; he presented innumerable speeches at Canadian universities and at municipal and regional conferences. He was also influential in the establishment of the Civic Improvement League for Canada in an attempt to stimulate citizen interest in urban planning. The League, inaugurated in 1916, was soon followed by the establishment of numerous similar organizations at the municipal level. And, in 1917, Adams completed a major book, *Rural Planning and Development: A Study of Rural Conditions and Problems in Canada,* which succeeded in attracting a good deal of national and international attention [32]. In this comprehensive analysis of Canadian development trends, Adams outlined the components which he considered necessary to maintain a healthy environment. By stressing the importance of considering social aspects within the planning process, Adams stressed that less value should be placed on economic gains than on social and environmental quality.

> National prosperity depends on the character, stability, freedom and efficiency of the human resources of a nation, rather than on the amounts of its exports or imports, or the gold it may have to its credit at a given time. . . . While the conservation of natural resources and the promotion of industries are important and the development of trade has possibilities of benefit, the conservation of life and ability in the individual workers is supreme. [33]

Adams' considerable education effort, however, proved ineffective in coming to grips with one of the central concerns of Garden City planning— the provision of housing for the working man and the poor. In fact, the suburban movement accentuated rather than alleviated the problem, for it led to further fragmentation of the city into rich and poor because only the more prosperous could take part in the move away from the congested urban cores.

The question of whether government at any level would get involved in providing housing was one of the key issues of the period. Garden City advocates like Adams constantly pushed for intervention on the British model, but provincial governments made clear their reluctance to enter this field; all provincial planning legislation excluded the provisions of the 1909 British Act which concerned 'The Housing of the Working Classes'. The earliest housing schemes were thus privately initiated, combining philanthropy and investment, a practice popular in the United States. For example, Herbert Ames, a Montreal businessman, built a small group of model apartments but his initiative was not imitated to any great extent by his business compatriots [34].

In spite of a lack of action by private enterprise, city authorities generally remained aloof, and when civic government did get involved, it proved to be extremely minimal. Experiments in Toronto in 1913 and 1920 are examples. In one case the city guaranteed the bonds of a limited-dividend scheme of a joint stock company. In the other, a housing commission was appointed with clear instructions not to lose any city money. Together these ventures built over 500 housing units, but this housing generally proved too expensive for low-income families [35]. More popular with city officials was the strategy of improving housing through codes and strict code enforcement. Regulations were designed to ensure proper sanitary conditions, to control the quality of tenement housing, and to check the spread of slums. Codes, unfortunately, did not provide more or better low-income housing; if anything, they increased the cost of housing and reduced the available supply [36].

The major government intervention in housing came, surprisingly, from the federal government, even though housing was a provincial jurisdiction. Between 1918 and 1925 the federal government operated a scheme to lend money to the provinces to encourage new housing construction. Most of the provinces participated; in Ontario, more than one hundred municipalities took advantage of the measures. Thomas Adams and other reformers hoped that this move signalled a new direction in government policy, but federal officials soon made it clear that it was a temporary measure to relieve the severe postwar housing shortages, especially for returning servicemen, and to reduce the threat of social unrest.

The accession of Arthur Meighen to the office of Prime Minister in 1920 cast the dye for a retreat from federal involvement. Symbolic of the federal move away from responsibility in the area was the abolition of the Commission of Conservation in 1921. The loan scheme was finally abandoned in 1923–24 and the federal government was not to return to the housing field until the crisis of the Depression in the 1930s [37].

As housing reform declined as a positive force in the early 1920s, the pendulum swung back to a business-oriented approach to planning. Efficiency became the practical goal of reform, with planning seen as a rational, scientific activity. Technical experts were brought in to provide technical solutions. The trend was away from large-scale comprehensive plans to zoning as a means of achieving efficiency. The segregation of land uses was established on a legal-administrative basis by provincial legislation during the interwar years, borrowing heavily from the United States Department of Commerce Standard Zoning Enabling Act [38]. The move to zoning was characterized by a close relationship between planners and the property industry [39]. In fact, political support for land-use restrictions through zoning was possible because it protected property values. Zoning became a good way of prohibiting the intrusion of industry and low-income tenements into the more prosperous neighbourhoods. A second justification of zoning was the protection of public health. An examination of some Canadian city zoning plans reveals, however, that this concern over public health was definitely secondary. In the Kitchener plan, for example, the city was zoned into four categories: industrial, commercial, institutional, and residential. Although no industrial uses were allowed in the areas fortunate enough to be zoned residential, residential uses were allowed in the industrial areas of the city. In other words, while it was deemed important to keep noisy and polluting industries out of existing residential areas for public health reasons, it was not seen as important to keep new residential construction— usually workers' housing—out of the industrial areas [40].

The extent to which public authorities and planners influenced the shape of early twentieth-century cities has been the subject of research only recently. A case study of Calgary indicates that the direction of development was determined by geography and the decisions of the railway company and speculators, but only marginally by civic planning. Subdivision was not regulated by a zoning by-law until 1932. The civic corporation's control was largely negative; it could, for example, discourage residential development in certain areas by withholding utility extensions [41]. In Toronto, planning before 1936 was limited to the relatively minor function of improving traffic flow, while zoning was largely a neighbourhood-based concern to prevent nuisances and protect property values [42]. It was only in the new resource towns of the period that planners, governments, and corporations were able to put the most advanced planning ideas into practice without the difficulties inherent in working with an existing community infrastructure. Some pulp and paper towns in particular were completely preplanned; in the case of Temiscaming, Quebec, with federal government advice; in the case of Kapuskasing, Ontario, by provincial planners [43].

## THE DISSOLUTION OF THE COMMISSION OF CONSERVATION

During the era from 1890 to the early 1920s, the Canadian public developed a growing planning consciousness and were exposed to a wide range of ideas in the related areas of conservation planning and urban planning. By the late 1920s, however, Canadian planning was floundering and it was to be some time before it even began to recover. There were many reasons for this crisis [44], but the dissolution of the Commission of Conservation in 1921 signalled most clearly the end of an era in Canadian planning history.

There are several reasons that explain the dissolution of the Commission of Conservation. The members of the Commission were very able men, as were their staff, but the terms of reference under which they operated were very restrictive. The Conservation Commission had been designed as an advisory and research body that could not actually carry out their projects but had to depend on other federal government departments or other levels of government to finish what they started. These projects were not always carried out to the Commission's satisfaction; sometimes the project was too long in being completed and some projects were simply not carried out. As the years passed, however, the Commission, anxious to get the job done, often overstepped the limits of its jurisdiction. This kind of activity soon caused friction between the Commission's staff and the civil service bureaucracy, particularly the Department of the Interior. Under Sir Clifford Sifton, a powerful figure in Canadian public affairs, the Commission's prestige was protected. But in November 1918 Sifton resigned in a dispute over staff salaries and the federal cabinet began to consider the possibility of dissolution [45].

The end of the Commission came in the spring session of Parliament in 1921 when a Bill was passed to repeal the Commission of Conservation Act. Prime Minister Meighen opened the debate. In the course of his remarks he was to present several arguments for ending the Commission. It was far too expensive, he stated, and it was duplicating work done by the regular departments of government and creating a good deal of ill-feeling within the civil service. Meighen also felt that it was logical that a Commission 'could only be of a temporary character' and that such a body, devoid of ministerial responsibility, was 'not consistent with our system of government'. He also noted that the creation of a department of pensions and public health, the development of the forest service, mines department, and other government branches, had made most aspects of the work of the Commission of Conservation redundant. Few speakers supported the Commission and the Bill to dissolve the body was passed [46].

The end of the Commission of Conservation did not, of course, herald an abrupt termination of planning activity in Canada. Indeed, though the life of the Commission was relatively short, it left a strong legacy that continued for many years to influence planning activity. Perhaps its most important achievement was in assuming the role of a national forum for the discussion and development of issues and ideas about resource policy and management. It stimulated argument and research into a whole range of problems associated with particular resources and it initiated national consideration of public health and town planning problems, leading to the establishment of a national health department and a national planning association. More significantly, through the work of Adams, it developed concepts of total resource use in the field of urban planning. In short, the Commission of Conservation did more than any other institution to draw attention to integrated resource development.

In the decades following the demise of the Commission, planning in both the conservation and urban areas, however, developed slowly. In the former, there was no examination of natural resources on the same scale again until the Reconstruction Conference of 1945, although problems of forest, water, soil, and wildlife resources were discussed during the 1920s and 1930s at conferences with limited frames of reference [47]. In general, though, there was little conservation planning during the period from 1921 to 1961;

instead, these were years of intense and rapid resource exploitation. The period was, in a sense, a return to the 'doctrine of usefulness' which had held sway in the years before 1900. The focus of conservation planning, such as it was, was on natural science. The social motivation that had been evident during the life of the Conservation Commission was modified by a concern for the conservation of physical resources more in the physical than in the economic sense: 'the object was to refine techniques to improve conservation . . . in the physical sense. . . . Conservation, or resource development, became a means to an end, an instrument of economic policy' [48].

The emphasis on resources for development was not to shift until at least 1961 when a major conference, 'Resources For Tomorrow', was convened. The papers and discussions published in the conference report indicated that concern was again shifting to include a concern for both social and economic aspects in conservation planning [49]. It was the beginning of a new conservation movement in Canada, but unlike the earlier one, it did not achieve quick recognition in the form of a government agency or department. The new conservation movement, however, did constitute a political force and eventually, in 1971, a federal Department of the Environment was created that brought together in a single ministry a host of agencies involved in the management of renewable resources and the natural environment. In the last decade, conservation planning has been evident in a growing body of environmental legislation at both provincial and federal levels and it promises to be a major force in the immediate decades ahead [50].

Urban planning also had a checkered existence in the years following 1921. Problems began in the 1920s when public interest turned from urban-oriented issues to provincial and national concerns. Cities particularly dropped in priority during the Great Depression and World War II [51]. One Canadian planner succinctly characterized the period:

> For us the economic depression of the thirties was a vacuum and a complete break with the past. . . . We had no public housing programs and none of the adventurous social experiments of the New Deal. . . . We withered on the stem. So in 1946 we almost literally started from scratch with no plans or planners, and we immediately hit a period of tremendous city growth. [52]

The federal government had returned to the housing field during the crisis of the 1930s and formalized its intervention with a new National Housing Act in 1944. A Crown Corporation, the Central Mortgage and Housing Corporation (CMHC), was established in 1945 to operate the Act. The number of new housing units financed under this scheme increased from almost 12,000 in 1946 to 65,000 in 1955. The long-term results of this federal intervention were twofold. CMHC's lending policies literally created a Canadian house-building industry which built thousands of these new homes, but little planning accompanied this rapid growth and cities sprawled into formless suburbs [53]. During the 1950s, CMHC was reoriented from its previous emphasis on suburban mortgage lending to a concern for the interior of cities through urban renewal by contributing fifty per cent of the cost of acquiring and clearing land for low-rental housing. The first major project was Regent Park South in Toronto, followed by the Jean Mance project in Montreal and Mulgrove Park in Halifax. What began with the enthusiasm of reform, however, soon became isolated monuments, for the expected tide of urban renewal failed to gather strength, leaving low-income people segregated in public-housing ghettoes [54].

The federal government's activities in the cities were paralleled by the institutionalization of local planning through the establishment of departments of planning in municipal governments. This trend tended to bring planning more directly under political control, at the expense of the older system of planning commissioners or boards, whose respectable members presumably had been above politics [55]. In searching for planners, both the CMHC and local departments recruited heavily in Britain. One result was that the 'British takeover of planning in the 1940s was massive' [56]. According to one critic, the consequences of this domination by British planners was a planning profession preoccupied with the physical details of land use and a relentless desire to centralize planning power at the expense of the public's involvement in the process [57].

While it is extremely difficult to generalize about recent trends in urban planning, at least two divergent directions are apparent. One represents a reaction to the centralizing policies of the federal agencies and city planning departments, and was symbolized by the citizen-oriented fight for local control of the Trefann Court project in Toronto. The issue was simply whether people who are affected by planning could have a major voice in that planning [58]. The other direction involved planning at an entirely different scale—the regional level—which was initiated with the studies leading to the concept of the Toronto-centred region. Metro Toronto combined with several departments of the provincial government in planning a parkway belt to accommodate future transportation and industrial development for a large section of southern Ontario, focused on Toronto. Both the local and regional planning concerns reflect a renaissance of urban consciousness. Ironically, this renewal is taking place in cities which no longer have the financial or political independence to determine their own destinies [59].

In general, then, both conservation and urban planning continued to develop, albeit haphazardly, in the years after 1921. But they developed along distinct and frequently unrelated lines. The interrelationship between conservation and urban planning, so evident during the era of the Commission of Conservation, was no longer present. This was the tragedy of Canadian planning. The Commission of Conservation had articulated and fostered an integrated view of resource planning and, for all their naïvete and failures, the advisers and members of the Commission had discovered the best possible approach to planning [60]. In the years after 1921, however, this approach was lost in a plethora of political, jurisdictional, and ideological disputes. At a time when the need for planning was greatest—during the crisis of the 1930s and the massive growth of the 1950s and 1960s—the response of Canadian planning was weak. If it is to succeed in the future, Canadian planning must learn from the successes and failures of the Commission of Conservation.

## NOTES

1. Canada was confederated under the terms of the British North America Act which came into force on 1 July 1867. The doctrine of usefulness is discussed in Brown, R. C. (1969) The doctrine of usefulness: natural resource and national park policy in Canada, in Nelson, J. G. (ed.), *Canadian Parks in Perspective.* Montreal: Harvest House, pp. 46–62.

2. Burton, T. L. (1972) *Natural Resource Policy in Canada: Issues and Perspectives.* Toronto: McClelland and Stewart, p. 42 and *passim.* For an excellent discussion of the role of staples in Canadian development see Buckley, K. (1958) The role of staple industries in Canada's economic development. *Journal of Economic History,* 18 (4), pp. 439–50.

3. Some of the earliest urban planning in Canada is briefly covered in Reps, J. W. (1969) *Town Planning in Frontier America.* Princeton, N.J.: Princeton University Press. See also Hugo-Brunt, M. (1968) The origin of colonial settlements in the Maritimes, in Gertler, L. O. (ed.), *Planning the Canadian Environment.* Montreal: Harvest House, pp. 42–83.

4. See Gidney, N. (1978) From coal to forest products: the changing resource base of Nanaimo, B.C. *Urban History Review,* 1, pp. 18–47; and Stelter, G. A. (1971) The origins of a company town: Sudbury in the nineteenth century. *Laurentian University Review,* 3, pp. 3–37. Numerous other examples could be cited, including Prince Rupert, B.C., planned in 1904 by a distinguished Boston firm of landscape architects for the Grand Trunk Pacific Railway Company. See Richardson, N. H. (1968) A tale of two cities, in Gertler, L. O. (ed.), *Planning the Canadian Environment.* Montreal: Harvest House, pp. 269–84.

5. See, for example, Doucet, M. (forthcoming) Speculation and the physical development of mid-nineteenth century Hamilton, and Ganton, Isobel (forthcoming) Land subdivision in Toronto, 1847–1883, in Stelter, G. A. and Artibise, A. F. J. (eds.), *Shaping the Canadian Urban Landscape: Essays on the City-Building Process, 1821–1921.*

6. For detailed statistics on Canadian urban growth see Plunkett, T. J. *et al.* (1973) *Urban Population Growth and Municipal Organization,* Local Government Reference Paper No. 1. Kingston: Institute of Local Government, Queen's University; or Stone, L. O. (1967) *Urban Development in Canada.* Ottawa: Dominion Bureau of Statistics.

7. See, for example, Artibise, A. F. J. (1975) *Winnipeg: A Social History of Urban Growth, 1874–1914.* Montreal: McGill-Queen's University Press; and Copp, T. (1974) *The Anatomy of Poverty: The Condition of the Working Class in Montreal.* Toronto: McClelland and Stewart.

8. Rutherford, P. (1977) Tomorrow's metropolis: the urban reform movement in Canada, 1880–1920, in Stelter, G. A. and Artibise, A. F. J. (eds.), *The Canadian City: Essays in Urban History.* Toronto: McClelland and Stewart, p. 368.

9. For an excellent collection of reformers' writings see Rutherford, P. (ed.) (1974) *Saving the Canadian City: The First Phase, 1880–1920—An Anthology of Early Articles on Urban Reform.* Toronto: University of Toronto Press.

10. Jacobs, Jane (1961) *The Death and Life of Great American Cities.* New York: Random House.

11. For an example, see Thomas Adams' comments in Commission of Conservation (1916) *Seventh Annual Report.* Montreal, pp. 118–19, and in Town planning and the housing problem. *Canadian Club Addresses,* Montreal, 11 January 1915. For a general discussion see Van Nus, W. (1977) The fate of City Beautiful thought in Canada, 1893–1930, in Stelter, G. A. and Artibise, A. F. J. (eds.), *The Canadian City: Essays in Urban History.* Toronto: University of Toronto Press, pp. 162–85.

12. Bartholomew, H. (1929) *A Plan for the City of Vancouver, B.C., Including Point Grey and South Vancouver and a General Plan of the Region.* Vancouver: Town Planning Commission. See also Gunton, T. (1979) The ideas and policies of the Canadian planning profession, 1909–1931, in Artibise, A. F. J. and Stelter, G. A. (eds.), *The Usable Urban Past: Politics and Planning in the Modern Canadian City.* Toronto: Macmillan, pp. 177–95.

13. Quoted in Tomovcik, V. (1977) The Greber Plan for Ottawa. Unpublished M.A. Thesis, University of Waterloo, p. 40.

14. Contemporary sources for this period of planning are particularly rich. These include the voluminous Commission of Conservation annual reports, 1910–19; the Commission's magazine, *Conservation of Life,* 1914–21; the Proceedings of the National Conference on City Planning, usually held in the United States, but held in Toronto in 1914; the dozens of speeches Thomas Adams and others gave to Canadian Clubs in Montreal, Ottawa, Toronto, Hamilton, Winnipeg and Vancouver, and published in annual volumes of Club *Addresses* by those respective clubs.

15. For a detailed discussion of the diffusion process see Saarinen, O. (1979) The influence of Thomas Adams and the British New Towns movement in the planning of Canadian resource communities, in Artibise, A. F. J. and Stelter, G. A. (eds.), *The Usable Urban Past: Politics and Planning in the Modern Canadian City.* Toronto: Macmillan, pp. 268–92.

16. Brown, R. C. and Cook, R. (1974) *Canada, 1896–1921: A Nation Transformed.* Toronto: McClelland and Stewart, p. 96.

17. Hays, S. P. (1959) *Conservation and the Gospel of Efficiency: The Progressive Conservation Movement, 1890–1920.* Cambridge: Harvard University Press.

18. Thorpe, F. J. (1961) Historical perspective on 'Resources for Tomorrow' conference, in *Resources For Tomorrow: Conference Background Papers.* Ottawa: Queen's Printer, pp. 2–3.

19. Armstrong, A. H. (1968) Thomas Adams and the Commission of Conservation, in Gertler, L. O. (ed.), *Planning the Canadian Environment.* Montreal: Harvest House, p. 18.

20. Commission of Conservation (1910) *First Annual Report.* Ottawa, p. 2.

21. Sifton was a logical choice as chairman. He had been a prominent member of the

Laurier Cabinet from 1896 to 1905 and had served as Minister of the Interior. In this position he had gained a thorough understanding of conservation issues. He had also attended the North American Conservation Conference and the National Conference on City Planning where he argued for a more systematic approach to conservation and town planning. See *Proceedings of the Sixth National Conference on City Planning, Toronto, May 25–27, 1914.* Boston, 1914, p. 136. See also Dafoe, J. W. (1931) *Clifford Sifton in Relation to his Times.* Toronto: Macmillan.

22. Lists of these publications can be found in the 1919 and 1920 *Canada Year Books.*

23. The best summary of the work of the Commission is Smith, C. R. and Witty, D. R. (1970, 1972) Conservation Resources and Environment: an exposition and critical evaluation of the Commission of Conservation, Canada. *Plan Canada,* 11 (1), pp. 55–71; 11 (3), pp. 199–216. A short overview is Renfrew, S. (1971) Commission of Conservation. *Douglas Library Notes,* 19 (3–4), pp. 17–26.

24. *Ibid.* See also Armstrong, A. H. (1968) Thomas Adams and the Commission of Conservation, in Gertler, L. O. (ed.), *Planning the Canadian Environment.* Montreal: Harvest House.

25. Commission of Conservation (1911) *Second Annual Report.* Montreal, p. 75.

26. Armstrong, A. H. (1968) Thomas Adams and the Commission of Conservation, in Gertler, L. O. (ed.), *Planning the Canadian Environment.* Montreal: Harvest House.

27. Smith, P. J. (1979) The principle of utility and the origins of planning legislation in Alberta, in Artibise, A. F. J. and Stelter, G. A. (eds.), *The Usable Urban Past: Politics and Planning in the Modern Canadian City.* Toronto: Macmillan, pp. 201–2.

28. Armstrong, A. H. (1968) Thomas Adams and the Commission of Conservation, in Gertler, L. O. (ed.), *Planning the Canadian Environment.* Montreal: Harvest House; and Saarinen, O. (1979) The influence of Thomas Adams and the British New Towns movement in the planning of resource communities, in Artibise, A. F. J. and Stelter, G. A. (eds.) *The Usable Urban Past: Politics and Planning in the Modern Canadian City.* Toronto: Macmillan. See also Wiesman, B. (1977) The development and nature of provincial planning legislation, 1912–1975. Unpublished paper presented to 'Canada's Urban Past', The Canadian Urban History Conference, University of Guelph.

29. Adams, T. (1917) *Rural Planning and Development.* Ottawa: Commission of Conservation, pp. 224–5. This problem is also discussed in some detail in a western Canadian context in Artibise, A. F. J. (forthcoming) Boosterism and the development of prairie cities, 1870–1913, in Stelter, G. A. and Artibise, A. F. J. (eds.), *Shaping the Canadian Urban Landscape: Essays on the City-Building Process, 1821–1921,* and in Artibise, A. F. J. (1979) Continuity and Change: elites and prairie urban development, 1914–1950, in Artibise, A. F. J. and Stelter, G. A. (eds.), *The Usable Urban Past: Politics and Planning in the Modern Canadian City.* Toronto: Macmillan, pp. 130–54.

30. Commission of Conservation (1919) *Tenth Annual Report.* Montreal, Appendix VII, pp. 109–11.

31. McCann, L. (1978) The changing internal structure of Canadian resource towns, *Plan Canada,* 18, pp. 46–59.

32. In addition to a constant round of Canadian Club speeches in major cities, Adams spoke at a variety of other gatherings. Examples are included in *Report of the Urban and Rural Development Conference, Winnipeg, May 28–30, 1917.* Ottawa.

33. Adams, T. (1917) *Rural Planning and Development.* Ottawa: Commission of Conservation, p. 2.

34. Examples of speeches on this subject are The Housing Problem. *Canadian Club Addresses,* Montreal, 24 February 1919, pp. 180–6; and *Report of the Preliminary Conference of the Civic Improvement League for Canada.* Ottawa, 1918, pp. 11–17. See also Rutherford, P. (1972) Introduction, to Ames,' Herbert Brown, *The City Below the Hill: A Sociological Study of a Portion of the City of Montreal.* Toronto: University of Toronto Press (reprint of 1897 edition).

35. Spragge, Shirley (1979) A conference of interests: housing reform in Toronto, 1900–1920, in Artibise, A. F. J. and Stelter, G. A. (eds.), *The Usable Urban Past: Politics and Planning in the Modern Canadian City.* Toronto: Macmillan, pp. 247–67.

36. Weaver, J. C. (1977) 'Tomorrow's metropolis' revisited: a critical assessment of urban reform in Canada, 1890–1920, in Stelter, G. A. and Artibise, A. F. J. (eds.), *The Canadian City: Essays in Urban History.* Toronto: McClelland and Stewart, pp. 403–9.

37. Grauer, A. E. (1939) *Housing. A Study Prepared for the Royal Commission on Dominion-Provincial Relations.* Ottawa: King's Printer; Saywell, J. T. (1975) *Housing Canadians: Essays on the History of Residential Construction in Canada.* Ottawa: Economic Council of Canada.

38. Wiesman, B. (1977) The development and nature of provincial planning legislation, 1912–1975. Unpublished paper presented to 'Canada's Urban Past', The Canadian Urban History Conference, University of Guelph.

39. Van Nus, W. (1979) Towards the City Efficient: the theory and practice of zoning, 1919–1939, in Artibise, A. F. J. and Stelter, G. A. (eds.), *The Usable Urban Past: Politics and Planning in the Modern Canadian City.* Toronto: Macmillan, pp. 226–46.

40. Gunton, T. (1979) The ideas and policies of the Canadian planning profession, 1909–1931, in *ibid.,* pp. 223–43.

41. Foran, M. (1979) Land development patterns in Calgary, 1884–1946, in *ibid.,* pp. 293–315.

42. Moore, P. (1979) Zoning and planning: the Toronto experience, 1904–1970, in *ibid.,* pp. 316–41.

43. Stelter, G. A. and Artibise, A. F. J. (1978) Canadian resource towns in historical perspective. *Plan Canada,* 18, pp. 7–16.

44. Gunton, T. (1979) The ideas and policies of the Canadian planning profession, in Artibise, A. F. J. and Stelter, G. A. (eds.) *The Usable Urban Past: Politics and Planning in the Modern Canadian City.* Toronto: Macmillan, pp. 223–43.

45. Thorpe, F. J. (1961) Historical perspective on 'Resources for Tomorrow' conference, in *Resources For Tomorrow: Conference Background Papers.* Ottawa: Queen's Printer; Armstrong, A. H. (1968) Thomas Adams and the Commission of Conservation, in Gertler, L. O. (ed.), *Planning the Canadian Environment.* Montreal: Harvest House.

46. Canadian House of Commons (1921) *Debates,* pp. 3958–71.

47. Thorpe, F. J. (1961) Historical perspective on 'Resources for Tomorrow' conference, in *Resources For Tomorrow: Conference Background Papers*. Ottawa: Queen's Printer; Burton, T. L. (1972) *Natural Resource Policy in Canada: Issues and Perspectives*. Toronto: McClelland and Stewart.

48. Thorpe, F. J., *ibid.,* pp. 11–12.

49. *Resources For Tomorrow: Conference Background Papers*, 2 vols. Ottawa: Queen's Printer, 1961. See also Dakin, J. (1968) Resources for Tomorrow, the background papers, in Gertler, L. O. (ed.), *Planning the Canadian Environment*. Montreal: Harvest House, pp. 119–36.

50. For an overview of the federal environment ministry and its concerns, see Environment Canada (1972) *Canada and the Human Environment*. Ottawa.

51. See, for example, Taylor, J. (1979) Relief from relief: the cities' answer to depression dependency. *Journal of Canadian Studies*, 14 (1), pp. 16–23.

52. Carver, H. (1960) Planning in Canada, *Planning 1960: Proceedings of the American Society of Planning Officials*. Chicago, 1960, p. 22. The history of urban planning since World War II has not been examined in detail but some useful guides are available. The most readable and full account is Humphrey Carver's humanistic autobiography, *Compassionate Landscape*. Toronto: University of Toronto Press, 1975. An outline of federal legislation as applied to housing and planning can be found in Bettinson, D. (1975) *The Politics of Canadian Urban Development*. Edmonton: University of Alberta Press, pp. 61–104. For an anti-establishment interpretation of recent events, see Clark, R. (1976) The crisis in Canadian city planning. *City Magazine*, 1 (8), pp. 17–24. Also useful are the historical sections of papers by Brahm Wiesman and Kenneth D. Cameron in Oberlander, H. P. (ed.) (1976) *Canada: An Urban Agenda*. Ottawa: Community Planning Press.

53. Carver, H. (1975) *Compassionate Landscape*. Toronto: University of Toronto Press, pp. 107–57; and Carver, H. (1962) *Cities in the Suburbs*. Toronto: University of Toronto Press.

54. For a detailed description of the reformist expectations and the administrative and political problems, see Rose, A. (1959) *Regent Park: A Study of Slum Clearance*. Toronto: University of Toronto Press; and Carver, H. (1975) *Compassionate Landscape*. Toronto: University of Toronto Press, pp. 134–48.

55. Gerecke, K. (1976) The history of Canadian city planning. *City Magazine*, 2 (3–4), pp. 14–15.

56. Adamson, A. (1973) Thirty years of the planning business. *Plan Canada*, 13, p. 7.

57. Clark, R. (1976) The crisis in Canadian city planning. *City Magazine*, 1 (8), pp. 22.

58. The major study of this struggle, when it still promised to be successful, is Fraser, G. (1972) *Fighting Back: Urban Renewal in Trefann Court*. Toronto: Hakkert. It should be noted that a federal Ministry of State for Urban Affairs was created in 1971. Smaller than the Environment Ministry, it was established to design and coordinate urban-oriented policies and programmes administered by other departments and agencies. Significantly, the MSUA was ended in April 1979, and federal involvement in urban planning was again spread over a variety of government departments and agencies.

59. See, for example, Nowlan, D. M. (1978) Towards home rule for urban policy. *Journal of Canadian Studies,* 13, pp. 70–9.
60. Humphrey Carver, a noted Canadian planner, wrote in 1975 that 'in retrospect, the creation of the Commission of Conservation appears as a brilliant flash of national insight, anticipating by more than sixty years the departments of environment set up by federal and provincial governments in the early 1970s'. Carver, H. (1975) *Compassionate Landscape.* Toronto: University of Toronto Press, p. 32.

# 3

# The origins of the German conservation movement

## STEFAN MUTHESIUS

This paper briefly surveys attitudes to the conservation of buildings and towns in the German-speaking countries *circa* 1900 which was a time of radical change and development [1]. The conservation movement grew out of the *Neu Romantik* (New Romanticism) philosophy which held *Kultur* more valuable than economics or politics; it rejected 'foreign', 'scientific' and 'democratic' ways of thinking in favour of ideas more emotional and more deeply rooted in the German lands and peoples [2]. The *Heimat Bewegung*— the meaning of *Heimat* lies somewhere between *Heim* (home) and *Vaterland* (fatherland)—was an important element of this movement and formed a focus of association for many other like-minded philosophies. It is now well-known that many of these led directly into the Third Reich but for the period just before the First World War we might be excused for treating them reasonably sympathetically, just as we can decide not to chide Max Weber's excursions into German nationalism (he was one of the many eminent supporters of the *Heimat Bewegung)* or Mies van der Rohe for designing a monument to Bismarck in 1912.

### Nineteenth-Century Beginnings

The beginnings of an appreciation of the past in Germany lie with the Romantic poets and the picturesque movement. In the 1850s Wilhelm Hierich Riehl put the study of the man-made landscape, of old towns and houses, and of old customs on to a sound antiquarian and socio-historical footing [3]. He may be considered the first *Volkskundler* (scientist of folklore) and founder of a subject that has since been taught in all schools and universities as *Heimatkunde* (local history and local geography). To Riehl, the old German order—at that time hardly touched by industrialization—was not only picturesque but socially sound and provided a guaranty of future well-being (figure 1). In the decades which followed, economic and social philosophers began to turn away from industrialization and town life and back towards agriculture. In particular, they developed programmes for land resettlement while more specifically, Adolf Damaschke's *Bodenreform* (reform of land tenure) movement demanded public ownership of the land and protection of natural resources for the enjoyment of the general public [4].

Public appreciation of natural landscapes increased rapidly during the second half of the nineteenth century. *Wandervereine* (walking and mountaineering societies) mushroomed from the 1860s and sociologists and botanists initiated more environmental approaches to their subjects. All types of landscape, including the ordinary and unspectacular, were now appreciated in their own right.

By the end of the century, conflicts arose between this newer view and the established picturesque attitude towards beauty spots like the Rhine which by then were being spoilt by growing numbers of tourists and modern paraphernalia like funicular railways and souvenir shops. Two early propagators of *Naturschutz* in the 1880s, Ernst Rudorff and Hugo Conwentz, pressed the case for the protection of natural monuments by law and tried to establish pressure groups to this end. The states of Hesse and Prussia were the first to enact legislation; in Prussia, for example, a law was passed in 1902 to prevent 'the disfigurement of outstanding parts of the landscape'. A state agency for *Naturdenkmalpflege* (protection of natural sites) was established in Berlin in 1906 [5]. In addition further impetus was provided by the *Wandervogel* youth organizations which appeared in the 1890s. They sought freedom from bourgeois restrictions and gripped the imagination of the sons of the middle classes. On the fringes of the environment debate, groups of naturists and vegetarians were established and flourished [6].

## HISTORIC BUILDINGS AND RURAL CRAFTS

Public interest and concern for historic buildings and other art objects also has many roots going back into the nineteenth century. The completion of Cologne Cathedral from about 1840 to the 1880s was a triumph never surpassed. Many universities appointed professors of art history and the *Technische Hochschulen* taught architectural history. Inventories of historic buildings, including farmhouses, were also compiled in the nineteenth century. In the applied arts, the Austrians from the 1860s and, from a little later on, the Museums in Berlin and Hamburg, showed a keen interest in the products of remote and 'uncorrupted' regional craftsmen [7]. In the 1890s, *Volkskunst* (popular art) became a truly popular concern for which from

FIGURE 3.1. Peasant; etching by Fritz Böhle, 1896. (From *Deutsche Kunst und Dekoration,* 35, 1914–15, p. 281)

about 1900 the term *Heimatkunst* was applied [8]. From 1902 the *Dürerbund,* an offspring from the *Kunstwart* circle, supported the preservation and encouragement of rural and amateur crafts on a large scale. Finally all conservation efforts were united in the *Bund Heimatschutz,* founded in 1904 by Rudorff, R. Mielke and P. Schultze-Naumburg [9]. The list of its members reads like a Who's Who of the art and intellectual circles of the period; the *Bund Heimatschutz* also provided links with other important groups such as the *Deutsche Werkbund,* founded a few years later [10]. In this context it is interesting to note the characteristic use of the traditional sounding word *Bund* (association) the equivalent of which in English would be 'guild'.

Opinions about the restoration and conservation of historic buildings changed markedly *circa* 1900. Many German restorers continued, until the

FIGURES 3.2 and 3.3. Good (above) and bad (below) examples of town planning by Cornelius Gurlitt. (From *Baukunst,* Berlin, c. 1905)

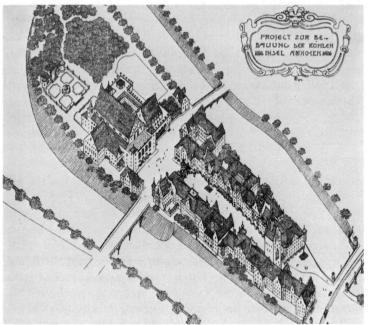

FIGURES 3.4 and 3.5. Unexecuted designs for Kohleninsel, Munich by Theodor Fischer. (From *Deutsche Bauzeitung*, 21 April 1900)

early twentieth century, with the nineteenth-century method of completing and perfecting an old building in an approximation of its period style (somewhat misleadingly called the 'puristic' approach). A *cause célèbre* was the proposal by the then elderly and generally very respected Carl Schäfer to 'complete' the Ott-Heinrichsbau of the Heidelberg Schloss. The anti-restoration lobby which won this battle maintained that modern imitations of old styles were always recognizable as such and argued that old buildings should be repaired, but otherwise left alone. The writings of the Dresden critic Cornelius Gurlitt in the late 1890s and the work of Morris and Ruskin from about 1897 onwards were important influences on this German anti-scrape movement [11].

Perhaps even more important in the evolution of conservation in Germany were changes in ideas about restoration associated with two new developments in architecture and town planning in the late nineteenth century. The first of these was a move towards the essential simplicity of 'Modern Movement' design. The second was Camillo Sitte's 'discovery' of 'space' in town planning in his book of 1889, *Der Städtebau nach seinen künstlerischen Grundsätzen* (City planning according to artistic principles) [12]. Sitte enthused about the feeling of enclosure provided by buildings in old squares or piazzas in contrast to that of 'modern', i.e. post-baroque and nineteenth-century, traffic-orientated junctions. The actual styles of the individual buildings did not seem to matter very much.

Relatively little is known about how Sitte developed his notions of form and space but sketches made by two young Berlin architects, Paul Wallot and Otto Rieth, in the mid-1880s provide a clue. They revived an almost Piranesian sense of picturesque space and massiveness. To this should be added the 'cosy' home notion of those decades which Sitte transferred to the larger environment of the small *Platz* (square).

### ALFRED LICHTWARK AND PAUL SCHULTZE-NAUMBURG

Many strands of artistic criticism and innovation gave rise to the notion that simple, 'monumental' (which does not necessarily mean large in size) forms were better than the over-elaboration prevalent in late nineteenth-century continental architecture. Alfred Lichtwark was perhaps the most influential critic in the field. In the mid-1890s he described the form of a small town in the Harz mountains in terms of 'the continuous walls of the houses of the market place . . .; the roof of the church with its large surface of green copper finds its correspondence in the solemn, simple mass of the walls . . .' [13]. The crucial effect of these notions was, in analogy with what has been said about preference in landscapes, that historic buildings or towns did not have to be outstanding or particularly ornate to be considered interesting; virtually every piece of undisturbed old surroundings had its aesthetic merits.

FIGURE 3.6. 'Evening' by Paul Schultze-Naumburg, 1898. (From *Dekorative Kunst,* 4 (4), 1901)

Lichtwark's publicizing did much to revive the architecture of simple old farmhouses but perhaps even more important in this respect were the writings of Paul Schultze-Naumburg. In his early life he worked as an artist depicting quiet rurality in the manner of Hans Thoma. From about 1900, Schultze-Naumburg travelled widely through Germany collecting and publishing photographs of 'good' old farmhouses and landscapes and contrasting them with 'ugly' nineteenth-century intruders. He went further than Lichtwark and identified a series of simple house types deeply rooted in the German race and soil [14]. He also stated, more clearly than anybody else at that time, his attitudes to modern technology. We need it in our houses, he said, but it does not have to be prominent in the form of the house but can quite easily be accommodated in simple, traditional house types. Of course we need reservoirs, but their forms and architecture can be designed to suit

FIGURES 3.7 and 3.8. Paul Schultze-Naumburg's examples of bad (above) and good (below) architecture. The suburban house is considered 'bad' because of the attempt to make it look picturesque by arbitrarily adding a gable. (From *Dörfer und Kolonien*, vol. 3 of *Kulturarbeiten*. Munich, 1903)

the landscape, not to disturb it. Schultze-Naumburg, in conjunction with his pupil, the architect Heinrich Tessenow, created the small German *Siedlungs* (estate) house. With its high-pitched simple roof it remained popular almost to the present day.

## PRESERVATION OF THE CHARACTER OF TOWNS

Preserving the character of old towns was much more difficult than ensuring the continuance of vernacular architectural styles. Sitte's formulae were only slowly accepted. A turning point was the acknowledgment of the danger of isolating outstanding historic buildings from their immediate environment as the earlier nineteenth century had done with Cologne Cathedral. Small old buildings provided an effective contrast and created picturesque viewpoints. But gradually German town planners, working alongside local pressure groups like the Hildesheim *Pinselverein* (art society), realized that they could use local by-laws as instruments for the preservation of historic streets. In the late 1890s, a number of design competitions were held to set standards for the rebuilding of street façades in a generalized old manner in Hildesheim. From about 1903 onwards, it was realized that one of the most effective ways of helping to preserve old streets was to enforce new kinds of *Fluchtlinien*

FIGURE 3.9. Competition entry for a design for reconstructing a square in Hildesheim. (From *Die Denkmalpflege*, 1901)

(building lines) which respected the old irregular patterns instead of regularizing them. What seemed to matter in rebuilding or extending old streets was to 'harmonize contours, the shape of roots, materials and colour'; with the details of design there was room 'for artistic freedom'. *Denkmalpflege* (the preservation of monuments) was not just a matter of arresting decay; 'a good copy may be worth as much as the old monument' [15]. Within a decade attitudes to restoration turned full circle away from anti-scrape and back to an appreciation of copies in some circumstances.

It is interesting to note that the *Heimatschutz* movement very soon caught the attention of social reformers. Paul Weber, a lesser known adherent of the *Bodenreform* movement, wrote in 1906 that the public had a right to study and enjoy old buildings even if the monument in question happened to be in private ownership [16]. From statements like this grew the demand for public ownership of land and buildings, or at least some extension of the powers of civic authorities in this field. In fact, state legislation and aid followed very soon. Hesse made a start in 1902 with its *Denkmalschutzgesetz* and Prussia followed suit in 1907 [17]. The main feature of the law in Hesse was the institution of a state council for the listing of monuments and their surroundings, comprising members from churches and historical societies. Public bodies were also held responsible for the upkeep of their listed monuments and those in private ownership could be expropriated if they fell into neglect.

## ENGLAND AND GERMANY COMPARED

In all matters of planning, architecture and design, the links between England and Germany were very close indeed. The traditional view is that around 1900 the new movements in architecture and the applied arts in Germany were strongly influenced by Morris and the 'Domestic Revival'; a view propagated by the Germans themselves, mainly in order to show that they had progressed, while the English, they thought, had come to a standstill, or were even regressing. This rather simplified view needs considerable amplification. Overall, at the turn of the century Germany presented a wider range of ideas than Britain, having lagged behind for much of the nineteenth century. There were the notions of rationalism in domestic design and planning which were shared by reformers in many countries, but there were no direct parallels in Britain to the way in which housing by-laws in Germany were incorporated in town planning laws. Indeed in this respect Germany was the country that influenced all others. Exchanges between England and Germany concerning garden cities are examples of cross-fertilization. On the one hand, German planners came in great numbers to England to look at early garden suburbs and garden colonies such as Port Sunlight and, on the other, English planners borrowed German notions and combined them with garden city ideas in the first town planning legislation of 1909. Another important Central European principle in town planning, the importance of 'space' developed by Sitte, had no early parallel in Britain and Raymond Unwin must be counted among Sitte's most understanding followers from 1905 onwards.

For some decades English architects and critics had felt a deep concern for vernacular architecture and their surroundings; but the more aggressive kind of mystic nationalism and racism of German critics from 1900 onwards can seldom be found in England, although there are some parallels in Unwin's and Schultze-Naumburg's praising of the old feudal order and its restraining effect on the decoration of the individual house. Thus there is no strict parallel to the early strong influence of the *Heimatschutz* societies and legislation. Not much notice seems to have been taken of Richardson Evans' 'National Society for Checking the Abuse of Public Advertising' set up in 1893; the Council for the Protection of Rural England was not founded until 1926 [18].

As has been noted earlier, we now know what all the then new German ideas of cultural nationalism led to. The vernacular revival was an international movement but it did imply the need to concentrate on one's own surroundings, on their aesthetic and cultural merits, and to cut oneself off from wider stylistic and cultural trends. Cultural nationalism in Germany was fuelled by the existing strong political nationalism.

Another point is also worthy of consideration here. During the period 1880–1910 the development of industrialization and urbanization was drastically and rapidly changing much of the German countryside, whereas in Britain the pace of industrial expansion had slowed down by this time and the effects of its associated urbanization were already being mitigated by picturesque suburbanism. In Britain industry was more localized and in many parts of the country, especially the south where most artistic critics lived, it could be claimed that the rural structure of the countryside had been hardly touched at all. The more hectic developments in Germany needed more drastic reforms. Today we can see again in Germany the beginnings of a strong conservation movement after the economic boom and pace of change of the last twenty years.

## NOTES

1. A more detailed account of these matters can be found in: Muthesius, S. (1974) *Das englische Vorbild, eine Studie zu den deutschen Reformbewegungen in Architektur, Wohnbau und Kunstgewerbe im späteren 19. Jahrhundert.* Munich: Prestel.
2. See, for instance, Stern, F. (1961) *The Politics of Cultural Despair. A Study in the Rise of the Germanic Ideology.* Berkeley: University of California Press.
3. Riehl, W. H. (1854–69) *Naturgeschichte des deutschen Volkes,* 4 vols. Stuttgart-Tübingen; see Weber-Kellermann, I. (1969) *Deutsche Volkskunde.* Stuttgart: Metzler.

4. Bergmann, K. (1970) *Agrarromantik und Grosstadtfeindschaft*, vol. 20 of Abendroth, W. (ed.), *Marburger Abhandlungen zur Politischen Wissenschaft*. Meisenheim am Glan: Anton Heim.

5. Schoenichen, W. (1954) *Naturschutz, Heimatschutz; Ihre Begründung durch Ernst Rudorff, Hugo Conwentz und ihre Vorläufer*, vol. 16 of Frickhinger, H. W. (ed.) *Grosse Naturforscher*. Stuttgart: Wissenschaftliche Verlagsgesellschaft.

6. Frecot, J., Geist, J. F. and Kerbs, D. (1972) *Fidus*. Munich: Rogner and Bernhard.

7. Riegl, A. (1894) *Volkskunst, Hausfleiss und Hausindustrie*. Berlin: Georg Siemens.

8. Kratzsch, G. (1969) *Kunstwart und Dürerbund*. Göttingen: Vandenhoeck and Ruprecht.

9. *Mitteilungen des Bundes Heimatschutz*, 1904 ff.

10. See Hermand, J. (1967) *Stilkunst um 1900*. Berlin: Akademie Verlag.

11. *Die Denkmalpflege*, 1899 ff (a companion publication to *Centralblatt der Bauverwaltung*).

12. Collins, G. R. and Collins, C. C. (1965) *Camillo Sitte and the Birth of Modern City Planning*. London: Phaidon Press.

13. Lichtwark, A. (1899) *Palastfenster und Flügelthür*. Berlin. Also in Mannhardt, W. (ed.) (1917) *A. Lichtwark, eine Auswahl aus seinen Schriften*. Berlin: Bruno Cassirer Verlag.

14. Schultze-Naumburg, P. (1903) *Dörfer und Kolonien*, vol. 3 of *Kulturarbeiten*. Munich: D. W. Callwey, pp. 134ff.

15. See *Die Denkmalpflege*; Blunck, E. (1913) *Denkmalpflege und Städtebau*, vol. 6, part 2 in series: *Städtebauliche Vorträge*. Berlin.

16. Weber, P. (1906) *Heimatschutz, Denkmalpflege und Bodenreform*, No. 26 in series: *Soziale Zeitfragen*, edited by A. Damaschke. Berlin.

17. Wieland, C. A. (1905) *Der Denkmal und Heimatschutz in der Gesetzgebung der Gegenwart*. Basle: Friedrich Reinhardt; Kneer, A. (1915) *Denkmalpflege in Deutschland*. München Gladbach.

18. Evans, R. (1893) *The Age of Disfigurement*. London: Remington.

# 4

# The origins and development of a conservation philosophy in Austria[1]

## PETER BREITLING

The term 'conservation' as used in the English-speaking world does not exist in German. The collective noun for the recording, protection and mainten-ance of historically-valuable buildings is *Denkmalschutz* (protection of monuments), or *Denkmalpflege* (preservation of monuments). Discussions have been going on for many years amongst architects, planners and the general public to find an alternative, which better reflects the greater awareness of conservation matters that now exists. There are a number of other new terms in the literature, such as *Rehabilitation* (rehabilitation), *Wiederbelebung* (revitalization), and *Erhaltende Erneuerung* (reinstatement as opposed to renewal) [2]. When dealing with whole settlements or town centres, one uses the term *Stadterhaltung* (town centre preservation) or *Altstadterhaltung* (historic town centre preservation). No German synonym has yet been found for the term 'integrated conservation' coined by the Council of Europe [3]. In his translation of the Council's manifesto, Alfred A. Schmidt uses the literal equivalent of the French and English terms *integrierte Konservierung,* although in German the term *Konservierung* does not imply the protection of buildings as it does in French and English [4].

The difficulty in defining what precisely is meant by the term conservation gives an interesting insight into the relationship of our society to its built heritage, and indeed into the whole question of how best to preserve existing form and structure.

It goes without saying that ever since the Industrial Revolution there have been popular movements in the German-speaking countries, dedicated to the preservation of architectural heritage, notwithstanding the reservations of certain 'progressive' circles. For example, there are a large number of societies referred to collectively, and rather misleadingly, as the *Heimatschutz* (homeland protection), or *Heimatpflege* (homeland preservation) societies [5]. However, both terms are somewhat tainted with the whiff of dilettanteism and parochialism and are somewhat denigrated by many intellectuals in both Germany and Austria, even though there are some well-known academics who have used both of them. Also, in the Federal Republic of Germany, some authorities now regularly consult *Heimatpfleger* (homeland preservationists) when drawing up development plans and action plans for individual communities [6].

Despite the somewhat ambivalent attitude of society as a whole towards conservation, the protection of monuments is now accepted without question, probably because the subject has always been academically respectable and well-documented. There is an academic tradition that for decades has concentrated on recording, evaluating and preserving outstanding architecture from the past, including 'monuments' in the more specific, narrow sense. The growing public interest in conservation since the beginning of the 1970s has not always been an undisguised blessing, and it could well be that the term *Denkmalpflege* (preservation of monuments) will be dropped as the collective noun for all conservation efforts and retained to refer only to *klassischen Denkmalpflege* (protection of classical monuments) [7].

To avoid any misunderstanding in what follows, I shall use the term *conservation* to refer to everything to do with the protection of the historic built environment and with the cultural landscape; the term *Denkmalpflege* to refer to those national and local government bodies and to those legal instruments concerned with conservation. I shall also leave the terms *Heimatschutz* and *Heimatpflege* untranslated.

## ORIGINS OF CONSERVATION IN THE NINETEENTH-CENTURY 'RESTORATION' MOVEMENT [8]

If the term conservation is interpreted very widely, it first appeared in the German-speaking countries as early as the eighteenth century with, for example, the moves to protect archives and to use historic building styles in contemporary developments. In 1769 the choir of the Benedictine church at Maursmunster was rebuilt in the Gothic style and many of the eighteenth and even seventeenth century Gothic pinnacles and finials on Cologne Cathedral were modelled on earlier designs. The first edict on the subject of the protection of archives in Austria was issued by Maria Theresia in 1769.

The first interest in conservation proper in Germany and Austria, as in the rest of Europe, goes back to the nineteenth century and stems from a concern for the historical value of all types of man-made artifacts. As early as the

Wars of Independence imaginative plans were drawn up as a direct result of the trends towards enlightenment and secularization. Sulpiz Boisserée and Karl Friedrich Schinkel pressed for a legally-binding undertaking to help protect historic buildings and even the ageing Goethe became an active supporter. In 1814 and 1816, Görres and Schinkel appealed for the completion of Cologne Cathedral. The time was not ripe however, and for all practical purposes these early efforts were of no significance. It is just possible that the detailed draft of a law for the protection of monuments in Greece, drawn up by the German Professor Maurer in 1834, was a direct outcome of these earlier efforts.

In Germany and Austria, as nearly everywhere else, the work of those two great neo-classical architects Viollet-Le-Duc and Sir George Gilbert Scott dominated the second half of the nineteenth century. The *Kaiserlich Königliche Zentralkommission zur Erfassung und Erhaltung der Baudenkmale* (Imperial Commission for the Recording and Preservation of Historic Buildings), founded in 1853, was charged by the statute of 1872/3 with the duty of restoring, or more precisely recreating the original Roman and more importantly, Gothic styles. Purity of style, rather than the flamboyance of later years was the overriding aim. The strongest personality at the Commission was Friedrich von Schmidt, a man brought up in the traditions of the building industry. He had been dedicated to the recreation of Gothic architectural styles ever since he had worked as chief architect at Vienna Cathedral. His search for stylistic purity and accuracy in every last detail forced him to sacrifice all his own judgements as a craftsman, although ironically this was one of the main distinguishing features of the work of stone masons in the Middle Ages.

Despite a certain aridity and uniformity, the major ecclesiastical buildings of the neo-classical period were an undoubted success. Buildings restored during this period have subsequently been widely denigrated, but it is a tribute to the quality of the work, that the names of even the best of the restorers of Gothic architecture, like Benzinger, Schmitz, Kemp, Steinbrecht and Hertel, are now almost totally forgotten. Hans Hormann has quoted a remark by Sir Frank Baines to the effect that the era of restoration in Germany was blessed with the light of a particularly lucky star, and that, as a result, the country's heritage of well-preserved monuments from the Middle Ages is the richest in Europe [9]. Although not so applicable to Austria, the same applies to some degree here as well.

The fact that St. Stephen's in Vienna and the cathedrals of Ulm, Cologne and Regensburg date in large part from the second half of the nineteenth century is unknown to all but a very few experts. It is possible that the enthusiastic reception given by the general public to the many examples of Gothic restoration staunched the kind of criticism, which today would label such work as simply barbaric. There was no equivalent in the German-speaking countries to the dismissive judgements of men like Ruskin, who

FIGURE 4.1. Left: the church at Klosterneuburg before restoration. Right: the same building after 'restoration' in the nineteenth century. Max Dvorak commented that all traces of its long history were destroyed and the church transformed to a Gothic building.

preferred that monuments be allowed to decay in the remnants of their former glory.

In other ways the influence of the ideas of Ruskin and Morris may certainly be detected in the Austrian protection of monuments movement. Although those opposing restoration in Austria did not cite any English or German sources, there are interesting parallels with statements made by the famous Englishmen and with statements made by the German protection of monuments and *Heimatschutz* movements.

Aside from a few spectacularly successful pieces of church architecture, conservationists now generally consider the restoration period as being rather unimportant for the development of conservation ideas. Nevertheless there are some extremely effective examples of contemporary infilling in the middle of groups of historic buildings. Towards the end of the century, many secular buildings of historic importance were torn down, in many cases to make way for the growing volume of traffic. There certainly was no general appreciation of the value of the built heritage and the less pretentious, everyday buildings and historic town layouts were completely ignored.

In the final analysis the enthusiasm of the 'Gothic revivalists' and the restorationists had a negative effect on conservation policy. Enlightened Austrian Emperors had preserved the traditional building form of plaster-

FIGURE 4.2. The town hall at Gaming, Niederöster-reich constructed in 1898 and demonstrating that the 'Imperial' style survived all the vicissitudes of the late nineteenth century.

FIGURE 4.3. One of the few Austrian examples of Sittesque housing layout is the Bachmann Siedlung at Graz laid out by Adolf Inffeld in 1910.

rendered brickwork and the *Biedermeier* appearance of new buildings. The style survived all the viscissitudes of the second half of the nineteenth century. Without prior knowledge, the more everyday buildings constructed in the 1890s in most Austrian provincial and market towns could easily be thought to be fifty or sixty years older, because the original style was rigidly retained by order of the Imperial civil service. Indirectly therefore, Imperial building policy led to continuity in architectural style and, in a very general way, to preservation policies. The Austrian building tradition has never recovered from the initial trauma caused by the onset of the Gothic restoration period, followed as it was by first secession and then the arrival of foreign architectural influences, which meant that there was little support from parallel trends in architecture for the protection of monuments. The 'romantic' period in architecture, which dominated the years from the turn of the century to the outbreak of the First World War was closely identified with the protection of monuments in Germany, but it has left hardly any traces in Austria. The trifling influence of Camillo Sitte's ideas in his own country is astonishing [10].

## THE 'CLASSICAL PERIOD': THE CONTRIBUTIONS OF ALOIS RIEGL AND MAX DVORAK

About the turn of the century new pressures for conservation began to appear in Austria. They originated in the 1880s and were closely associated with the names of Alois Riegl and Max Dvorak. In a pamphlet produced by the Central Commission, entitled 'The Cult for Contemporary Monuments', Riegl argued the case which produced the decisive change of attitude [11]. He defined two sets of measures for assessing the value of monuments; on the one hand whether there was any historic, artistic or art historical value, on the other whether there was any novelty, economic or antique value. Even today his approach still underpins the basic philosophy behind the protection of monuments, in particular the idea that a monument can be an historical document in its own right. The individual sets of measures still form the basis of the protection of monuments policy in Austria.

Walter Frodl has rightly claimed that Riegl's measures enabled the type of restoration practised previously to be abandoned as official policy. The old system in its pursuit of stylistic uniformity and purity had often led to falsification of the built record, thus, in a sense, making it guilty of forging 'documentary' sources [12].

Max Dvorak pursued Riegl's ideas further and contributed greatly to their general dissemination through the publication of a popular pamphlet entitled 'A Catechism for the Protection of Monuments' [13]. The enduring importance of Dvorak's ideas is shown by the strong similarity, even in matters of quite small detail, between them and the proposals in the papers published to mark the occasion of European Conservation Year in 1975.

The approach adopted in the catechism for the protection of monuments strongly resembled the 'cultural good deeds' of Paul Schultze-Naumburg, particularly in its use of vivid examples and counter examples [14]. In practice, however, Dvorak paid more attention to the protection of monuments as such, than Paul Schultze-Naumburg and the other supporters of a comprehensive conservation policy.

The time was quite obviously ripe for Riegl's and Dvorak's ideas to be enthusiastically espoused and pressure from art historians led to fundamental changes in the way in which monuments were protected in Austria. The Imperial Commission, which had previously been a collective voice including a number of layman, but which had lacked government authority, was reorganized and expanded to include a tightly-organized professional executive. The new organization comprised a central committee, the National Monument Office, the Monument Advisory Service, and the Institute for Art History with Max Dvorak as its first Director. In the individual states the functions of the National Monument Office were carried out by state conservators. In his history of the protection of monuments in Austria, Walter Frodl wrote that,

There was now a well-established organization with a guaranteed budget, which was actually part of the public service and geared to those specific requirements. It had at its disposal the most up-to-date knowledge from all the relevant academic disciplines and, through the new Institute for Art History in the National Monument Office, had access to a unique body, which still, as far as I know, does not exist in this form anywhere else in the world. [15]

In spite of the reforms, a law dealing with the protection of monuments did not follow immediately, even though it had long been accepted as an urgent necessity. There were several unsuccessful attempts to promote one, but the national political upheaval that began in 1918 eventually led to the passing of the Austrian Protection of Monuments Law in 1923. The concept of a strong, centralized organization which had been accepted under the Empire, was retained in the Republic and actually strengthened in the 1920 constitution. This is in sharp contrast to the situation in Germany where even today there is no central government policy on the protection of monuments.

## NOTES ON AUSTRIAN CONSERVATION LAW

On 25th May 1923 Abgeordnete Dr. Angerer introduced a motion proposing a protection of monuments law into the *Nationalrat*—the Austrian Parliament. It was interesting in a number of respects, although it made no detailed proposals, only putting forward general arguments about the need for legal regulations. Angerer argued that there was an urgent need for the law,

> at this particular time, when those classes of people who had traditionally seen it as their task to care for the nation's historical conscience and to preserve its heritage ... faced the prospect of certain financial ruin and for the first time needed to earn money for themselves ... they should still be able to hold up their heads. ... Nearly every advanced nation in the world ... has a law for the protection of monuments. ... In Austria, thanks to the inspiration of men like Riegl and Dvorak, the administrative system for protecting monuments is much more efficient than in other advanced European countries. However, although we have played a pioneering role from both an academic and an organisational point of view, we do not have a law of our own for the protection of monuments. Largely as a result of political oversight, an appropriate bill has never been introduced. [16]

What the *Nationalrat* managed to achieve was extremely important for, despite the fact that the law was watered down considerably during the Parliamentary debate, it has remained in force almost unaltered to the present, except for some rather retrograde modifications made during the period of the *Anschluss* to Germany. Even the most recent amendment has only resulted in minor changes.

As in most other European countries, legal protection for the built environment is restricted to old buildings of historic, artistic or cultural importance, which in the opinion of the appropriate authorities—in this case the *Bundesdenkmalamt* (Office of National Monuments)—are worth preserving in the public interest. It is automatically assumed that it is in the public interest to protect all buildings either wholly or predominantly owned by the State, by a province, by other public bodies, or by recognized church and religious communities. This remains in effect permanently, unless the owner successfully petitions to the contrary.

It goes without saying that in a situation where public buildings are protected *ex lege,* but privately-owned ones only when their value as monuments has been officially recognized by the authorities, those elements deemed to be of 'lesser historical importance' in the fabric of the built environment are gravely at risk when there is a high level of economic activity.

Austrian law does not provide for the protection of whole villages, or areas within towns as a part of the protection of monuments; it is something that is outside the competence of the central government. To overcome this deficiency some of the individual states have passed so-called 'protection of historic centre laws' and 'protection of townscape' laws so that the whole of historically-important city centres and villages may be included. However, with the exception of the preservation laws in Salzburg and Graz, they are very recent and their long-term effect cannot yet be judged with any certainty. Certainly the *Altstadterhaltungsgesetz* (Historic City Preservation Law) in Graz has provided much better protection both for individual buildings and for the historic city centre as a whole, than the general Protection of Monuments Law. Of particular significance is the fact that every building application within the preservation zone must be scrutinized by an independent committee of experts, thus removing almost totally any chance of the decision being affected by political influences [17].

## INTEGRATED CONSERVATION AND TOWN PLANNING IN AUSTRIA AND GERMANY TODAY

The laws pertaining to the protection of monuments in virtually all European countries contain the following ground rules for assessing the historic value of individual buildings and sites. They must date from an earlier period; they must be of either historic, artistic, scientific or cultural importance; and their preservation must be in the public interest [18]. From a legal point of view these three key characteristics—age, importance and degree of public interest—are very hard to define, any assessment being heavily dependent on the particular attitudes and values existing at the time. In the last few years there has been a definite tendency to stretch the limits of both age and importance and, as a result, there has been an increase in what needs to be protected in the public interest. What started as a concern for the future of individual buildings has now spread to include ever larger groups of buildings. Initially only buildings of outstanding historical, or art historical importance were considered, but now architecture that can only be described as run-of-the-mill is being included. Some of it is old, dating from the distant past, but some is relatively recent, sometimes less than a generation old. There are many examples that could be used to illustrate the new trend, but the decision of the *Deutsche Nationalkomittee fur Denkmalschutz* (German National Committee for the Protection of Monuments) on 6th August 1974 is typical,

> The protection of monuments should include individual buildings, groups of buildings, streets and squares. A whole quarter in a town, or exceptionally even the whole of the town can be worth preserving and it must be remembered that even a group of the simplest old houses can be crucial for determining the overall quality of the townscape. Buildings from the nineteenth and twentieth centuries must also be protected today. In some cases it will not be sufficient to protect selected neighbourhoods, the whole cultural landscape will have to be included. [19]

In addition to extending what is meant by the protection of monuments, conservation is now no longer considered a purely defensive activity. Today it incorporates not only the protection of monuments and the organization of this work, but also such things as the modernization of buildings, the improvement of living conditions, questions of land use and economics, as well as several other similar concerns.

The most all-embracing definition of the town conservation produced so far is contained in Resolution 7628 of the Council of Europe, which deals with integrated conservation and the architectural heritage. The 'aim' of this resolution was 'to ensure that the heritage contained in the built environment was not destroyed, that proper provision was made for the upkeep of major buildings and natural features, and to make sure that what was conserved was adapted to the needs of society. Such measures are not merely a matter of conservation, they are essential for reviving and rehabilitating the environment'. It will be clear from what has been said that integrated conservation is seen as an indivisible part of town and country planning, or in the words of the resolution, is 'one of the fundamental ingredients of land use planning' [20].

It goes without saying that the almost unlimited proliferation of conservation-related tasks implied in the Council's resolution makes the phrase 'protection of monuments' as defined in the Austrian Protection of Monuments Law virtually irrelevant. It is of fundamental importance to decide whether this comprehensive strategy for preserving everything of historical importance is to be referred to as the protection of monuments or urban renewal. In any case the new definition of conservation has some interesting implications for the future of town planning. Speaking on this very subject at the fourth Council of Europe Symposium in Berlin in 1976, Leonardo Benevolo said that,

> Today one is faced with the task of renewing historic town centres, starting at the periphery; tomorrow the periphery will have to be renewed, starting at the historic town centre. In the last analysis it is not a question of creating a privileged special zone within the town, but rather a search for an overall concept around which the whole future of the town can be built, so that eventually it can be called 'modern'. [21]

*Conservation integrée* and town planning gave a strong new impulsion to the preservation and protection of the built heritage. The town planning situation in which we now find ourselves at the beginning of the 1980s can, in some ways, be compared with that at the end of the 1880s when Camillo Sitte inveighed against the formlessness and dullness of contemporary urban suburbs in his book of 1899, *City Planning according to Artistic Principles,* and received widespread support for his views [22].


## AUSTRIAN ARCHITECTS' VIEWS ON THE ARCHITECTURAL HERITAGE

A peculiarity in the Austrian situation is that architects, who as a profession did not come down on one side or the other in this issue initially, have recently come out strongly against protection and are vehemently opposing the efforts of some individual provincial governments to pass local townscape protection laws. Austrian architects do sometimes admit that almost everything that has been built to replace the historic fabric in the last twenty years is unsatisfactory, as are the new additions that have been made to existing villages and towns. However, they always qualify such an admission by claiming that the main fault with any given plan was that it did not have the benefit of the 'right' architects; had better architects been employed, they always maintain, a most satisfactory result could have been achieved.

Serious attempts to define what would be accepted as good architecture in an historic environment, or what makes for the best kind of infilling within an historic group of buildings, have so far not been attempted in any of the German-speaking countries. All the relevant meetings and conferences have so far been satisfied with the somewhat tautological answer, that 'good' is what 'good' architects think to be 'good' [23].

Revised standards for a new approach to architecture will never emerge from discussions amongst architects alone. Provincial governments stick rigidly to the official interpretations of local conservation laws and, in questions of design, rely almost entirely on the opinions of 'the educated man in the street', who is taken to be the official legal arbiter in such matters in all the German-speaking countries. The best general commentary on this state of affairs was made some seventy years ago in 1911, in the introduction to the official plan for Hellerau Garden City near Dresden:

> If there were such a thing as a generally accepted artistic tradition in all matters architectural and, in particular, in house design and town planning, then building proposals with only minority approval would be acceptable. A dynamic and architecturally educated way of thinking about building, imbued with a general sense of social responsibility, would make it possible to abandon official guidelines and allow towns to grow up as villages and towns did in the old days. They would be good and safe, and secure as expressions of a new culture and new customs.
>
> At the present time we are still a long way from such a goal—indeed there must be grave doubt whether it would ever be attainable. Postwar society has almost self-consciously rejected its antecedents, but has still not decided what it wants from the future, let alone how it is going to satisfy its aspirations in an appropriate way. Nor has it decided what kind of education and civilization it is striving for. The whole issue is still a matter for debate and, all too often, parochial self-interest is allowed to dominate the wider needs of the community as a whole. The absence of agreed cultural values also provokes again and again the rigour of the authorities. [24]

It may seem regrettable that in matters of conservation and preservation Austria is unwilling to override the power of the bureaucrats. It may be that this very inability will itself eventually be the touchstone in a search for new standards. For the search to be successful, it would have to be completely unpatronizing and free of any taint of élitism. It might, however, eventually lead to the creation of a formal terminology, free of both pomposity and artistic snobbery. It might also make people more patient with the attempts made by our politicians to explain, in their own way, the spirit of our times. 'To be able to inherit, that is the very essence of what we call culture' Thomas Mann once said. Even if one only accepts this point of view in principle, it follows that governments and parliaments have to be allowed to participate in this neglected aspect of architectural planning as they see fit.

I believe that the way Austrian architects denounce every draft of every conservation law as the product of small-minded parochialism, and the way they plead for exceptions to be made for the 'good architects', does their cause more harm than good. No local preservation law can be phrased so narrowly that it completely stifles professional flare; in any case it is up to the professionals to rise to the challenge of such limitations.

It is arguable that conservation laws would not have been necessary at all, had architects been more successful in finding that natural order, which is the key to the relationship between man, nature, towns and history.

NOTES

1. Translated from the German by Mark Blacksell, Department of Geography, University of Exeter.

2. I have made several attempts to 'naturalize' the term *Rehabilitation* in German as, for instance, in (1973) Gefährdet Sanierung die Individualität unserer Städte. *Deutsche Kunst und Denkmalpflege,* 31 (1), p. 140; on *Wiederbelebung* see Foramitti, H. and Leisching, P. (1971) *Wiederbelebung historischer Stadtviertel, die Lösung in Frankreich als mögliches Vorbild,* Graz: Styria Verlag; and on *Erhaltende Erneurung* there is Deutsches Nationalkomitee für Denkmalschutz und Deutsche UNESCO Kommission (1974) *Historische Städte, Städte für Morgen.* Köln: Deutsche UNESCO Kommission.
3. Council of Europe (1976) *Résolution sur l'adaption des systèmes législatifs et réglementaires aux exigences de la conservation integrée du patrimoine architectural.* Strasbourg: Council of Europe.
4. Professor Alfred A. Schmid is Chairman of the Committee for Monuments and Sites of the Council of Europe and has recommended the use of the term 'integrated conservation' in a number of papers and conferences.
5. See Stefan Muthesius' article 'The Origins of the German Conservation movement' in this volume.
6. Consultation of advocates of public interests has been legally fixed as a rule in the 1960 German Town Planning Act, and some states recognize the *Heimatpfleger* as such.
7. Durian-Ress, S. (1975) Klassische Denkmalpflege, in Bayerisches Landesamt für Denkmalpflege (ed.), *Eine Zukunft für unsere Vergangenheit.* München: Prestel Verlag.
8. A comprehensive survey of the development of Austrian conservation policy is in Pötschner, P. (ed.) (1970) *Denkmalpflege in Österreich 1945–1970.* Wien: Selbstverlag des Bundesdenkmalamtes; Hocke, N. (1975) *Denkmalschutz in Österreich.* Wien: Jupiterverlag; and Gebessler, A. (1975) Zur Geschichte der Denkmalpflege. *Das Münster,* 1 and 2.
9. Hörmann, H. (1937) *Methodik der Denkmalpflege.* München: Neuer Filserverlag.
10. Collins, G. R. and Collins, C. (1965) *Camillo Sitte and the Birth of Modern City Planning.* London: Phaidon Press.
11. Riegl, A. (1903) *Wesen und Entstehung des modernen Denkmalkultus.* Wien: Verlag der K. K. Zentralkommission.
12. Frodl, W. (1970) Die staatliche Denkmalpflege in Österreich, in Pötschner, P. (ed.) *Denkmalpflege in Österreich 1945–1970.* Wien: Selbstverlag des Bundes-denkmalamtes, p. 13.
13. Dvorak, M. (1918) *Katechismus der Denkmalpflege,* 2nd ed. Wien: Anton Schroll.
14. Schultze-Naumburg, P. (1901–17) *Kulturarbeiten,* 9 vols. München: D. W. Callwey.
15. Frodl, W. (1970) Die straatliche Denkmalpflege in Österreich, in Pötschner, P. (ed.), *Denkmalpflege in Österreich 1945–1970.* Wien: Selbstverlag des Bundes-denkmalamtes, p. 14.
16. Helfgott, N. (ed.) (1979) *Die Rechtsvorschriften für den Denkmalschutz.* Wien: Mannsche Verlags und Universitätsbuchhandlung, p. 6.
17. Breitling, P. (1978) Wie man eine Altstadt rettet. *Merian,* 31 (9), p. 19.
18. Hingst, H. and Lipowschek, A. (eds.) (1975) *Europäische Denkmalschutzgesetze,* vol. II. Neumünster: Karl Wachholtz Verlag.
19. Beschluss uber die Konzeption für das Europäische Denkmalschutzjahr 1975, in Bayerisches Landesamt für Denkmalpflege (ed.) (1975) *Eine Zukunft für unsere Vergangenheit.* München: Prestel Verlag.

20. Council of Europe (1976) *Résolution sur l'adaption des systèmes législatifs et réglementaires aux exigences de la conservation integrée du patrimoine architectural.* Strasbourg: Council of Europe.
21. Benevolo, L. (1976) Denkmalschutz und Städtebau, Versuch einer Bilanz. Unpublished mimeographed paper, p. 5.
22. Sitte, Camillo (1965) *City Planning according to Artistic Principles,* translated by George R. Collins and Christiane C. Collins. London: Phaidon Press and New York: Random House.
23. Some proof for this tendency is to be found in an exhibition prepared by German and Austrian Architects Associations entitled, 'New Buildings in Historic Areas'. The only rule which can be discerned in its documentation is a statement in the introduction to the catalogue requiring exclusivity for the 'good architect' in urban infilling. See, Bayerische Architektenkammer (ed.) (1978) *Neues Bauen in alter Umgebung.* München: Selbstverlag der 'Neuen Sammlung', p. 5.
24. Quoted from Hartmann, K. (1976) *Deutsche Gartenstadtbewegung.* München: Moos Verlag, p. 49.

# 5

# Camillo Sitte reappraised

## GEORGE R. COLLINS
## and
## CHRISTIANE C. COLLINS

It is the intention in this paper to up-date the conclusions to be found in the book that we published in 1965: *Camillo Sitte and the Birth of Modern City Planning* [1]. The first three sections (pp. 63–7) are written by GRC and the fourth (pp. 67–71) by CCC.

This title still seems to us to be appropriate. Sitte's book in its German and French editions flourished during the years 1889–1921, precisely the decades of formation of the international profession of city planning. Sitte's little volume, his subsequent individual essays, and his posthumous periodical *Der Städtebau* were a substantial contribution to the young profession, but in what ways specifically remains somewhat ambiguous, in part because the principles he enunciated, once expressed, became truisms; many individuals who were later to make essentially the same points were unaware that Camillo Sitte was the ultimate source of such ideas.

In fact, the precepts concerning city planning that were articulated by Sitte are so basic as to be obvious. Are they obvious, however, because they had inevitably to arise given the urban conditions of late nineteenth-century Europe, or is it because they are constituent elements of planning at all times, surfacing periodically throughout history?

### APPROACHES TO THE PLANNING PROCESS

Looked at in a certain way it might be said that approaches to the planning process are of two contrasting characters. On the one hand, there is the large schematic or abstract plan, sometimes geometrical and often regional in scope. On the other hand, there is its opposite—essentially what Sitte advised—of architectural, landscaping, or city-building scale, which in comparison is more adaptive, *ad hoc*, or even of a 'tinkering' nature.

The first of these tends not to be detailed, although a 'master plan' may be accompanied by more detailed schematics embracing smaller geographical areas but of the same sort of generalized character. Examples of this attitude would be Daniel Burnham's overall Chicago plan of 1909, Arthur Comey's continental triangulation of 1923 (which did indeed focus down in seven stops, but remained schematic), Frank Lloyd Wright's Broadacre City of 1932, Le Corbusier's *cité industrielle linéaire* of the late 1930s, or Archigram's Plug-In City of the 1960s. These are obviously all on too grand a scale for the perception of any human conditions such as construction or context, and certainly no aesthetic judgments could be made of the area encompassed in the plan unless from a satellite. The rendered plan itself often does involve an aesthetic, however, which makes it somewhat suspect.

The second approach proceeds from utterly different assumptions: How does one design or reform an urban space or street so as to fit the particular needs of its users? How does one design a dwelling and its immediate vicinity; i.e., how does one furnish the surroundings (not the interior) of a dwelling? How does one formulate the appearance of a structure that is to be inserted into an existing gap in a street wall or plaza wall? How, in architectural parlance, does one 'turn a corner', viz., relate what one is doing to what was earlier there or is adjacent?

Needless to say these two basic attitudes toward planning are nearly always present and should, one would think, be able to be combined—the universal plan and the specific working details—but perhaps because planning is so often fraught with polemics, this seldom if ever occurs, and instead the two tendencies seem to see-saw cyclically over time. It may be that the entire history of planning in the West can be seen as a fluctuation between these two attitudes.

We can say that the second type persisted almost exclusively in planning until Greek times when the gridiron plan became popular, when the Romans applied it with centuriation, and when a geometrically-perfect city plan was described in the Book of Revelation.

Such aspects of the first (i.e., regularized) type as existed in the ancient world presumably disappeared (except for some of the bastides) during the medieval period. In any case, medieval times are held up as a model of the second type of planning. Sitte, like his earlier contemporary Viollet-le-Duc with respect to architecture, explained the apparent casualness of design in the Middle Ages as being essentially rational, i.e., carried out with foresight.

The Renaissance in the West saw the re-emergence of schematic planning, in theory at least, although only in towns of limited size and not as regional planning. These plans were decidedly geometric, favouring the radiocentric polygon as if the Renaissance were regularizing or schematizing the natural town growth patterns of the later Middle Ages. In the Baroque period such plans were extended out from their geometrically-designed nuclei, often through regular landscaping. In fact, it might be said that from this time on a number of formularized schematics began to be applied in routine ways, especially in the nineteenth century, and this led to those circumstances that Sitte was to castigate, although he was generally enthusiastic about Baroque design and used the piazza of St. Peter's in Rome as his book's frontispiece. In fact, as we have pointed out [2], Sitte's *Der Städtebau* can be considered an early example of the late nineteenth-century Baroque revival of which a culminating instance was Daniel Burnham's Chicago plan, previously mentioned.

Although this universal history that has been outlined here may be overly simplistic, like a schematic plan itself, it does suggest that although *ad hoc* and abstract planning dominated, respectively, in extended cycles throughout history, the really large abstract planning procedure that is described at the outset has been primarily a development of modern times when technology became sufficiently sophisticated for such plans to be visualized in terms of other than cosmic order.

If we take Sitte to be a reaction to the mechanical application of the abstract plan, the question then arises as to whether he represents a unique modern phenomenon in the realm of city planning or whether he was merely playing out the recurring cyclical history that we have here abstracted. When we translated him and wrote our book about him in the early 1960s, we thought the former to be the case, but now we are less sure.

It may be that when Sitte registered his surprise in the preface to the second printing of his book, that was necessary only a month after it had first appeared, and later remarked that 'a literary work can provoke such an effect only when the whole matter is already in the air' [3], the explanation was that his little volume had simply triggered a sudden switch in the cycles of rapidly increasing frequency. The manner in which the cycles have continued to speed up, particularly in the last decade or so, would tend to substantiate this.

### SITTE'S TOWN PLANNING PHILOSOPHY

What, in most basic terms, was the thrust of Sitte's book? He himself said retrospectively in the preface to his edition of 1901, 'to go to school with Nature and the old masters also in matters of town planning' [4]. By this he did not mean, however, to 'copy' in the usual nineteenth-century sense of revivalism or historicism. Here was an architect who, in the very heyday of eclecticism—when its doctrine had hardened into what we call 'speaking architecture' in which certain styles had been crystallized into symbols (or signs) for one programme or another (classic banks, medieval churches, Baroque public buildings, and the like)—had the courage to say: away with specific styles! Let us see what lies behind it all, what are the effective organizational principles that operate in the whole of which individual buildings are a part? What are the relevant virtues of the different methods of the past—medieval layouts, Renaissance–Baroque layouts, modern grids? What sort of equilibrium should be sought between technician and artist or between engineer and architect in these matters?

In the decades that followed, many a romantic absurdity was perpetuated in the tradition of Sitte's reverence for the past. We find little basis for this, however, in the writing of Sitte himself:

> Modern living as well as modern building techniques no longer permit the faithful imitation of old townscapes, a fact which we cannot overlook without falling prey to barren fantasies. The exemplary creations of the old masters must remain alive with us in some other way than through slavish copying; only if we can determine in what the essentials of these creations consist, and if we can apply these meaningfully to modern conditions, will it be possible to harvest a new and flourishing crop from the apparently sterile soil. [5]

Sitte was ultimately concerned with the crisis that the resident in an urban setting was experiencing *vis-à-vis* his immediate surroundings:

> What counts in this is the position of the spectator and the direction in which he is looking. [6]
> Only that which a spectator can hold in view, what can be seen, is of artistic importance. [7]

While here expressed in purely aesthetic terms, his ultimate purpose was more social in nature; he was, for instance, fighting a tendency about which he commented 'the life of the common people has for centuries been steadily withdrawing from public squares, and especially so in recent times' [8]. This has accelerated since his time. It was not long after Sitte's book appeared that Georg Simmel, the German philosopher-sociologist, in his 'The Metropolis and Mental Life', was also to personalize the urban experience by seeking the rules that operated behind the appearances in social conduct of individuals [9].

By the early twentieth century one might say that Sitte's ideas had been considerably elaborated upon and that the movement in architectural planning that he had initiated had come to embrace quite a variety of interests. On the one hand, individuals like A. E. Brinckmann submitted 'classic' plaza groupings to more extended analysis [10] and on the other hand, a new picturesque aesthetic developed—especially with respect to an enthusiasm for medieval and/or local vernacular styles. The latter are exemplified by Camille Martin's influential French edition of Sitte's book of 1902 and 1918 and by the publications of such writers as the architect Paul Schultze-Naumburg who enthused over ethnic German streetscapes [11]. And, finally, Werner Hegemann's *Civic Art* of 1922 interprets Sitte as an adherent of Renaissance/Baroque principles [12]. As Sitte himself stressed principles rather than stylisms, these varied interpretations of his argumentation are not surprising.

One could take the 1920s and 1930s, however, as a period of relative suppression of the Sittesque tradition (although as Nikolaus Pevsner has pointed out both Christopher Hussey's *The Picturesque* and Kenneth Clark's *The Gothic Revival* were published at the very peak of the austere modern style—1927/28 [13]). Typical of what happened to Sitte was his negative treatment at the hands of Le Corbusier who, an enthusiast for Sitte's way in his youth, then turned on him (calling it 'the pack donkey's way') in favour of the geometries that characterize Corbusian planning of the 1920s and 1930s. The Sittesque did not again move into a dominant position until the mid-1940s with the appearance of Eliel Saarinen's book *The City* in 1943 and the American translation of Sitte in 1945 [14]. This coincided with the first stirrings of the British Townscape movement in the pages of *The Architectural Review*, a movement that quickly attained a crescendo. Then in the later 1960s the Sittesque tended to become somewhat recessive (although Townscape was still strong) because of the flourishing of visionary architecture and planning which tended to stress technology and authoritarian utopianism to the point of megascale [15]. By the mid-1970s, however, the Visionaries were faltering. In part owing to environmentalism, the preservation movement, and the energy crisis, the Sittesque has taken over again, now bearing new names—collage, adhocism, recycling, contextualism—as part of a backlash that is currently belabouring the functional, the neat, the large scale, and the big plan in design.

## THE TOWNSCAPE MOVEMENT

A brief survey of the chronology and particular circumstances of the postwar Townscape movement and of the contextual revival of today, neither of which was discussed at length in our Sitte book, might be appropriate.

Townscape ideas in the twentieth century actually have other and earlier sources than Sitte; in fact, some of its practitioners were possibly unaware of him. Townscapes are to be seen in the oldest pictorial paintings, mosaics, and reliefs; over the heads and shoulders of figures in the Middle Ages; in the Renaissance and Baroque as full paintings; attaining great popularity in the eighteenth century among *veduta* painters. Pugin's *Contrasts* and Ruskin's diatribes against the new metropolises are ancestors of the movement as were the popular nineteenth-century travel books with their elaborately detailed illustrations from which Sitte himself borrowed. In fact, Sitte opens his book with the following words:

Enchanting recollections of travel form part of our most pleasant reveries. Magnificent town views, monuments and public squares, beautiful vistas all parade before our musing eye, and we savor again the delights of those sublime and graceful things in whose presence we were once so happy. [16]

The twentieth-century movement that bears the name Townscape originated in the January 1944 issue of *The Architectural Review* with a piece on 'Exterior furnishing or sharawaggi: the art of making urban landscape', with a subtitle 'How to let Bill Brown see what he is going to get' [17]. This was followed in time by similar articles, but the term 'Townscape' was not coined until five years later in the same periodical, at which point the 'Townscape Casebook' began [18]. Meanwhile Thomas Sharp's *Anatomy of the Village* and J. M. Richards' *The Castles on the Ground* of 1946 and Frederick Gibberd's '3-D aspects of housing layout' of 1948 made similar noises in high places, architecturally speaking [19].

The 1950s were too dense with related publications to begin to list them here, but we might cite the psychologist James J. Gibson's *Perception of the Visual World* of 1950, Steen Eiler Rasmussen's *Towns and Buildings* of the following year, Frederick Gibberd's *Town Design* of 1953, G. Kidder Smith's *Italy Builds* and Gordon Logie's *Urban Scene* of 1954 [20]. That same year Nikolaus Pevsner in his 'C20 picturesque' drew attention to the latent picturesque tendencies in the International Style, to which we have referred.

In the 1960s a number of extended book-length studies entitled 'Townscape' appeared: Gordon Cullen's first edition of that name in 1961, Ivor de Wolfe's *Italian Townscape* in 1963, and Carlos Flores' 'Townscape español' in 1966 [21]. And the movement began to shift from the aesthetics of perception to more social issues with Kevin Lynch's *Image of the City* of 1960 and Jane Jacobs' *Death and Life of Great American Cities* in 1961; it internalized itself with E. T. Hall's *Hidden Dimension* of 1966, and an entire history of the city à la Townscape was provided by Edward Bacon in 1967 [22]. Polemical architectural tracts were published by Lawrence Halprin in 1963, Bernard Rudofsky in 1964, and Theo Crosby in 1965 [23]. Still vigorous, but now decidedly over-shadowed by the Visionaries, the Townscape movement had been broadened from a largely pictorial aesthetic into promotion of pedestrianization of the city and study of the social nature of the street and of the relation of behaviour to environment; all of which extended decidedly its architectural origins and, incidentally, expanded on the very precepts enunciated by that now distant figure, Camillo Sitte.

Although it did not surface until somewhat later, the mode of 'contextualism' (read 'neo-Sitte') apparently was born at the Cornell University School of Architecture in the mid-1960s, stimulated in part by a renewed interest in the Viennese planner. It represents a growing concern, in design, with the individual physical surroundings of any project, i.e., its context. It is more of a design process than an aesthetic attitude, but that is precisely what Sitte's book had turned out to be: a German magazine which delayed for a year (i.e., until 1890) to review it found that it had to report on the changes wrought by the book rather than on the book itself [24]. Exponents today of this renewed Sittesque, not all of whom call it contextualism, include Tom Schumacher in a special issue of *Casabella* in

1971, Stuart Cohen (a co-inventor of the term) in *Oppositions 2* of 1974, Colin Rowe and Fred Koetter, who call it 'Collage City' in *The Architectural Review* for August 1975, and Rob Krier—out-and-out neo-Sitte—with his book about his Stuttgart plan of the same year [25]. Associated with this is the adhocism of Charles Jencks and Nathan Silver (1972) [26] insofar as it deals with urban environment, and the consortium of recent books and articles heaping abuse on the functionalism of the 1920s and 'modernism' in general. Both Brent Brolin's *The Failure of Modern Architecture* and Charles Jencks' *The Language of Post-Modern Architecture* seem to be seeking a type of harmony or 'fit' and are essentially faced with the problem of whether at any time in history *one person* has ever succeeded in designing a streetscape in other than a uniform manner [27]. The answer is Yes: Main Street, U.S.A. at Disneyworld', but that hardly solves the problems that they pose. Adhocism is, of course, a process and a critique—launched against the very type of large schematic (type one) planning with which this paper began. We have, in a sense, come full circle.

So we could conclude—or step aside—with the original question still haunting us: is the Sittesque as a mode of analysis and planning endemic, surfacing from time to time in history in cyclical fashion, or is it a uniquely modern phenomenon, the search for a retrospective urban aesthetic that only survives in the Old World and places like Boston, Massachusetts? It is an attitude that has been negated by modern city development everywhere, but yet is periodically entertained in our century as perhaps the only hope of making the individual at home in the urban environment.

## THE RELEVANCE OF SITTE'S *STÄDTEBAU*

There are other things that make Camillo Sitte's *Städtebau* vital to us today that were not as clear when we published the work in 1965.

One is Sitte's upholding the ideal of vernacular architecture and planning. In some passages in his book he is frankly anti-professional, making 'engineers' and other technicians responsible for the failure of the contemporary urban environment. He sought salvation through some 'artistic' architect/planner who might be able to recreate what had grown up anonymously over centuries. Sitte was attracted by the innate sense of place and scale in plazas and streets that had been created by those who were actually using these spaces and were adapted by them over periods of time to fit the changing needs (figures 5.1 and 5.2).

As we puzzle today over the theoretical attractions and practical pit-falls of citizen participation in the planning process, we are drawn to vernacular building; in studying it systematically for its aesthetic merits, Sitte was a pioneer. His analysis of plazas and streets is akin to study of the arts and crafts. We must remember that although he was a practising architect, he spent most of his career as the head of art schools: first the State School of

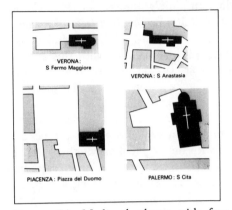

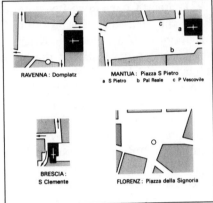

FIGURE 5.1. Medieval plazas with free centres.

FIGURE 5.2. Older enclosed squares.

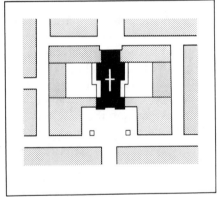

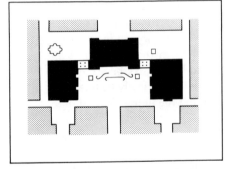

FIGURE 5.3. Sitte's own plan for the setting of a church.

FIGURE 5.4. Sitte's own plan for the setting of a theatre.

Applied Arts in Salzburg, and later he organized the new Kunstgewerbe-schule in Vienna. He published extensively on subjects related to the interests of such schools.

This brings us to another point. Analysis of folk art and ornament leads to an awareness of pattern—pattern that can be abstracted out and thereby becomes universal. Sitte's analysis of town plans—which he viewed in a detached manner from towers, high towers that he would ascend—can be compared to the study of design in such arts; for instance, he published a study of Islamic ornament. From this it was just another step to his attempt to discover universal principles in planning, universal and timeless language that could be applied to contemporary and future situations.

*Der Städtebau* is then a pattern book in two basic meanings of the term 'pattern': first as a model, guide, plan, or paradigm; and secondly as an arrangement of form, disposition of parts or elements (figures 5.3 and 5.4).

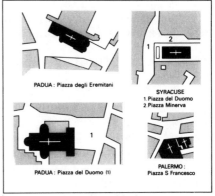

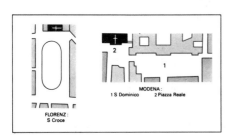

FIGURE 5.5. A deep and broad plaza.          FIGURE 5.6. Irregular old plazas.

Recent fascination with pattern, such as the semiotic analysis of ornament and of individual elements within a whole, makes us especially receptive to Sitte's analysis.

Rob Krier's *Stadtraum in Theorie und Praxis,* and *A Pattern Language* by a team under the leadership of Christopher Alexander are clearly evolved from Sitte's approach of reducing the complex to working principles that can, hopefully, be applied to solving problems in different situations [28].

These pattern principles of Sitte's are timeless and universal: they are chosen from a wide geographical area and range chronologically from Roman times to his day (figures 5.5 and 5.6). They also relate, like compositional elements in tiles or textiles, to the contiguity of such elements, and the pattern will lose meaning without this relationship. We have to think of Sitte's diagrams of plazas within a context of place as well as possessing the ability of enduring within a process of urban change. Quoting from *A Pattern Language:*

> . . . no pattern is an isolated entity. Each pattern can exist in the world only to the extent that it is supported by other patterns: the larger patterns in which it is embedded, the patterns of the same size that surround it, and the smaller patterns which are embedded in it. This is a fundamental view of the world. It says that when you build a thing you cannot merely build that thing in isolation, but must also repair the world around it, and within it, so that the larger world at that one place becomes more coherent, and more whole; and the thing which you make takes its place in the web of nature, as you make it. [29]

Let us look, then, at these patterning principles of that late nineteenth-century Viennese as a way toward an evolving unity and universality in planning.

NOTES

1. Collins, George R. and Collins, Christiane C. (1965) *Camillo Sitte and the Birth of Modern City Planning.* London: Phaidon Press and New York: Random House.

2. *Ibid.*, note 95.
3. Sitte, Camillo (1901) *Der Städte-Bau nach seinen künstlerischen Grundsätzen,* 3rd ed. Vienna: Graeser and Leipzig: B. G. Teubner, Preface.
4. *Idem.*
5. Sitte, Camillo (1965) *City Planning according to Artistic Principles,* translated by George R. Collins and Christiane C. Collins. London: Phaidon Press and New York: Random House, p. 111.
6. *Ibid.*, p. 39.
7. *Ibid.*, pp. 91, 92.
8. *Ibid.*, p. 106.
9. A lecture of about 1908 (?), translated in Wolff, Kurt H. (1950) *The Sociology of Georg Simmel.* New York: The Free Press.
10. Brinckmann, Albert E. (1908) *Platz und Monument.* Berlin: Wasmuth. Further editions 1912, 1923.
11. Sitte, Camillo (1902) *L'art de Bâtir les Villes.* Notes et Réflexions d'un Architect traduites et completées par Camille Martin. Geneva: Ch. Eggiman & Cie. and Paris: Librairie Renouard, 2nd ed. 1918; Schultze-Naumburg, P. (1906) *Städtebau,* Vol. 4 of *Kulturarbeiten.* Munich: D. W. Callwey, 2nd ed. 1909.
12. Hegemann, Werner, and Peets, Elbert (1922) *The American Vitruvius: An Architects' Handbook of Civic Art.* New York: Architectural Book Publishing Co.
13. Pevsner, Nikolaus (1954) C20 picturesque. *Architectural Review,* 115 (688), pp. 227–9.
14. Saarinen, Eliel (1943) *The City, its Growth, its Decay, its Future.* New York: Reinhold; Sitte, Camillo (1945) *The Art of Building Cities,* translated by Charles T. Stewart. New York: Reinhold.
15. Collins, George R. (1979) *Visionary Drawings of Architecture and Planning: 20th Century through the 1960s.* Cambridge, Mass.: MIT Press.
16. Sitte, Camillo (1965) *City Planning according to Artistic Principles,* translated by George R. Collins and Christiane C. Collins. London: Phaidon Press and New York: Random House, p. 3.
17. De Wolfe, Ivor (1944) *Architectural Review,* 95 (565), pp. 3–8.
18. De Wolfe, Ivor and Cullen, Gordon (1949) *Architectural Review,* 106 (636), pp. 355–74.
19. Sharp, Thomas (1946) *Anatomy of the Village.* Harmondsworth: Penguin; Richards, J. M. (1946) *The Castles on the Ground: The Anatomy of Suburbia.* London: Architectural Press. Revised 1973; Gibberd, Frederick (1948) 3-D aspects of housing layout. *Journal of the Royal Institute of British Architects,* 55, pp. 433–42.
20. Gibson, James J. (1950) *Perception of the Visual World.* Boston: Houghton Mifflin; Rasmussen, Steen Eiler (1951) *Towns and Buildings Described in Drawings and Words.* Cambridge, Mass.: Harvard University Press. There had been a Danish edition in 1949. The MIT Press published it in paperback in 1969; Gibberd, Frederick (1953) *Town Design.* London: Architectural Press, many later editions; Smith, George Kidder (1954) *Italy Builds.* New York: Reinhold; Logie, Gordon (1954) *The Urban Scene.* London: Faber and Faber.
21. Cullen, Gordon (1961) *Townscape.* London: Architectural Press. Reissue in concise paperback 1971; De Wolfe, Ivor (1963) *The Italian Townscape.* London:

Architectural Press; Flores, Carlos (1966) Townscape español. *Hogar y Arquitectura,* no. 65, special issue.

22. Lynch, Kevin (1960) *Image of the City.* Cambridge, Mass. MIT Press; Jacobs, Jane (1961) *Death and Life of Great American Cities.* New York: Random House; Hall, E. T. (1966) *The Hidden Dimension.* New York: Doubleday; Bacon, Edmund N. (1967) *Design of Cities.* New York: Viking Press, revised 1974.

23. Halprin, Lawrence (1963) *Cities.* New York: Reinhold; revised, Cambridge, Mass.: The MIT Press, 1972; Rudofsky, Bernard (1964) *Architecture without Architects: An introduction to Non-pedigreed Architecture.* New York: Museum of Modern Art; Crosby, Theo (1965) *Architecture: City Sense.* London: Studio Vista.

24. Collins, George R. and Collins, Christiane C. (1965) *Camillo Sitte and the Birth of Modern City Planning.* London: Phaidon Press and New York: Random House, p. 76.

25. Schumacher, Tom (1971) Contestualismo: ideali urbani deformati. *Casabella,* 35 (359–60), pp. 78–86, also in English; Cohen, Stuart (1974) Physical context/ cultural context: including it all. *Oppositions 2,* pp. 1–40; Rowe, Colin and Koetter, Fred (1975) Collage city. *Architectural Review,* 158 (942), pp. 66–91, see also Rowe, Colin and Koetter, Fred (1979) *Collage City.* Cambridge, Mass.: MIT Press; Krier, Rob (1975) *Stadtraum: Theorie und Praxis.* Stuttgart: Karl Kramer Verlag.

26. Jencks, Charles and Silver, Nathan (1972) *Adhocism: The Case for Improvization.* New York: Doubleday.

27. Brolin, Brent C. (1976) *The Failure of Modern Architecture.* New York: Van Nostrand Reinhold; Jencks, Charles (1977) *The Language of Post-modern Architecture.* London: Academy Editions. Updated in *Architectural Design,* January, 1978, and separately.

28. Krier, Rob (1975) *Stadtraum: Theorie und Praxis.* Stuttgart: Karl Kramer Verlag. Alexander, Christopher and others (1977) *A Pattern Language.* New York: Oxford University Press.

29. *Ibid.,* p. xiii.

# 6

# The reconstruction of Kalisz, Poland, following its destruction in 1914

## TERESA ZAREBSKA

The Polish town of Kalisz with a population of just over 80,000 today has much to interest conservation planners. It suffered terrible destruction during the First World War but is now one of the showpieces of Polish restoration architecture. Many of the principles of reconstruction developed at Kalisz were later applied to the rebuilding of Warsaw after World War II.

### THE HISTORY AND TOPOGRAPHIC DEVELOPMENT OF KALISZ TO 1914

Kalisz is situated in the preglacial valley of two small rivers, the Prosna and the Swedrnia. During the Roman Empire the so-called 'amber route' led through Kalisz; about 200 archaeological sites have been recorded in the town and its close vicinity, and many Roman remains have been discovered [1]. Evidence of very ancient settlement has been confirmed in the northern, western and south-eastern districts of the present town [2].

In the south-eastern district a ducal castle was built between the two rivers in the ninth century AD [3]. Close by the castle a small settlement grew up comprising a fortified borough, an open borough and a trading centre [4]. A number of villages located up to about twenty kilometres around the borough completed the settlement system of this area at the end of the early Middle Ages (the eleventh and twelfth centuries) [5] (figure 6.1).

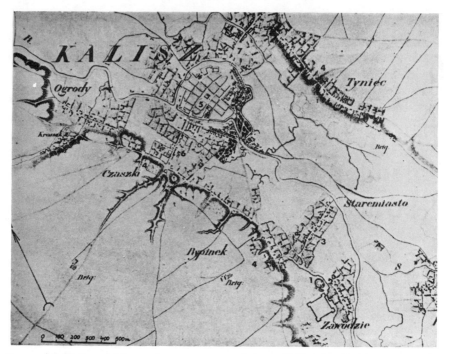

FIGURE 6.1. Kalisz and its environs on a map of about 1820 (after H. Münch). *1* is the old castle destroyed in 1233; *2* the settlement which grew up by the castle; *3* the commercial settlement or Old Town of Kalisz; *4* dependent villages founded in the early Middle Ages; *5* New Kalisz founded in the middle of the thirteenth century; *6* the Wroclaw suburb; *7* the Toruń suburb.

The town was first reconstructed in the high Middle Ages when Poland was subdivided into a number of autonomous duchies. The Duchy of Kalisz was relatively small and remained independent for less than a hundred years. The old castle and borough were destroyed in 1233 and soon after this the town was rebuilt to a plan with all the features of a large city scaled down for a provincial capital. A town centre was created on an artificial island, peripheral quarters were arranged round it, and it was joined to the ducal castle [6] (figure 6.2). The island and defence walls were almost circular, only the western part of the fortifications was rectangular and this protected a district separate from the rest and known as the 'Jewish town'. In 1264 this obtained separate legal status [7].

A single thoroughfare ran across the island and after entering the town gates it forked to produce an elliptical network of streets with a market place in the centre, quite typical of the Wielkopolska (Great Poland) Province and neighbouring Silesia. The two main streets leading to the town gates were the focus of business and service activities. There was also a north-western thoroughfare leading to the castle and passing through the market square and

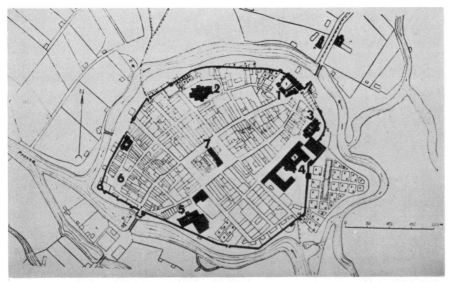

FIGURE 6.2. Plan of Kalisz in 1785 (after H. Münch). *1* is the castle built in 1233; *2* the thirteenth-century parish church; *3* the fourteenth-century collegiate church; *4* the Jesuit church, monastery and college dating from the last quarter of the sixteenth century; *5* the church and monastery of St. Francis, thirteenth century; *6* the Jewish quarter; *7* the main market place and medieval town hall.

the Jewish quarter. This roughly concentric street system was truncated by three streets at right-angles which defined the market place. The whole town was surrounded with a rampart in the thirteenth century, and in the fourteenth century high, defensive brick walls with two gates were constructed. Along two roads running below the terraces of the Prosna river valley, the two suburbs of Town and Wroclaw grew up in medieval times. In the Middle Ages residential houses in the town were built of wood. In the sixteenth and early seventeenth centuries, i.e. in the period of the town's greatest prosperity [8], they were replaced by two- and three-storey brick houses surmounted by attics [9]. The town hall erected in the centre of the market place was particularly remarkable for its ten-storey tower [10].

The late seventeenth and early eighteenth centuries were tragic years in the history of Kalisz. Wars and natural disasters decimated its population and destroyed its buildings. There was a period of rapid development in the years 1815–31, when the authorities of the Polish Kingdom, set up by the Congress of Vienna, granted the town the status of *voivod* (regional capital) and initiated a substantial investment campaign. Part of an old Jesuit college was adapted to house the *voivod* administration and new squares were laid out in the north-eastern zone of the town. All this activity resulted in the destruction of what had remained of the ducal castle, the town gates and a large part of the defensive walls. No important changes occurred in the layout

FIGURE 6.3. The town hall
and market place of Kalisz.
(Engraved in 1797 and
published in 1835)

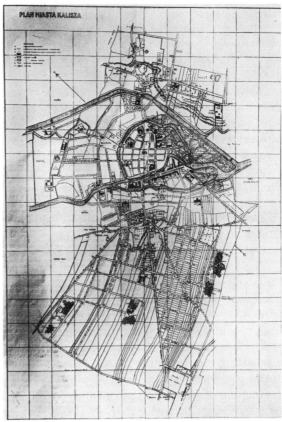

FIGURE 6.4. Plan of Kalisz
in 1907 showing the extension to the south towards
the railway. (Source: The
Polish Academy of Sci-
ences, Warsaw, Institute
of Art)

of the town from then until the beginning of the twentieth century when, as a result of industrialization, the population of the town increased to 25,000 [11]. Densities were increasing in the central area, and peripheral industrial and working-class districts had grown up (figure 6.4). The rapid expansion of the town is evidenced by the growth of its population to 51,000 in 1910 and 70,000 by 1914 [12]. Housing investment failed to keep pace with such rapid population growth. To highlight the appalling housing conditions the Kalisz branch of the Warsaw Hygienic Society surveyed the housing situation. They found that fifteen per cent of the population of Kalisz lived in basements not designed for residential purposes [13]. Housing conditions became even worse after the outbreak of war.

THE DESTRUCTION OF THE TOWN AND THE PROBLEM OF ITS RECONSTRUCTION

Kalisz was destroyed at the very beginning of the First World War. Between 7th August and 22nd August 1914 it was subjected to continuous shelling by a Prussian army regiment [14]. This tactic of deliberate destruction razed almost the whole of the central residential districts and a part of the Wroclaw suburb to the ground. West European war correspondents often referred to Kalisz as the most devastated of all European towns [15].

This act of barbarity took on a symbolic meaning for the Polish

FIGURE 6.5. Devasted buildings in the area of the market place. (Source: The Polish Academy of Sciences, Warsaw, Institute of Art)

population; it was seen as an assault on Polish culture and national tradition, as well as on a town with a special role in history and which was still a lively cultural centre. It was an act of vandalism to which the unanimous reaction was to vow to rebuild. The 'renascent' Kalisz had to be returned to its former splendour without losing anything of its historic value; it was to be a monument to the national culture and at the same time a town with new functional and aesthetic values. To attain this goal the effort of the whole population was needed, and especially the cooperation of the finest Polish architects. Their organization, the Warsaw Architects' Circle, launched a competition for a master plan for the reconstruction and expansion of Kalisz by the end of the first year of the war. The competition was organized in cooperation with the National Committee for the Reconstruction of Kalisz.

Activity in the town itself was particularly difficult as it was still occupied by the Germans; the occupation authorities supervised the municipal authorities and the town's building department and so controlled and limited the initiatives of the Polish administration. To start reconstruction it was necessary to make an inventory of the devastation in the town centre. This revealed that almost all the residential and commercial buildings in the market place had been destroyed but that churches and most public buildings remained intact. Exceptions were the town hall, theatre and a few other public buildings. The destruction of residential fabric was almost total. Only a few buildings could be erected on their old foundations or ground floor walls [16]. The problem of finding a plan to govern all the necessary rebuilding had to be tackled quickly.

## THE ARCHITECTS' CIRCLE COMPETITION

A design competition was held to solve this problem. The commission that worked out the conditions of the competition had to take a stand on the fundamental question of whether the former physical plan was to be restored, or the opportunity taken for general modernization. The opinion of the commission was unanimous; the town had to be rebuilt to its historical form. For this reason the conditions of the competition contained basic information about the history of the town, the functions of its districts and quarters, and an evaluation of the transportation network and suggestions for its improvement [17]. The commission also adopted a suggestion put forward by the municipal council to enlarge the two main streets to eighteen metres wide so that a tramway might be run along them [18]. As the competition embraced not only reconstruction but also further expansion of the town, its terms of reference included the location of future industrial quarters and contained other recommendations relating to the physical development of the town.

The announcement of the competition received widespread press coverage. An appeal to the competitors by Jozef Dziekonski, doyen of Polish architects, was particularly influential [19]. He wrote, 'Old towns should preserve their traditional character. If they do not, their citizens should be blamed for narrow-mindedness and ignorance'. To preserve their character, streets had to be narrow, winding and short, and irregular building lines preserved with their characteristic masses and details. Architectural monuments needed particular care. All these elements were enshrined in the basic provisions of the competition.

The result of the competition was particularly promising; ideas put forward by the participants proved valuable not only in this local situation, but also advanced the wider theory of Polish town planning. The chairman of the Architects' Circle, Jan Heurich, stated, when announcing the results of the competition, that work on the reconstruction of Kalisz 'will serve as a model and example to other towns, demonstrating how to start work on a correct reconstruction of the Polish town' [20]. The competition was a new experiment for the Warsaw group of architects and it stimulated their efforts to find theoretical principles applicable to towns damaged by hostilities. Fifteen teams of architects took part, and included most of the distinguished architects of the day. The team headed by Tadeusz Zielinski won the first prize for a plan satisfying all the conditions of the competition; the second prize went to Zdzislaw Kalinowski for a design which, in the opinion of the jury, was remarkable for its 'artistic approach and successful realization of the ideas of preserving the character of a Polish town' [21]. In the group of works that won honorary distinctions Tadeusz Tolwinski's was placed top. He was appointed head of town planning at the new Department of Architecture at Warsaw Technical University in the same year [22].

All these authors gave priority to reconstructing the centre of the town. Zielinski pointed out that the guiding principle of his plan was to be faithful to the past not only by basing reconstruction work on the old plan of the town, but also by carefully restoring and preserving the surroundings of historical monuments. He warned against the demolition of buildings adjoining ecclesiastical architecture because 'setting apart the old walls of a monastery could deprive it of the romantic aura old churches have when surrounded by old houses and narrow streets'. His care not only for architectural monuments but also for the authenticity of the whole of the urban fabric is in accord with modern ideas but was quite revolutionary at the time of the First World War.

## KALINOWSKI'S PLAN FOR KALISZ

The text accompanying Kalinowski's plan contains a comprehensive account of the method of architectural design in an historical environment [23]. He points to the need to study the history of town planning principles 'beginning with ancient times . . . and on to Howard'. In his opinion architects had a duty

FIGURE 6.6. Kalinowski's design for rebuilding the town hall and market place. (From *Przeglad Techniczny,* 1916)

to study the history of a town if they intended to affect its future development. He thought that understanding the history of a place would help avoid the production of sterile, schematic designs bearing little relation to a town as a living organism. He warned against 'transplanting ideas born in England, France or Germany to Poland where historical development, character of the people and the economic structure are very different'. He reminded his readers that towns in the past were built not as a result of haphazard but happy coincidence (as it sometimes popularly supposed at present), but as a result of consistent and conscious effort on the part of individuals or governing groups.

Returning from theory to practical considerations, Kalinowski referred in his studies to written documents and cartographic material relating to the history of town planning in Kalisz. He regretted that the short closing date of the competition precluded a more thorough historical study as it was his idea that new development at Kalisz should be 'born of the bone' of the town centuries ago, and not be an 'artificially added appendage'.

Kalinowski's studies of engravings of the silhouette of this 'town on an island' suggested that prominence ought to be given to the town hall with its tower rising up over all the other buildings in the town. He also thought it important to rebuild all the late Renaissance merchants' houses as they were very characteristic features of Polish towns. He gave them, though, ground floor arcades which obviated the need to widen the streets leading into the market place which would have spoiled its sense of closure. While keeping the streets as narrow as in the past in the immediate vicinity of the town centre squares, Kalinowski accepted that streets could be widened outside this most sensitive area, although his overall plan for the centre of the city is clearly related to early pictorial representations of Kalisz [24].

The maturity of Kalinowski's opinions concerning the principles of the reconstruction of historic towns and restoring historic values deserves particular emphasis. He appreciated the need to integrate the work of conservationists and town planners at all scales from compiling a master plan down to the detailed planning of the Old Town and the treatment of single architectural monuments. His principles of encouraging the organic development of old towns in harmony with their tradition and topography and his search for the individual character of a town and cultivating its particular features are all as relevant today as in 1914.

## TADEUSZ TOLWINSKI AND GARDEN CITY PLANS

Tadeusz Tolwinski, author of a plan that won an honorary distinction, was just beginning his career as an architect at the time of the competition. Later on he founded the Warsaw School of Town Planning, and the present town planning professors in the Faculty of Architecture of Warsaw Technical University are Tolwinski's pupils. Twenty years after the competition, he wrote a textbook on town planning which is still used by students today [25].

FIGURE 6.7. Sketch of the northern part of the town by Tolwiński, indicating the Russian orthodox church. (From *Przeglad Techniczny,* 1916)

FIGURE 6.8. Plan submitted to the rebuilding competition by Dygat, Kozlowski and Zurkowski, which gained an honorary distinction. It is one of a number of 'garden city' plans, both the inner area of the Old Town and the new extension are surrounded by green belts.

He considered the reconstruction of Kalisz particularly important not only because of the historical value of the town itself, but also because it could serve as a precedent, as an example to be followed, when starting the reconstruction of other Polish towns. So he was careful to 'preserve and respect the old features, to seek to create "genuine" forms'.

Attention should be drawn to the caution Tolwinski displayed when deciding on changes to the existing structure of the town. In his project the Old Town district 'remains unchanged'. He even planned to make use of a huge Orthodox church erected by the Russian administration in the square situated at the northern entrance to the town. Most other participants in the competition demanded that it be demolished as a symbol of political oppression, but they did not consider the effects of removing such an architectural mass separating two squares [26]. Tolwinski adopted the Jesuit College as his focus for planning the town and he developed it into a vast complex of buildings to house the town's cultural services [27]. He surrounded the historic town centre with a belt of planted open space and relieved it from through traffic.

Authors of other projects which won prizes or distinctions tackled different aspects of reconstruction and protection of the Old Town [28]. In the main, however, their attention was concentrated on problems of the expansion of the town rather than its reconstruction; in particular they sought solutions to the pressing housing problem. Many works sent in to the competition attempted to find the most appropriate structure for the various residential quarters of new Kalisz. A number of types of 'Garden City' development were suggested (figure 6.8). The idea of garden cities was particularly popular in Poland at that time; after 1900, Ebenezer Howard's book was frequently reviewed in the Polish literature [29]. People also became acquainted with Howard's ideas at lectures and in press articles and an exhibition of garden cities was opened in Warsaw in 1910. A competition for a master plan of a garden city at Zabki near Warsaw was launched in 1912 [30]. Among the champions of these ideas was Wladyslaw Dobrzynski, a physician and cofounder of the International Garden Cities and Town Planning Association [31]. When Howard arrived in Cracow in August 1912 he was given an enthusiastic reception when he lectured [32]. The many suggestions for the layout of new quarters in Kalisz according to Garden City principles were further evidence of the popularity that Howard's ideas enjoyed in Poland.

## The Kalisz Competition in the Wider Context of the Protection of Historic Towns in Poland

To assess the achievements of the competition for the reconstruction and expansion of Kalisz it is necessary to survey briefly general ideas on the protection of historic urban areas in Polish towns at the time.

The idea of preserving the traditional Polish character of towns and their historic pasts grew up in the Polish community as a protest against the cultural policy of the three super powers which had partitioned Poland and ruled the occupied country. In the world of architects on the other hand, the growing preservation movement was founded on concepts similar to those in other European countries. Historic towns were viewed as artefacts shaped by history according to the artistic ideas of the past. In contrast, towns built in the period of industrialization were supposedly characterized by schematic conformity. Camillo Sitte's book was as valuable a contribution to the discussion of town planning and the protection of historic towns in Poland as it was elsewhere in Europe [33].

In the southern part of the country under Austrian rule, two associations for the protection of historic monuments were set up as early as 1888. These were the Western and Eastern Galicia groups of Conservators centred in Cracow and Lwow respectively. In 1902, the Society for the Protection of Polish Historic Artefacts and Culture was set up which soon extended its scope of interest from single buildings to groups [34]. The Society was not only interested in public buildings, churches and palaces, but also in merchants' houses, particularly those built in market places and main town streets [35]. 'A step forward has been taken', the Polish architect Wladyslaw Ekielski wrote in 1909, 'from the conservation of single buildings to attempts to preserve the character of whole historic urban areas' [36]. The growing concern for the preservation of the essential values of historic layout and for the harmonious physical development of new or recently incorporated zones of cities was evident when a competition was launched in 1910 for a plan of Greater Cracow. This can be considered a turning point in the development of modern methods of town planning in Poland [37]. Many articles published in the period when the Cracow master plan was being developed demonstrate that architects were aware of their responsibility for the protection not only of the most outstanding historic towns, but also of small provincial settlements which contributed to the specific character of Polish landscapes and townscapes [38].

In the early twentieth century, the protection of historic monuments was extended to the part of Poland under Russian domination. In 1906, the Society for the Protection of the Monuments of the Past was founded. A special commission of the Society was set up for the protection of the Old Town of Warsaw. Many articles published in *Przeglad Techniczny* (Technological Review) testify to the interest of the Warsaw Architects' Circle not only in the purely technical problems of the reconstruction and modernization of towns, but also in their historic past and the aesthetic and legal problems connected with the protection of this past [39]. An analysis of the physical structure of Warsaw by Alfred Lauterbach was the first of a number of studies by members of the Architects' Circle leading up to the completion of the Greater Warsaw Plan in 1916 under the coordination of Tadeusz Tolwinski [40]. In the same year the Architects' Circle organized its competition for the reconstruction and expansion of Kalisz.

The Kalisz competition was an important contribution to the development of the theory of the protection of historic monuments in Poland for a number of reasons. Its participants had been educated in a variety of architecture schools both at home and abroad and they tended to maintain regular contacts with these institutions. This is confirmed by frequent reviews, reports of trips, travels, conferences, and exhibitions in *Przeglad Techniczny*. The Kalisz competition provided an opportunity not only to tackle an important and difficult town planning task, but also to exchange opinions and to construct theories. This is why the descriptions of the designs sent in for the competition are so long and detailed. They contain general statements and are really manifestos of their authors' views relating to the protection of historic urban areas.

Ideas contained in the Kalisz competition entries were also incorporated in textbooks dealing with the principles of town planning. It is difficult to demonstrate the direct borrowing of ideas, but it is a fact that the three earliest Polish textbooks on town planning were very much influenced by the ideas of the architects' teams competing at Kalisz. Ignacy Drexler's *Reconstruction of Villages and Towns in Our Country* (1916), Roman Felinski's *Town Building* (1916), and a book by Artur Kuhnel published in 1918 entitled *Principles of Building Small Towns and Townships* went some of the way to help those concerned with reconstructing towns damaged or destroyed during the hostilities.

The plans sent in to the Kalisz competition also had an effect on Polish legal regulations concerning the protection of historic monuments. As early as 31st October 1918, the Regency Council issued a decree on the protection of historic relics and monuments. Krzysztof Pawlowski has recently emphasized the fundamental importance of that document, pointing out that it was a pioneer Act [41]. It was republished in 1928, with minor amendments, as a Decision of the President of the Polish Republic on the protection of historic relics and monuments. It served as a basis for conservators' work not only in the interwar years but also during the campaign to rebuild Polish towns after the Second World War. It was only repealed in 1962 when a Law on the Protection of Historical Monuments was passed.

The 1918 decree laid down principles which governed the scope of the protection of historic monuments for nearly half a century. It considered that *groups* of buildings were particularly valuable as also were the street plan, the survival of historic street names; ornamental gardens, and surviving avenues of trees. The decree stated that 'immovable monuments cannot be demolished, damaged, remodelled, renovated, reconstructed, ornamented or supplemented without permission of the relevant conservator's authority'. A commentary on the decree issued by the Ministry of Art and Culture in 1920 emphasized that 'care and protection of historic monuments should extend to groups of buildings, the layout of streets and town quarters, and to the character and fundamental elements of the town plan' [42]. It also warned against leaving historic monuments intact but lessening their value by transforming their immediate environment by designing aggressive new buildings discordant with the old ones.

The principles of the protection of urban historic areas were codified by architects who collaborated with the Ministry of Art and Culture, the Ministry of Religious Denominations and Public Education, and the Ministry of Public Works [43]. The rebuilding of Kalisz after the war was, then, an experiment in which theoretical principles and legal provisions were tested in practice. At the end of the war, some four years after the destruction of the town, only two houses had been rebuilt and six repaired. Preliminary work had started on forty-eight building plots, leaving 370 on which nothing had been done by the end of the war. Despite such insignificant progress in reconstruction, the war years marked a very important stage in the development of the *idea* of reconstruction.

### PLANS FOR THE RECONSTRUCTION OF KALISZ MADE BEFORE THE END OF THE WAR

The German occupation authorities in Kalisz, like the Polish municipal council and its building department, intended to rebuild Kalisz according to its historic plan and proportions. The endeavours of the German authorities in this field were once considered an act of appeasement after destroying the town but recent studies have shown that they were interested in reconstruction work because of their plans to incorporate the 'Polish border belt' into the German state [44]. The 'belt' was to include territory along the Russian–German frontier belonging to Russia before 1914, and Kalisz was situated within this area [45]. German architects' designs for the market place have a uniform appearance, lack detail, and were clearly inspired by early twentieth-century German buildings. During the preparations for the Architects' Circle competition, the district commander forbade the municipal council to contact the Architects' Circle, which as a Polish organization might have been expected to enhance the Polish traits of the town during rebuilding. But this did not prevent the municipal building department from taking advantage of the works sent in for the competition when suggesting amendments to the plan of the town. In fact, the 'Plan for the regulation of Kalisz central district' drawn up in the early months of 1916 refers quite· explicitly in its descriptive section to the rich fund of ideas which the competition provided and of which 'advantage has been taken when designing the detailed plan'.

Improvements on the plan executed by the district administration related first and foremost to improving the very inefficient transport network. Main

FIGURE 6.9. One of a number of designs produced by the German occupation authorities for rebuilding houses in the market place. (Source: The Polish Academy of Sciences, Warsaw, Institute of Arts)

streets were to be widened slightly on those sides where buildings had been too seriously destroyed to be restored. New building lines had to be fixed as soon as possible so that credits could be granted and permissions issued to proprietors wanting to rebuild. A plan completed in 1917 was to serve as the basis for reconstruction. It shows the area in the town where streets were to be enlarged, the new building lines on the main squares and defines the height of buildings. In the three widest streets and the market place the height was fifteen metres (four storeys), and in other streets twelve metres (three storeys). At the same time a building law was approved, defining construction principles. This document was particularly important as it was approved again by the Polish authorities in 1919 and governed the later stages of the reconstruction of the town [46].

The law required a strict adherence to building lines, and allowed for very few deviations. On the other hand, it was thought that the interiors of deep street blocks could be densely built-up to help alleviate the desperate housing situation in the town. But this produced a legacy of badly structured infilling which is still a problem today.

The provisions of the law relating to the reconstruction of public buildings in the historic urban area were excellent. No industrial buildings were allowed near them and strict height limits were fixed for blocks of flats adjoining them. No cellars for residential use were allowed, and only twenty per cent of attics could be used for housing purposes. The pitch of roofs and all roofing materials used on buildings fronting on to the street were also subject to control and new buildings had to be decorated with restraint. One of the law's articles reads: 'excessive use of machine-made architectural parts of plaster, plaster of Paris, cement, etc. is not allowed... sign-boards, advertisements and inscriptions placed on buildings for advertisement purposes should not be offensive, and should be placed in such a way as not to obscure important architectural elements'. It is to the credit of the provisions of this building law that the rebuilt town did constitute an harmonious whole.

The plan and the building law provided the guidelines for rebuilding but their implementation was not all plain sailing. Realizing the difficulty of designing the market place and town hall and being aware of the importance of architecture in this central part of the town, the municipal council approached the Architects' Circle asking it to announce another competition. The Municipal Building Commission prepared the conditions of the competition early in 1918 and the result was announced in May of the same year [47]. Although as many as thirty-one entries were received, none was considered adequate. The three first prizes were awarded to Z. Kalinowski, K. Tolloczko and T. Zielinski. While the results of the earlier competition were published and the original submissions preserved at least in part, the second competition is known today only from a few documents, notably about a dozen drawings probably made on the occasion of one of the three

FIGURE 6.10. Kalinowski's entry to the 1918 competition for a town hall and market place design. (Source: The Polish Academy of Sciences, Warsaw, Institute of Arts)

FIGURE 6.11. Zielinski's design for the town hall, submitted to the 1918 competition. (Source: The Polish Academy of Sciences, Warsaw, Institute of Arts)

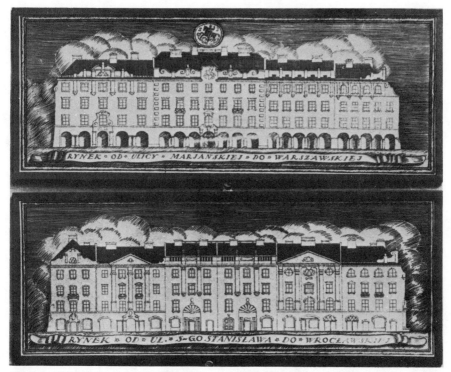

FIGURE 6.12. Zielinski's competition entry—market place elevation. (Source: The Polish Academy of Sciences, Warsaw, Institute of Arts)

exhibitions at which the designs were displayed [48]. The designs that have survived are very interesting studies showing various kinds of eclecticism and attempts to revive and modernize local and regional architectural traditions.

The achievements of the building department of the Kalisz municipal council in the years of the war proved to be very important for ideas that were developed further in the postwar years. On the other hand, practical implementation was particularly difficult during the war. The period of effective construction begins after 1918.

## POSTWAR RECONSTRUCTION

In the first postwar months public work was started employing over 2500 people to clear away rubble. At the same time efforts were made to raise enough money for a large-scale building campaign. Early in 1919, the municipal council submitted a memorandum on the reconstruction of the town to Parliament, and asked the relevant ministries for assistance. In reply to this request, the Minister of Public Works visited Kalisz with two of his heads of department. The Minister of Art and Culture sent the distinguished

FIGURE 6.13. A present-day
view of the town hall.

historian, Jozef Raciborski to Kalisz as municipal conservator. Raciborski
published a series of articles on the history of the town in the local press,
organized an exhibition 'Kalisz Past and Future', and convened a conference
of specialists to discuss the many problems still unsolved.

The proceedings of this conference were published as a book and illustrate
one of the themes of his essay which is that work at Kalisz was of much more
than local importance and made significant methodological contributions to
the preservation debate [49]. In its publication the municipal council stated
'in our town whose central district was almost completely destroyed, it will be
easier to apply the latest achievements of technology, public health, culture
and art than in other towns, and when all these have been put into effect,
Kalisz will perhaps serve as a pattern for other towns'.

The master plan for the town was the first item on the conference agenda.
The consensus adopted was that to carry out improvements necessary in the
Old Town it would be necessary to enlarge the field of analysis and to work
on the whole of the town at once. Municipal architects were offered
assistance in the form of consultations with the Town Regulation Office set
up at the Ministry of Public Works [50]. Next followed discussion of detailed
problems like exposing the medieval defensive walls wherever they

remained, the management of the three main Old Town squares and finally the reconstruction of the town hall and the theatre. It was also decided that old street names should be retained within the Old Town and wherever they had been changed, the oldest known names should be restored. The tragic destruction of the town was to be commemorated by leaving one building in a state of ruin; a decision that was not, perhaps, happily, put into effect.

The designs of apartment blocks also had to be approved, this time by a commission set up by the municipal council [51]. Many of the minutes of this commission have been preserved in land ownership records and show that its members were careful to ensure that the provisions of the building law were observed. Landlords certainly tried to evade the law whenever possible to locate shops, workshops and even flats in basements. A firm stand by the commission prevented such evasions from occurring. It also took a very hard line with street frontages; designs were frequently returned to proprietors for amendment to bring them in line with the regulations or to make them more sympathetic with the character of neighbouring houses. Buildings adjoining historical monuments could not be constructed without the approval of the conservator of historic relics and monuments.

Not all the problems were, however, successfully solved. An old factory that survived the war is still in operation close to the market place but is scheduled for demolition soon. Odd empty plots as in Sukiennicza Street still await new buildings and some mistakes were made with rebuilding the old Jesuit college buildings. Nevertheless, the reconstruction of the historic area of Kalisz can be considered an outstanding achievement. Further, it provided an opportunity for methodological debate and helped formulate principles and influence legislation. In recent years the reconstruction of Kalisz has perhaps been overshadowed by the rebuilding of towns after the Second World War but many of the ideas it gave rise to are still as valid today as when they were formulated in the difficult days of the First World War.

## NOTES

1. Dabrowski, K. (1960) Kalisz starozytny (ancient Kalisz), in *Szkice z dziejów Kalisza (Essays on the History of Kalisz)*. Wroclaw, p. 13.
2. Drewko, M. (1953) Slady osady z czasów cesarstwa rzymskiego na Tyńcu w Kaliszu (traces of a Roman settlement in Tyniec, Kalisz). *Wiadomości Archeologiczne*, 19, pp. 198–206; Dabrowski, K. (1970) *Z przeszłości Kalisza (From the History of Kalisz)*. Warsaw, pp. 67–71.
3. Wasowiczowna, T. (1960) Topografia wczesnośredniowiecznego Kalisza, in *Szkice z dziejów Kalisza, op. cit.*, p. 37.
4. Münch, H. (1946) *Geneza rozplanowania miast wielkopolskich w XIII i XIV w (Origins of town plans in the Wielkopolska province in the thirteenth and fourteenth centuries)*. Cracow, p. 64.
5. Trawkowski, S. (1962) Geneza regionu kaliskiego (the origins of the Kalisz region), in *Osiemnaście wieków Kalisza*, vol. 3. Kalisz, p. 7 ff.

6. Młynarska, M. (1962) Proces lokacji Kalisza w XIII w i I poł. XIV w (the process of the foundation of Kalisz in the thirteenth and early fourteenth centuries), in *ibid.*, vol. 1, pp. 105–31.
7. The history of the physical layout of Kalisz is described in an unpublished town planning study of 1959 preserved by the *voivod* conservator of monuments in Poznań. The chapter dealing with the physical development of the town in the Middle Ages was written by Z. Kaczmarczyk.
8. Reconstruction and growth of the town is discussed by Herbst, S. (1962) Kalisz renesansowy (renaissance Kalisz), in *Osiemnascie wieków Kalisza,* vol. 3. Kalisz, pp. 91–105.
9. The problem of the reconstruction of Kalisz in modern times is also discussed by Nalepa, J. (1959) Historia układu przestrzennego miasta od końca XV w do pocz. XX w (the history of the physical development of the town from the end of the fifteenth to the early twentieth centuries) in unpublished town planning study of 1959 preserved by the *voivod* conservator of monuments in Poznań.
10. Documentary evidence etc. is discussed by Ruszczynska, T. (1962) Materialy ikongraficzne do historii zabudowy Kalisza (pictorial sources for the history of architecture in Kalisz) in *Osiemnaście wieków Kalisza,* vol. 2. Kalisz, pp. 91–125.
11. In 1897 the population was 21,680 and in 1902, 26,103 according to a memorandum sent from the Kalisz magistrate's office to the Land Office in Warsaw on 12 June 1923.
12. Zakrzewska, J. (1936) *Odbudowa Kalisza po wielkiej wojnie (Reconstruction of Kalisz after the Great War).* Kalisz, p. 13; according to municipal records the population numbered 50,903 in 1910; Raszewska, J. (1969) Rozwój zaludnienia miasta Kalisza w latach 1793–1939 (population growth in the town of Kalisz in the years 1793–1939). *Rocznik Kaliski,* 2, p. 34. The author estimates population on the eve of the outbreak of the Second World War at 64–70,000.
13. Koszutski, B. (1912) Stan sanitarny mieszkań piwnicznych w mieście Kaliszu (sanitary condition of basement flats in the town of Kalisz). *Zdrowie,* 5, p. 5.
14. The course of events in Kalisz during the war has been related many times and recently by Wrotkowski, H. (1970) *Rocznik Kaliski,* 3, pp. 165–215.
15. They compared the destruction of Kalisz to that of Belgian towns, particularly Liège. See Dabrowski, K. (1960) Kalisz starozytny (ancient Kalisz), in *Szkice z dziejów Kalisza* (Essays on the History of Kalisz). Wroclaw, p. 247.
16. Many drafts prepared by building inspection commissions have survived in land ownership files.
17. See the conditions and programme of the forty-eighth competition announced by the Warsaw Architects' Circle on 3 December 1915.
18. They were adopted by the council on 14 December 1915 and published in *Przeglad Techniczny* in 1916.
19. Dziekonski, J. (1915) Konkurs Koła Architektów na odbudowe m. Kalisza (The Architects' Circle competition for the reconstruction of Kalisz). *Przeglad Techniczny,* p. 475.
20. *Przeglad Techniczny,* 1916, p. 260.
21. The authors were Zielinski, T. and Wojcicki, W. with a contribution by Bystydzienski, M. and it was given the reference number 9; see also competition entry number 12.
22. See competition entry number 10; Filipkowski, S. (1962) Professor Dr

honoris causa Tadeusz Tolwinski, an Architect. *Kwartalnik Architektury i Urbanistyki*, 7, p. 7.

23. It was published with minor abridgements in the competition publications. The full text and original descriptions of all the prize-winning entries are in the archives of the Municipal Town Planning Department, Kalisz.

24. Particularly relevant in this context is a view of the town in the background of an early eighteenth-century painting of St. Paschalis in the parish church.

25. Tolwinski, T. (1934) *Urbanistyka*, 1.

26. Orthodox churches were demolished in Warsaw and many Polish towns, Kalisz included, after the First World War.

27. This altered the axis created by H. Marconi in the first half of the nineteenth century between a prison built in the valley and the front elevation of the administrative seat of the *voivod*.

28. A full list is in a more comprehensive study of this topic published by the present author. See Zarebska, T. (1977) Sprawa odbudowy zabytkowego centrum Kalisza po zniszczeniu w 1914 roku (The problem of reconstructing the historic area of Kalisz after the 1914 disaster). *Rocznik Kaliski*, 10, pp. 121–77.

29. They are discussed at length in, Ostrowski, W. (1975) *Urbanistyka współczesna (Contemporary Town Planning)*. Warsaw, pp. 30–2 and Ostrowski, W. (1968) *L'urbanisme contemporain, des origines à la Charte d'Athenes*, 1st ed., Paris, p. 47; and Pawlowski, K. K. (1969) Poczatki polskiej myśli urbanistycznej (The beginnings of Polish town planning theory), in *Sztuka około 1900 (Art about 1900)* Warsaw, p. 67 ff.

30. T. Tołwiński won first prize in this competition and his work also attained a distinction in the Kalisz competition.

31. Pawlowski, K. K. (1969) Poczatki polskiej myśli urbanistycznej (The beginnings of Polish town planning theory), in *Sztuka około 1900 (Art about 1900)*. Warsaw, p. 82.

32. Ostrowski, W. (1975) *Urbanistyka współczesna (Contemporary Town Planning)*. Warsaw, p. 37.

33. The first review of this book appeared as early as 1890. See Wdowiszewski, J. (1890) Artystyczne zasady budowy miast (Artistic principles of town planning). *Czasopismo Towarzystwa Technicznego Krakowskiego*, 7, p. 68.

34. In 1909, for example, a study of medieval canon houses near Tarnów cathedral was made. See Pawlowski, K. (1977) Ochrona walorów zabytkowych miast a geneza polskiej nowoczesnej szkoły urbanistycznej (The protection of historic monuments in towns and the rise of the modern school of Polish town planning), in *Przeszłość a jutro miasta (The Past and Future of a Town)*. Warsaw, p. 165.

35. S. Tomkowicz frequently emphasized the need to protect all historic towns. See, for example, Tomkowicz, S. (1909) *Szpecenie Kraju (Spoiling the Beauty of a Town)*. Cracow; and his (1909) *Piekność miast i jej ochrona (The Beauty of Towns and Its Protection)*. Cracow.

36. Ekielski, W. (1909) Dwie konserwacje (Two conservations). *Architekt*, p. 19 as cited in Pawlowski, K. K. (1969) Poczatki polskiej myśli urbanistycznej (The beginnings of Polish town planning theory) in *Sztuka około 1900 (Art about 1900)*. Warsaw, p. 167.

37. Pawłowski, K. K. (1972) Geneza i działalność T.U.P. w latach 1923–39 a rozwoj

mysli urbanistycznej w Polsce (The origin and work of the Polish Town Planning Society 1923–39 and the development of town planning theory in Poland), in *Towarzystwo Urbanistów Polskich*. Warsaw, p. 16.

38. Pawłowski, K. (1977) Ochrona walorów zabytkowych miast a geneza polskiej nowoczesnej szkoły urbanistycznej (The protection of historic monuments in towns and the rise of the modern school of Polish town planning), in *Przeszłość a jutro miasta (The Past and Future of a Town)*. Warsaw, reviews a number of these articles and other publications on this subject like Luskina, E. (1910) *To the Defence of the Beauty of the Country*. Cracow.

39. For instance, regulations concerning the aesthetics of towns issued by the Duchy' of Baden and the 1909 Saxon law 'to forbid despoiling the beauty of towns and villages', were analysed. Based on West European examples the municipal authorities of Poznań issued a regulation in 1909 'to prevent changing the appearance of the town'. See Rymaszewski, B. (1970) The origin of the protection of historic areas in Poland. Unpublished manuscript; Pawłowski, K. (1977) *ibid.*, p. 172.

40. Lauterbach, A. (1915) *Zabytkowych miast potrzeby estetyczne Warszawy (Warsaw's Aesthetic Needs)*. Warsaw.

41. Pawłowski, K. (1977) *op. cit.*, pp. 187–9.

42. Ministerstwo Sztuki i Kultury (1920) *Opieka nad zabytkami i ich konser wacja (Protection and conservation of historic monuments and relics)*. Warsaw. Pawłowski, K. (1977) *ibid.*, provides a detailed analysis and commentary on the decree.

43. For example, Professor Juliusz Klos and the art historian Dr. Alfred Lauterbach; Jarosław Wojciechowski, head of the Department of Artistic Historical Monuments and Museums; Roman Feliński, head of the Department of Town Regulation and others.

44. Memorandum sent from Kalisz Magistrates' Office to the Land Office in Warsaw on 12 June 1923.

45. Geise, I. (1964) *The So-called Polish Border Belt, 1914–18*. Warsaw, p. 166 and 226, cited in Wrotkowski, H. (1970) *Rocznik Kaliski*, 3, p. 174.

46. The law was approved by the district head on 10th November 1917.

47. Report of the sitting of the municipal council on 31st January 1918 in *Gazeta Kaliska*, 7th February 1918.

48. The first was held in Kalisz on 26 September 1918 and the second, also in Kalisz, on 5th August 1919. The third took place in the Architecture Department at Warsaw in 1919. cf. SARP (Society of Polish Architects) (1970) *Architectural Competitions in Poland, 1918–39*, Wroclaw. Information supplied by G. Luba.

49. Report dated 1st September 1919 of the meeting of representatives of ministries on 15–16th August 1919 concerning the reconstruction of the town of Kalisz.

50. In 1922 Sylwester Pajzderski produced a master plan for the town which in 1925 was modified and produced in a new version by the Town Regulation Office.

51. The activity of the commission and the progress of building work in Kalisz are extensively discussed by this author in Zarebska, T. (1977) Sprawa odbudowy zabytkowego centrum Kalisza po zhniszcozeniu w 1914 roku (The problem of reconstructing the historic area of Kalisz after the 1914 disaster). *Rocznik Kaliski*, 10, pp. 121–77.

# 7

# Planning for nature conservation: a struggle for survival and political respectability

ANDREW W. GILG

This paper discusses the underlying philosophy of and arguments for nature conservation. The germ of this movement appeared about a hundred years ago; its growth and development since then has been aided and supported by a number of factors. For convenience these are grouped under the headings 'aesthetic', 'scientific' and 'preservationist'. The main theme of this paper is a discussion of the role and effectiveness of these three approaches in making nature conservation an area worthy of government attention and legislation. The development of nature conservation in Britain and elsewhere is well documented, so only a brief account is necessary here to provide some context for the following discussion [1].

In Britain the earliest concern about nature was based on 'scientific' interest. For example, the foundation of the Royal Society in 1663 was based partly on an interest in plant classification which was further developed with the formation of the Linnean Society in 1788. It was not until the nineteenth century, however, that a more widespread interest in nature was reflected in the growth of natural history societies, although their attention was confined mainly to preventing cruelty and the mass destruction of wildlife for museums, private collections and clothing. For example, the Society for the Prevention of Cruelty to Animals was established in 1824 (the RSPCA from 1840) and the Society for the Protection of Birds in 1889 (the RSPB from 1904).

The period from 1860 to 1940 saw a widening of approach to embrace the education of public opinion, the acquisition of further legal powers and the establishment of nature reserves. Education was considered essential for unless a majority of the rural population was in favour of wildlife preservation, enforcement would prove difficult. Indeed, only 1052 prosecutions were made between 1896 and 1920 under the 1896 Wild Birds Protection Act. Further legal powers were also provided during this period, extending the range of species protected and introducing more closed seasons for the field sports. Finally, the Society for the Promotion of Nature Reserves, often acting in concert with the National Trust, began to acquire a number of nature reserves.

By the end of the 1930s the impact of publicity about wildlife loss was sufficient to catch the attention of the government and wildlife became one of the subjects of the great wartime debates concerning the restructuring of Britain after the end of the war. For example, in its report on *Nature Conservation in Great Britain* (1943) the Nature Reserves Investigation Committee advanced the cause of nature conservation generally and that of nature reserves specifically [2]. Its arguments centred on the premise that once the natural heritage was destroyed it could not be replaced. The heritage aspect of the argument was also stressed by the botanist A. G. Tansley in his book *Our Heritage of Wild Nature* (1945) where he argued for nature reserves on the grounds of natural beauty and serenity, scientific value and as instruments of education [3]. This last point had already been given expression by the foundation in 1943 of the Field Studies Council, which had by 1948 acquired three field study centres at Flatford Mill in Suffolk, Juniper Hall in Surrey and Dale Fort in Pembrokeshire.

The work of the wartime Nature Reserves Investigation Committee was followed up by the postwar Huxley Committee which produced what is probably the most important document in the history of British nature conservation [4]. This document, simply titled *Conservation of Nature in England and Wales* (1947) led to the formation in 1948 of the Nature Conservancy, which has since become the model for many other countries to follow. It has, however, had to struggle against political opposition and interference and twice, in 1965 and 1973, it has had its organization and funding disrupted by governmental changes. It was renamed the Nature Conservancy Council in 1973.

As well as the expansion of the Nature Conservancy, the postwar period has also seen a very rapid growth in the membership of organizations connected with the preservation or enjoyment of wildlife. For example, membership of the Royal Society for the Protection of Birds rose from 7000 in 1950 to 205,000 in 1975, and of County Nature Conservation Trusts from 800 in 1950 to 107,000 in 1975, while the number of such Trusts rose from three in 1950 to forty in 1977 [5].

In the United States the development of nature conservation was not as straightforward, for although Frederic Law Olmsted produced a California State park management plan for Yosemite in 1865 and Congress created the

Yellowstone National Park in 1872, the same period also saw the slaughter of some six million buffalo and the settlement and devastation of vast areas of prairie and woodland [6]. This conflict between commercial exploitation inherent in the 'American Dream' and a powerful conservation ethic which had been originally inspired by the founders of the constitution, George Washington and Thomas Jefferson, has been apparent ever since. From time to time in this century this conflict of interest has been highlighted by natural (albeit human-induced) disasters like the Dust Bowls in 1934–35 and then the growth of recreational over-use and pollution in the 1960s and 1970s. A similar picture is revealed by Jane Foster in her history of wildlife conservation in Canada between 1880 and 1920. She shows how the Canadian government was slow to realize the importance of wildlife conservation [7]. This was due largely to the myth of 'superabundance' which has been described by S. Udall as, 'the intoxicating profusion of the American continent which induced a state of mind that made waste and plunder inevitable. A temperate continent, rich in soils and minerals, and forests and wildlife, enticed man to think in terms of infinity rather than fact, and produced an overriding fallacy that was nearly our undoing—the myth of superabundance' [8]. However, the resource was not infinite and in 1892 a Royal Commission on Fish and Game reported: 'On all sides, from every quarter, has been heard the same sickening tale of merciless, ruthless and remorseless slaughter. Where but a few years ago game was plentiful, it is hardly now to be found' [9].

Because nature is no respector of international frontiers, international progress is also important but once again has often been erratic. In Europe, the first attempt to coordinate conservation planning across borders was made as early as 1910 when at the Eighth International Zoological Congress at Graz a committee was formed to establish an international commission for the protection of nature. This led in 1913 to the suggested foundation of a Consultative Commission for the International Protection of Nature. Unfortunately the First World War intervened and the proposal fell into abeyance and subsequent attempts to form an International Office for the Protection of Nature also failed to bear fruit before the outbreak of the 1939–45 war. After the war, the Swiss government did achieve a break-through by helping to found a provisional International Union for the Protection of Nature in 1947. Further progress was made in the 1960s when the Council of Europe, worried by the dilatory nature of much European cooperation, founded the European Committee for the Conservation of Nature and Natural Resources in 1963. This was a rather weak body since many governments accepted the political kudos of agreeing to the laudable aims of the Committee but then did little about it in their own countries. Greater progress was made in 1967 when it was decided to mark 1970 as 'European Conservation Year'.

While progress was being made in Europe, worldwide international cooperation had also been achieved by a number of conferences which particularly helped the protection of birds. The foundation of FAO and UNESCO in the late 1940s helped provide a solid foundation for further progress and in 1956 the International Office for the Protection of Nature changed its name to the now familiar IUCN, the International Union for the Conservation of Nature and Natural Resources, and has used international conferences held every three to four years to advance its cause. For example, at the 1961 Tanganyika conference, Julius Nyerere the President of Tanganyika made the Arusha declaration:

> The survival of our wildlife is a matter of grave concern to all of us in Africa. These wild creatures amid the wild places they inhabit are not only important as a source of wonder and inspiration but are an integral part of our natural resources and of our future livelihood and well-being. In accepting the trusteeship of our wildlife we solemnly declare that we will do everything in our power to make sure that our children's grandchildren will be able to enjoy this rich and precious inheritance. [10]

From this brief introductory history it is perhaps possible to identify three main philosophies which underpin nature conservation. These might be called the 'ethical/aesthetic', the 'scientific/educational' and the 'self-preservationist/disaster' approaches. These are now considered in turn, in order to make an assessment of how effective they have been in persuading governments to provide funds and powers for nature conservation.

### The 'Ethical/Aesthetic' Approach to Nature Conservation

The relationship between man and nature is an obvious place to begin a discussion of the role of nature conservation in modern society. A central question is whether man should be considered as a part of nature or somehow a creature apart. This relationship has been explored in some literary detail by John Passmore [11]. He rejects the once traditional idea that the Book of Genesis gave man *carte blanche* to deal as he pleases with nature. For although Genesis and the Old Testament tell man that he is, or has the right to be, the master of the earth and all it contains, it also insists that the world was 'good' before man was created and that it exists to glorify God rather than to serve man. As a result of first Greek influence and then the work of Renaissance scientists like Bacon and Descartes an interpretation more favourable to man evolved. In this, nature was considered a 'system of resources' which man could modify and transform as he pleased. An alternative interpretation held that man was God's steward but nonetheless acknowledged the 'passive role of nature'. With growing scientific control over the world, the view that nature was subservient to man became predominant and was absorbed not only into Western capitalist societies but also into Marxist doctrines. However, opposition to this rather cavalier view had already begun in the eighteenth century first with Malthus' projections of world population growth exceeding food supply and then in 1864 with the first work detailing the effects of man's destructiveness, G. P. Marsh's *Man and Nature*.

Marsh drew attention in his book to the crucial fact that nature in its original state, as man inherited it, was not able to support civilization. In order to civilize the world man was forced to transform nature, for example, by clearing land for crops. Where man had been in error, Marsh argued, was in supposing that he could act with impunity. Unfortunately Marsh descended into the sort of polemic that has been used to browbeat nature conservationists ever since when he wrote,

> the ravages committed by man subvert the relations and destroy the balance which nature had established between her organised and her inorganic creations; and she avenges herself upon the intruder, by letting loose upon her defaced provinces destructive energies hitherto kept in check by organic forces destined to be his best auxiliaries, but which he has unwisely dispersed and driven from the field of action. [12]

Marsh's views did not receive wide attention again until the 1960s when a discernible political and philosophical ideology which has been loosely termed the 'environmental movement' emerged. A notable manifestation of this movement was student unrest in Paris and California in the late 1960s where for a short while 'flower power' was proposed as an alternative to the brutality of war and in particular the defoliant sprays used to lay waste to the jungles of Vietnam.

From this over idealistic and simplistic beginning a new ecology movement grew so fast that in 1972, E. Anderson said that, 'during the last few years, conservation and environment issues have moved from obscurity to prominence in the United States' [13]. Anderson attributed this growth to the activities of young radicals and to the increased public activity of leading scientists, particularly biologists. A new feature of the movement was that the environmental problem was seen as a symptom of a deeper malaise which could only be solved by major changes in the economic, social and ideological fabric of the modern world.

D. Ratcliffe, the chief scientist of the British Nature Conservancy Council, also points to changing attitudes to the environment when he argues that most intelligent people have a very deep need for a sense of purpose in life [14]. Formal religions that once provided this are on the decline, leaving a void in many peoples lives. Ratcliffe also notes that,

> ... a growing problem is that as leisure and affluence increase, and the difficulty of actually making a living declines, an increasing number of people appear to have little left to live for, and do not know how to fill their lives. Psychiatrists have to deal increasingly with this problem of the 'existential vacuum'. Many people have found that the world of natural history can provide

an abiding sense of purpose from the infinity of experience and interest which it offers. [15]

... nature conservation and its meaning penetrates far beyond the rational and conscious into the emotional and unconscious. It touches the roots of human nature and is ultimately to do with being and feeling. [16]

This kind of metaphysical argument for nature conservation is by no means fully accepted and many commentators would ascribe a higher priority to economic growth and human welfare than to the spiritual enjoyment to be gained from nature conservation. For example Passmore concludes in his review of man's responsibilities for nature that nature conservationists have had to fight against two philosophical traditions. First, that man is the sole finite agent and nature a vast system of machines for man to use and modify as he pleases. Second, that critics of economic progress and its inevitable disruption of wildlife are unscientific sentimentalists who wish to stand in the way of man's material development [17]. Nature conservationists have thus had to show that man is not a creature apart, but fundamentally a part of the wildlife system, and then to demonstrate this interrelationship by scientific analysis. The next section shows how nature conservationists have used the 'scientific/educational' approach to advance their cause.

## THE 'SCIENTIFIC/EDUCATIONAL' APPROACH TO NATURE CONSERVATION

In common with the idea that man might have a moral responsibility for nature, the idea that wild plants and animals could be a source of scientific instruction or of educational value in their own right claimed but few adherents in the seventeenth and eighteenth centuries. M. Blackmore describes how the great estates of the period, though vigorously managed, aimed at providing timber, pleasant landscapes and food for the table [18]. Nonetheless, naturalists had been adding to the store of knowledge about nature since Gilbert White began his detailed study of the wildlife of Selbourne in Hampshire in the seventeenth century. This approach was followed for the next two centuries, and impetus was given to it in the nineteenth century by the opening up of new parts of the world in which to classify and record wildlife. Darwin's four year voyage of collection in the *Beagle* and Veitch's expeditions to the Himalayas and Far East are examples. This approach was, however, rather sterile and sought to describe rather than explain. A wider approach did not develop until this century when the new science of ecology was founded. Dudley Stamp has traced the growth of ecology, from the translation into English in 1903 of A. F. W. Schimper's *Pflanzgeografie,* through the first publication of the *Journal of Ecology* in 1912, to A. G. Tansley's revolutionary concept of the ecosystem which he first presented in 1935 [19].

The science of ecology introduced two new ideas into nature conservation. These are, the need to consider all species, rather than single species in isolation, and to replace the artificial environment of the zoo with the natural one of the nature reserve. Nonetheless, Stamp still acknowledged the value of single species preservation in the zoological garden environment when he wrote,

> Some plants need protection if they are to survive, many animals and birds certainly do. . . . Let us face the issue fairly and squarely. A large number of animals and plants now have little or no hope of survival in the wild. . . . Half of all the Hawaian geese in the world are at Slimbridge Wildlife Reserve. [20]

Apart from these special cases, ecologists in the 1940s began to realize that more value could be obtained from studying wildlife in its natural competitive state, and so they developed the concept of the 'Nature Reserve', not just as a means for preservation, but also to facilitate scientific research and education. Max Nicholson observed that the practical application of ecology in the 'Nature Reserve' concept is 'one definition of conservation, and not a bad one' [21].

Even when in the 1940s nature reserves were officially recognized in Britain as being politically worthwhile the idea that nothing more had to be done than to find supposedly 'natural' areas and put ring fences around them, died hard. Fortunately, the views of the committee and staff of the newly created Nature Conservancy prevailed and since then A. G. Tansley's thesis that true conservation of nature and the environment flows naturally from ecological understanding has become the nearly universal doctrine.

Unfortunately, scientific knowledge has not yet caught up with the breadth of the ecosystem concept and in 1974 it was still possible for E. Duffy to write, 'the ecological knowledge required for the successful scientific management of wildlife communities and species is still rudimentary and research must not be allowed to lag behind the growing needs of the future' [22].

Another problem with the ecosystem approach is how to assess the two-fold role of man. First, man interferes with the so-called natural evolution of nature and second, he has introduced new species into most areas of the world. In Britain, for example, introduced species outnumber indigeneous species many times over. A further problem concerns the reconciliation of access to land by the public with preservation of protected habitats. To some extent this can be overcome by the development of nature trails which can combine scientific research and educational use. In 1977 the British Tourist Authority listed several such trails for each county in Britain [23]. The general public's continued attraction to wildlife has been demonstrated by a number of surveys. For instance, a survey of a forest in northern England showed that three-quarters of visitors hoped to see some form of wildlife, although there were wide variations between the popularity of different forms of wildlife. Deer and orchids are popular; insects and reptiles are unpopular [24].

Ironically, at the same time that it has become necessary to preserve wildlife in reserves as natural habitats have been destroyed by the pressure of economic growth, the suburban habitat has grown in value. In 1975, J. Owen and D. Owen found that suburban gardens covered 405,000 hectares, or 2.7 per cent of the total land area of England and Wales and that they supported an enormous variety of wildlife making them the most important nature reserve in the country [25]. Their value is further enhanced by the fact that they are in no danger of disappearing and will on the contrary probably spread.

Suburban gardens with their mass of alien species really do highlight the previously-noted scientific dilemma of how to deal with the problem of introduced species. By definition, introduced species must upset any idea of naturally-developing ecosystems based on the pure Tansley model. This problem was examined in detail at an important symposium on 'The Changing Flora and Fauna of Great Britain' in 1973. The majority view was that a liberal attitude was needed, particularly when so many botanical introductions had been made in the last century and are now to all intents and purposes wild plants. Indeed, K. Mellanby in his summary of the symposium, concludes that the conservation of ecosystems is more important than the merely systematic sectional approach based on individual species which tends to give exaggerated attention to rare species which are not necessarily any more scientifically valuable than common species [26].

The hope that the ecosystem approach will lead to the successful conservation of ecosystems in nature reserves has been dealt a savage blow by recent worldwide research reported by J. Diamond in his seminal paper on the 'Island dilemma' in 1975 [27]. He begins his paper by pointing out that natural habitats throughout the world are undergoing two changes. First, the total area occupied by natural habitats and by species adversely affected by man is shrinking, and secondly, formerly continuous natural habitats and the distributional ranges of man-intolerant species are being fragmented. By and large, the smaller the wildlife island the fewer species will survive and the quicker they will become extinct. But, the situation is not quite as simple as this. For example, different species will decline at different rates while some species may actually increase. The crucial points that Diamond makes are that nature reserves cannot by themselves preserve the existing pattern of wildlife and that wildlife conservation must be conducted at a global scale. Diamond's thesis leads logically to the third main approach to nature conservation identified in this paper which is that man's erosion of wildlife habitats threatens his own survival by undermining the life support systems of his own personal habitat.

## The 'Preservationist/Disaster' Approach to Nature Conservation

The third approach to nature conservation focuses on man's instinct for self-preservation which has brought him apparent control over the natural world. It is only recently that it has become respectable to criticize this view of all powerful man, although the preceding discussion has outlined the views of some early but generally isolated critics like Thomas Malthus and G. P. Marsh. It can be argued that the turning point in modern times came in 1963 with the publication of Rachel Carson's *Silent Spring* [28]. This often over-dramatic but politically-effective book paved the way for a host of doom-laden forecasts about the consequences of treating nature insensitively. Carson states that man's attitude to plants is a singularly narrow one. 'If we see any immediate utility in a plant we foster it. If for any reason we find its presence undesirable or merely a matter of indifference, we may condemn it to destruction forthwith' [29]. This view is further developed by J. Dorst, who points out that the real question is not whether man has the moral right to exterminate plants or animals, but whether it is in his interest to do so [30]. He considers that nature will never be saved from the actions of man. Rather, the real problem today is to save man from himself. To do this, Dorst argues that man must first curb population growth and secondly prevent land waste. In the longer term we need to sign a new pact with nature which will permit us to live in harmony with nature and not against it.

A central theme of this new school of thought is that man is not only destroying wildlife in small pockets as before, but is fundamentally altering the entire world ecosystem leading to irreversible declines in both the quality and quantity of living organisms as pollution worsens and the range of life able to exist on earth narrows. A chain of survival is envisaged, with the simplest organisms at the bottom of the chain being eliminated first, followed by successively more sophisticated animals and plants, as pollution works its way inexorably up until it reaches man at the top. The worldwide nature of the issues is neatly expressed by the botanist Nicholas Polunin.

> Even if, as many of us believe, 'there is time to avoid the abyss' of non-survival, there is no time for complacency. Rather there is need for eternal vigilance, scientific monitoring, international legal and other enlightened controls and often very costly action. For Man is inexorably changing the world, though often insidiously and quite unintentionally. Already he has the knowledge and wherewithal to control his numbers, effects, and very destiny, maintaining the biosphere for himself and to some extent for Nature; but has he the collective wisdom? And what are the limits of his folly? [31]

The present worldwide acceptance of this view by some specialists is confirmed by the collective views of 152 consultants, drawn together by B. Ward and R. Dubos for the 1972 United Nations Conference on the environment held in Stockholm. They summed up the general viewpoint as follows:

> In short, the two worlds of man—the biosphere of his inheritance, the technosphere of his creation—are out of balance, indeed, potentially in deep

conflict. And man is in the middle. This is the hinge of history at which we stand, the door of the future opening on to a crisis more sudden, more global, more inexorable and more bewildering than any ever encountered by the human species . . . [32]

SUMMARY OF APPROACHES TO NATURE CONSERVATION

The previous three sections have discussed the three main arguments advanced in favour of nature conservation. These have been summarized by the British Nature Conservancy Council,

> The conservation of wildlife is essential, because it safeguards resources which have economic, scientific, educational and aesthetic value. The nation has an obligation to hand on to future generations the richness and diversity of natural wealth which it has received from the past, and whenever possible to enhance it. . . . For the first time in the history of our country our resources of wildlife will be reduced unacceptably unless we plan to maintain them and pay more for them. We have had them virtually free for so long that this is a hard fact to accept. [33]

This neat exposition reintroduces the role of the nation state in nature conservation and reminds us that an argument put forward, even persuasively and authoritatively, does not necessarily lead to political action. The late 1960s and 1970s have, however, seen a number of government statements and international agreements in the field of nature conservation. A good example of a justification for wildlife conservation is provided by the British government's submission to the United Nations Conference on the Human Environment held in Stockholm in 1972 which listed eleven reasons for preserving wildlife [34]:

1. as a contributory component of ecological stability;
2. as a monitor of environmental pollution;
3. for the maintenance of genetic variability;
4. for the provision of a source of renewable biological resources;
5. for the needs of scientific research into the environment;
6. for its cultural and recreational value;
7. as a component of the aesthetic quality of the landscape;
8. for environmental education;
9. for the economic value of its resource, scientific and recreational components;
10. to provide future generations with a wide choice of biological capital;
11. for moral and ethical reasons.

The submission also recommended that, 'the government must develop a wildlife conservation policy which integrates the countryside as the habitat of wildlife with its uses for agriculture, forestry and recreation' and that the government should introduce legislation which could enable all forms of wildlife to be protected [35]. The rest of this paper discusses the responses to these arguments by governments around the world, before concluding with an assessment of the effectiveness with which the case for nature conservation has been made.

## NATIONAL AND INTERNATIONAL RESPONSES TO THE NATURE CONSERVATION CAUSE

In Britain, the work of the Nature Conservancy Council is well known and fully documented by its annual reports to Parliament, the source of its funds. Briefly, the Council conducts its work by managing national nature reserves (which it may own or rent), by conducting and commissioning research and by educating the public into the need for nature conservation. Since 1973 its work has been divided so that the Council looks after the nature reserves, finances and advice side, while the newly founded Institute of Terrestrial Ecology conducts scientific research. Throughout its existence the Council has been kept short of funds and has not been able to carry out as full a programme as it would have liked. Fortunately a number of vigorous voluntary organizations also conduct similar work to the Nature Conservancy Council and they often receive the blessing of the government through the medium of grants and favourable tax provisions. The best known of these is the National Trust.

Although the National Trust is primarily interested in buildings and landscapes, there are a number of cases where the conservation of plant, animal and insect life takes precedence [36]. For example, where rare species are present they are protected by prohibiting access except to *bona fide* naturalists. Although the Trust regrets this restriction, it argues that rare species may in due course spread outwards from their reserve and be seen by the general public again. The Trust often uses outside help to manage its reserves; the Nature Conservancy manages Scolt Head and the Field Studies Council manages Malham. In the specialist area of bird protection, the Royal Society for the Protection of Birds plays a very valuable role in attracting funds, maintaining public interest and in acquiring nature reserves. Other specialist bodies are also important, for example, the numerous field sport associations. Although primarily interested in hunting, shooting and angling, they are also concerned that stocks and habitats are maintained.

At a local level the County Naturalists Trusts have become increasingly important since the first one was formed in 1945. By 1977, there were forty County Naturalists Trusts fulfilling an important role, notably in consulting with planning authorities about plan making and planning permission. Unfortunately the transfer of planning control to district authorities in 1974 weakened this role and a survey in 1977 found that few district planning authorities were consulting the Trusts about planning applications, and were thus ignoring a potential source of expertise [37].

Notwithstanding the growth of nature conservation organizations throughout the 1950s and 1960s, it was still possible to argue in 1973 that official and voluntary organizations dealing with wildlife suffered from a lack of substantial financial support and a lack of sympathy and help when facing direct conflict with other interests, especially economic ones [38]. Clearly then, the case for nature conservation in Britain has yet to be fully accepted by the British government in spite of its statement in 1977 that,

> the general survival of the nation's wildlife cannot be achieved solely by site protections but depends on the wise management of the nation's land resources as a whole. Consequently, nature conservation has a place in all activities affecting rural land use and planning. [39]

In Sweden, T. Larsson argues that nature conservation has developed as a response to the opening up and exploitation of previously remote areas [40]. Until the last decade or so large areas of the country were protected by their inaccessibility but since the war, industry and other changes including better communications have begun to threaten all parts of the country. Real progress was made when the 1964 Nature Conservancy Act, which safeguards valuable areas and provided protection concerning land-use change, was amended to increase the role of nature conservation in forestry practice, to prevent shoreline housing development, and to forbid cross-country driving and shooting from off-road vehicles. In addition, 1.7 million hectares have been set aside for protection as national parks, nature reserves and wildlife sanctuaries. These can be established for both recreational and scientific purposes, although access to wildlife sanctuaries may be restricted in the breeding season. Larsson concludes that nature conservation in Sweden is, as elsewhere, largely a defensive process reacting to changes often outside its real control.

Italy is another country where nature conservation while theoretically strong is in practice weak. F. Cassola and S. Lovaro state that nature conservation is accorded low status in Italy and blame the central government for this [41]. They argue that the State has not established a new national park for forty years and has failed to manage correctly the few that already exist. Part of the blame is attached to sterile battles for political power over conservation fought between the central and regional governments. The State is now beginning procedures to create six new national parks and Cassola and Lovaro hope that national and international public opinion will encourage the Italian government to establish many more protected territories and to provide the resources for realistic management.

A final example of the gap between apparently thorough legislation and action on the ground is provided by Spain. In 1975, the Protected Natural Spaces Act defined four kinds of area: integral reserves of scientific interest, national parks, natural places of national interest and natural parks. But as Viedma and Ramos reported in 1977, none of the former protected areas which now qualified for designation under the Act had in fact been re-scheduled, and even the regulations relating to it had not been drawn up [42].

Ramos has also criticized the Spanish Institute of Nature Conservancy which deals with the fifty per cent of Spanish land that is uncultivated. He believes the Institute suffers from being only a department within the Ministry of Agriculture, from a growing dissociation between academic work and real-life decisions and finally, from a lack of real executive power [43]. Not only does the Institute lose out within the Ministry of Agriculture to pressures for agricultural expansion, as for example over draining the marshes of the River Guadalquivir, but the Ministry of Agriculture in turn loses out to the more powerful Ministries of Industry, Public Works or Tourism when economic developments affecting rural land are proposed. Finally, C. Carrasco criticizes the small amount of cash spent on Spanish national parks (only twelve million pesetas in 1974) and contrasts this with the much greater sums (124 million pesetas) spent on providing hunting and fishing reserves where benefits are enjoyed by only a few people [44].

The situation outside Europe is even worse where, because of public opinion or lack of finance, many of the world's nature reserves are virtually unmanaged. Also, many suffer from poaching, deforestation and other forms of encroachment or incursion. It is probable that this attitude of benign neglect will continue, at least in tropical countries, for the foreseeable future. Accordingly, models of the effects of lax management and the biological consequences of insularity have been constructed. One of these for East Africa shows that the pace of extinctions is inversely related to reserve size, but that even the largest reserves would lose most of their large species in a few centuries [45].

The extinction of many large species has already occurred in North America. Indeed, nowhere was the destruction of large species achieved more rapidly than in the exploitation of wildlife in the United States in the nineteenth century. In this period, wildlife was in the anomalous position of theoretically belonging to everybody and, therefore, to nobody [46]. Only later did the people through their political representatives assume a responsibility for wildlife. The first steps taken towards the end of the nineteenth century were to restock the country by a combination of nature reserves and by controlling the rate at which species could be killed. Many species were quickly controlled in this way, but in this century restocking and preservation were undermined by a decline in the numbers of many species of protected animals, because of habitat changes elsewhere. For example, species in a reserve may depend for their survival on other unprotected species that migrate across the reserve. If these fall in number then the pro-tected species may be endangered. Conversely, techniques of producing hunt-able species have so improved that vast quantities of wildlife, like deer and pheasants, are now reared for hunting. In fact, the sporting motive is a major force behind wildlife preservation in the United States as it is in Europe.

In Europe the two main bodies involved in conservation, the Council of Europe and its European Committee for the Conservation of Nature and Natural Resources have had to fight against the entrenched hunting lobby to achieve their two main aims [47]. These are first, to inform the public of changes in European wildlife and secondly, to pressure national governments into agreeing to international cooperation. The first aim has been achieved by the publication of twelve books in the series 'Nature and Environment' between 1962 and 1976. Recent examples include, *Threatened Mammals in Europe* (1976) which lists thirty-six endangered species and *The Effects of Recreation on the Ecology of Natural Landscapes* (1977) which highlights the uncoordinated nature of research in this area and recommends that member countries set up study groups to report on the location and extent of the areas used for outdoor recreation, their existing and predicted use, their amenity and ecological characteristics and the nature of potential problems.

Perhaps the most significant Council of Europe wildlife publication is *The Integrated Management of the European Wildlife Heritage* (1975) which, after outlining the causes of wildlife decline and the rather sketchy agreements concerning the international protection of wildlife, draws up a thirteen point plan of action as shown in the table. The Council of Europe plan recognizes that none of the national measures shown will achieve fundamental success without international agreement. C. Klemm has reviewed the degree of international cooperation so far achieved in the management of wildlife [48]. At a global scale, as a result of the 1972 Stockholm conference on the

*The Council of Europe's plan of action for the conservation of European wildlife.*

| |
|---|
| 1.  Draw up a European plan laying down priorities for various species |
| 2.  Each national state to draw up a national wildlife plan |
| 3.  Conduct an inventory of European species |
| 4.  Make periodical reviews of the wildlife situation |
| 5.  Assess the effects of products harmful to wildlife |
| 6.  Assess the need for further preservation of habitats |
| 7.  Consider the further implementation of protected areas |
| 8.  Draw up a list of rare or threatened species |
| 9.  Review the control of hunting and shooting interests |
| 10. Draw up specific international plans for migratory species |
| 11. Consider further controls over the trade in, keeping of and introduction of animals |
| 12. Continue to promote education of the public |
| 13. To develop further relations between the Council of Europe and other international organizations |

environment, the UN set up the United Nations Environment Programme with headquarters in Nairobi. Amongst its other roles this has a duty to protect wildlife and its habitats. UNESCO and FAO also have programmes for wildlife management, most notably the creation of a coordinated world network of protected areas known as 'biosphere reserves'.

There are also a number of non-governmental organizations at the world scale. For example IUCN is a private organization, although it counts nation states among its members. It works through specialized commissions and publishes the *Red Book,* a world list of endangered species. The World Wildlife Fund (founded in 1961) is an executive organization which raises funds to finance urgent projects which it selects in cooperation with IUCN. This enables it to intervene rapidly in order to save a threatened species or habitat. Other organizations include the International Council for Bird Preservation, the International Waterfowl Research Bureau and the International Hunting and Shooting Council. In addition there are a number of international regulations which governments have agreed to follow, albeit with varying degrees of enthusiasm. The 1950 Paris Convention which protects all birds during the breeding period and rare bird species throughout the year has only been ratified by a small number of countries.

CONCLUSION: A DEVELOPING CASE?

It is relatively easy in reviews of this kind to produce a seemingly logical progression of events, but history is rarely that simple. It is the purpose of this final section to assess the extent to which conservation has achieved political responsibility over the past hundred years. For reasons of space this review is confined to Britain, but it is clear from the preceding analysis that progress outside Britain has been similar, if somewhat slower, and so similar conclusions may be drawn.

Sheail shows how the first part of the period from 1870 to 1940 was characterized by a move away from the idea of creating national parks as wildlife sanctuaries towards a concept of the 'multi-purpose area' advocated by Dower in 1945 [49]. As late as 1931 the Addison report on national parks concluded that there was no alternative but to create two kinds of park, one primarily for outdoor recreation situated near large urban centres and the other for the preservation of scenery and wildlife [50]. These types of argument failed to excite the official imagination and in 1939 a government report on *The Preservation of the Countryside* still barely mentioned wildlife, except for referring to the lack of powers for preserving trees [51]. Even the 1942 'Scott Report' on land use in rural areas contains very little on wildlife, but it did recommend the setting up of nature reserves with prohibition of access as a first consideration [52].

There is thus little outward evidence in official circles of a growing interest in conservation between 1870 and 1940. Much work had been done, however, behind the scenes and the wartime debates of the national coalition government gave nature conservationists a unique chance to put forward their views in an apolitical climate. They did this brilliantly, particularly in evidence to the wartime Nature Reserves Investigation Committee [53]. After the war the new-found momentum was carried on by the work of the Huxley Committee whose report *Conservation of Nature in England and Wales* (1947) emphasizes two distinct lines of argument for a political recognition for nature conservation [54]. The first of these, the 'aesthetic' approach, is based upon preserving the characteristic beauty of the landscape and providing ample access and facilities for open-air recreation. The second, the 'scientific' approach, is primarily directed to the advancement of knowledge, without necessarily understanding the importance of aesthetic values. The committee believed it was wrong to suppose that there was any essential conflict between these two sets of interests, although their special requirements may differ. For these and other reasons the Committee recommended that the government should take a general responsibility for the conservation and control of the flora and fauna of the country and for the protection of features of geological and physiographical interest. A number of other considerations were also put forward in favour of nature conservation. First, the highly intricate and involved series of interactions which bring about the balance of nature are far from being completely understood and are sometimes of a most unexpected kind. Secondly, man is potentially the most destructive of all animal species and through ignorance and neglect frequently destroys things of great value to his own material, mental and spiritual advancement and thirdly, these islands are already crowded and demands for further development of land are increasing.

The political success of the report can be judged from the growth of the Nature Conservancy which was set up in 1948. This success was something of a double-edged weapon; by 1964 there was a feeling that much of the problem had already been tackled by the legislative action of the late 1940s and the designations of nature reserves and other protected areas in the 1950s. Indeed in 1964 a conference on 'The Countryside in 1970' put forward only one specific point out of twenty-five on the need for greater powers for nature conservation [55]. Furthermore, this was rather weakly worded and only called for a review of the legislation for the protection of nature and in particular for more adequate protection for sites of special scientific interest.

This feeling of complacency (albeit tinged with the caution of new environmental threats from land-use change and pollution) was reinforced by Max Nicholson of the Nature Conservancy. He pointed out the progress achieved not only in Britain, but by the British in helping to set up the World Wildlife Fund in 1961, and argued that, 'In these and other ways the once weak and dispersed efforts of the nature movement in Britain are being transformed into a new, strong and united drive at the pace which the modern world demands' [56]. Nicholson further echoed the need for nature conservation to be politically respectable when he continued,

> While supporting the growth of a strong and effectively organised nature movement, the Nature Conservancy have been mindful of the perils of narrow, intolerant or uncompromising attitudes in a world where mutual understanding and give and take are absolutely necessary. The Conservancy have therefore tried hard to understand the problems and attitudes of other interests which might conflict with conservation and to reach agreements with them for constructive partnership, ... [57]

The period of the mid-1960s was a time of positive optimism, but this was soon to be disturbed by the shock waves of the 'ecodisaster school' and then the economic crisis of the 1970s, which although slowing the engines of pollution also reduced even more the amount of resources for nature conservation and led to a growing realization that much remained to be done. For example, as part of its continuing struggle to gain further funds and control over habitats, the Nature Conservancy Council published the results of a review of sites of conservation importance in 1977. This reveals that roughly 950,000 hectares (700 key sites) are worthy of protection, but that only 120,000 hectares (153 sites) are actually protected by a full national nature reserve designation [58]. Accepting that not all these sites could be acquired in the near future, the Council put forward various proposals for public comment. Farmers and voluntary bodies are identified as the key groups to influence if wildlife is to be preserved outside of officially protected reserves and species.

An obvious conclusion to be drawn from their survey is that nature conservation is still struggling to survive and become politically acceptable, for in spite of the fact that wildlife conservation groups have experienced a rapid growth in membership in the postwar years and although they have appreciated the power of concerted lobbies and coordinated action, their effect on Whitehall has been slight, since many civil servants have tended to regard their members as socially unrepresentative, unworldly and possibly somewhat eccentric [59]. Furthermore, they have little of the power of the economically-based groupings of employers and trade unionists who deal directly with the government. This lack of power relegates the group's role to that of fighting a rearguard action rather than positively influencing policy formulation. For example, the group's most successful use of Parliament has been through the medium of sympathetic MPs, who have used the traditional back benchers weapons of Parliamentary questions, motions and adjournment debates to get publicity for their cause and remind Ministers of their presence. Occasionally, a private member's Bill may be introduced by an MP lucky enough to have won the ballot; a number of Bills for the protection of wild creatures have been adopted in this way. In the opinion of S. Brookes and J. Richardson, further progress will be made only if certain techniques and methods appropriate in a British situation are adopted, *viz:* the effective exploitation of crisis situations, establishing alliances of conservationist groups and related interest groups and changing the ground rules which have strengthened the power of anti-conservationist groups [60].

It is reasonably clear then that the battle for political respectability has been only partly won. Although government does now offer more than lip service to the aims of nature conservation, it does not always place it above goals like economic growth. The battle, let alone the war, will not be won while the scientific argument for nature conservation is still not fully accepted by the scientific world. Even D. Ratcliffe, chief scientist at the Nature Conservancy Council, has said that many scientists see nature conservation as irrelevant to their interests and are critical of its hasty, slip-shod methods [61]. He further states that the species that attract most conservation attention are those most popular with the general public or those on the verge of extinction but not necessarily the most worthy of investigation. He is sufficiently pessimistic to regard wildlife conservation as a defensive rearguard action against the inexorable advance of overwhelming superior forces.

In summary, the preceding discussion suggests that nature conservation has but limited political appeal in spite of the fact that public opinion is now generally favourable to wildlife preservation for its own sake, that some scientific arguments can be made in favour of conservation for research purposes, and that man cannot live on this planet without other creatures to support him. None of this, however, answers the ultimate and somewhat paradoxical question that nature conservationists have yet to face squarely.

Stated simply the paradox is this. In order to have the time and resources to care for nature man must provide an economic surplus, but at the same time growing population totals throughout the world have forced man to put ever increasing pressure on space to produce this surplus. Accordingly, wildlife in its natural state is pushed into ever smaller and smaller enclaves, until it can no longer survive. In these terms conservation and economic growth are ultimately incompatible. The only solution, bar catastrophe, is for wildlife to co-exist with man. Although some first attempts have been made to allow modern agriculture and wildlife to co-exist in the British lowlands, much work remains to be done if nature conservation is to move further along the road which in the past hundred years has progressed from museums to artificial zoological gardens, through the idea of nature reserves to the concept of a globally managed ecosystem. Unless this last step is taken the long-term survival of all life as we know it on this planet is in danger.

NOTES

1. Sheail, J. (1976) *Nature in Trust: The History of Nature Conservation in Great Britain*. Glasgow: Blackie.
2. Nature Reserves Investigation Committee (1943) *Nature Conservation in Great Britain*. London: HMSO.

3. Tansley, A. G. (1945) *Our Heritage of Wild Nature.* Cambridge: Cambridge University Press.
4. Ministry of Town and Country Planning (1947) *Conservation of Nature in England and Wales,* Cmd. 7122. London: HMSO.
5. Gilg, A. W. (1978) *Countryside Planning.* Newton Abbot: David and Charles.
6. Nicholson, M. (1970) *The Environmental Revolution.* London: Hodder and Stoughton.
7. Foster, J. (1978) *Working for Wildlife.* Toronto: University of Toronto Press.
8. Udall, S. (1963) *The Quiet Crisis.* New York: Holt, Rinehart and Winston, p. 54.
9. Royal Commission on Fish and Game (1892) *Report.* Toronto: Queen's Printer, p. 189.
10. Nicholson, M. (1970) *The Environmental Revolution.* London: Hodder and Stoughton, p. 203.
11. Passmore, J. (1974) *Man's Responsibility for Nature.* London: Duckworth.
12. Marsh, G. P. (1864) *Man and Nature.* Harvard: Harvard University Press, p. 43.
13. Anderson, E. N. (1972) Radical ecology: Notes on a conservation movement. *Biological Conservation,* 4 (4), p. 285.
14. Ratcliffe, D. A. (1976) Thoughts towards a philosophy of nature conservation. *Biological Conservation,* 9 (1), pp. 45–53.
15. *Ibid.,* p. 49.
16. *Ibid.,* pp. 52–3.
17. Passmore, J. (1974) *Man's Responsibility for Nature.* London: Duckworth.
18. Blackmore, M. (1974) The Nature Conservancy: Its history and role, in Warren, A. and Goldsmith, F. (eds.), *Conservation in Practice.* London: Wiley.
19. Stamp, L. D. (1969) *Nature Conservation in Britain.* London: Collins.
20. *Ibid.,* pp. 123–4.
21. Nicholson, M. (1974) Foreword, in Warren, A. and Goldsmith, F. (eds.), *Conservation in Practice.* London: Wiley, p. v.
22. Duffy, E. (1974) *Nature Reserves and Wildlife.* London: Heinemann, p. 116.
23. British Tourist Authority (1977) *Nature Trails.* London: The British Tourist Authority.
24. Everett, R. F. (1978) The wildlife preferences shown by countryside visitors. *Biological Conservation,* 14 (1), pp. 75–84.
25. Owen, J. and Owen, D. F. (1975) Suburban gardens: England's most important nature reserve? *Biological Conservation,* 2 (1), pp. 53–9.
26. Hawksworth, D. L. (ed.) (1974) *The Changing Flora and Fauna of Great Britain.* London: Academic Press.
27. Diamond, J. M. (1975) The island dilemma. *Biological Conservation,* 7 (2), pp. 129–46.
28. .Carson, R. L. (1963) *Silent Spring.* London: Hamish Hamilton.
29. *Ibid.,* p. 52.
30. Dorst, J. (1970) *Before Nature Dies.* London: Collins.
31. Polunin, N. (1974) Thoughts on some conceivable ecodisasters. *Environmental Conservation,* 1 (3), p. 187.
32. Ward, B. and Dubos, R. (1972) *Only One Earth.* London: Andre Deutsch, p. 47.
33. Nature Conservancy Council (1977) *Nature Conservation and Agriculture.* London: The Nature Conservancy Council, pp. 33 and 34.
34. Department of the Environment (1972) *Sinews for Survival.* London: HMSO.
35. *Ibid.,* p. 66.

36. Fedden, R. (1974) *The National Trust: Past and Present.* London: Jonathan Cape.
37. Beynon, J. and Wetton, B. (1979) Planning for nature conservation. *The Planner,* 65 (1), pp. 6–7.
38. Kelcey, J. (1973) A guide to nature conservation. *Built Environment,* 2, pp. 639–41.
39. Department of the Environment (1977) *Nature Conservation and Planning,* Circular 108/77. London: HMSO, paragraph 24.
40. Larsson, T. (1977) Nature conservation in Sweden. *Biological Conservation,* 11 (2), pp. 129–43.
41. Cassola, F. and Lovaro, S. (1976) Nature conservation in Italy. *Biological Conservation,* 9 (3), pp. 243–57.
42. Viedma, M. G. and Ramos, A. (1978) A commentary on Spain's 1975 Protection of Natural Spaces Act. *Biological Conservation,* 14 (1), pp. 13–23.
43. Ramos, A. (1976) Natural landscapes in Spain. *Landscape Planning,* 3 (1), pp. 7–8 and 25–33.
44. de Vera Carrasco-Munoz, C. (1977) Les parcs nationaux d'Espagne. *Biological Conservation,* 11 (1), pp. 5–11.
45. Soule, M. E., Wilcox, B. A. and Holtby, C. (1979) Benign neglect: A model of faunal collapse in the game reserves of East Africa. *Biological Conservation,* 15 (4), pp. 259–72.
46. Dasmann, R. F. (1968) *Environmental Conservation.* New York: Wiley.
47. Smit, C. J. and Wijngaarden, A. (1976) *Threatened Mammals in Europe.* Strasbourg: Council of Europe (HMSO).
48. Klemm, D. C. (1975) *The Integrated Management of the European Wildlife Heritage.* Strasbourg: Council of Europe (HMSO).
49. Dower, M. (1945) *National Parks in England and Wales,* Cmd. 6378. London: HMSO; Sheail, J. (1975) The concept of National Parks in Great Britain 1900–1950. *Transactions of the Institute of British Geographers,* 66, pp. 41–56.
50. Addison, C. (1931) *Report of the National Parks Committee,* Cmd. 3851. London: HMSO.
51. Ministry of Health (1939) *Report on the Preservation of the Countryside.* London: HMSO.
52. Ministry of Works and Planning (1942) *Committee on Land Utilisation in Rural Areas,* Cmd. 6378. London: HMSO.
53. Nature Reserves Investigation Committee (1943) *Nature Conservation in Great Britain.* London: HMSO.
54. Ministry of Town and Country Planning (1947) *Conservation of Nature in England and Wales,* Cmd. 7122. London: HMSO.
55. Nature Conservancy (eds.) (1964) *The Countryside in 1970.* London: HMSO.
56. Nicholson, M. (1964) quoted in *ibid.,* p. 204.
57. *Idem.*
58. Nature Conservancy Council (1977) *A Nature Conservation Review: Towards Implementation.* London: HMSO.
59. Brookes, S. K. and Richardson, J. J. (1975) The environmental lobby in Britain. *Parliamentary Affairs,* 28 (3), pp. 312–28.
60. *Idem.*
61. Ratcliffe, D. A. (1977) Nature conservation: Aims, methods and achievements. *Proceedings of the Royal Society of London B,* 197 (1), pp. 11–30.

# 8

# The early campaign for a national park in the Lake District[1]

## FRANCIS SANDBACH

A number of recent studies have reviewed the National Parks campaign in the interwar period [2–4]. There remains, however, much uncertainty as to the actual influence of pressure groups and the contribution of economic and political factors. The web of amenity societies, with multiple membership of influential individuals, can give rise to misleading interpretations if research is confined to the official reports of those groups and government alone. Moreover, the credit for initiating negotiations and achieving settlements is often given to the group with status and assumed influence where in fact others deserve it. This is found to have been the case during the early years of the National Parks campaign.

After the First World War there was mounting concern about preserving the countryside in the face of virtually unplanned urban growth and ribbon development, an accelerated growth of electricity generation with its associated amenity problems of pylons and overhead wires, as well as other features such as motor transport, petrol-filling stations, telephone wires, afforestation, skywriting and caravan encampments. In 1926 the Council for the Preservation of Rural England (CPRE) was formed to bring together national and local interest groups concerned with the countryside. Its task was to coordinate the promotion of relevant legislation, seek voluntary agreements to preserve important features of the landscape, and to advise landowners, developers and individual members of the public. During the interwar period various aspects of preservation warranted special attention from the voluntary amenity movement; of these the campaign to obtain national parks was one of the most significant.

The National Parks campaign can be traced back to a series of unsuccessful Bills aimed at gaining public access to mountain areas. The first of these was introduced by J. Bryce in 1884, and six more Bills were introduced between 1924 and 1931. During the 1920s, the aims of preservation and improved access to the countryside were combined in the first formulations of national park proposals. Impressed by American and Canadian national parks after a visit in 1925, Lord Bledisloe, the Parliamentary Secretary to the Ministry of Agriculture, began a personal publicity campaign for national parks in Britain [5]. In 1928 he wrote to the Prime Minister advocating the Forest of Dean as a national park, and at the same time offered part of his estate in the Forest for this purpose. One year later the CPRE submitted a memorandum to the Prime Minister, Ramsay MacDonald, calling for an enquiry into the need for national parks in Britain. After referring this memorandum to the First Commissioner of Works and to the Minister of Agriculture, the Prime Minister agreed to set up an official interdepartment National Park Committee under the chairmanship of C. Addison, Parliamentary Secretary of the Ministry of Agriculture.

The Addison Committee on National Parks reported in April 1931 [6]. It recommended the setting up of a National Parks Authority with an annual spending power of £100,000 or £10,000, dependent upon economic circumstances, and the establishment of executive regional planning in the Lake District and other potential national park areas. The report failed to bring about national parks in the 1930s, and it was not until the National Parks Act of 1949 that this became possible [7]. Despite this failure, there were some achievements of a comparatively limited nature. For example, there was the creation of a few national forest parks, first in Argyllshire in 1936 and then later in the Forest of Dean in 1939, and Snowdon in 1940. In some potential national park areas, notably in Dovedale, there was much success in securing land for the National Trust. However, the Addison Committee proposals formed the basis of the National Parks movement throughout the 1930s. Moreover, the membership of the Standing Committee on National Parks (SCNP), the voluntary body responsible in the main for leading the campaign from 1936 onward, was confined, apart from a few co-opted members, to representatives of those societies that had given evidence to the Addison Committee in 1929 and 1930 [8].

There was general agreement amongst pressure groups over the desirability of the Addison Committee proposals, but there was not the same degree of consensus about which areas in particular should have special preservation treatment and so become national parks. Moreover, there was much disagreement over the type of campaigning tactics to be adopted, and the relative merits of agitation, publicity, education and reconciliation. Despite the attempt to bring different interest groups concerned with the countryside together, first under the CPRE in 1926 and then again under the SCNP, conflict existed amongst the main propagandists: the CPRE; the

National Trust; the Ramblers' Organizations; the Commons, Open Spaces and Footpaths Preservation Society (COSFPS), and the Friends of the Lake District (FLD).

The extent of cooperation and conflict, and some of the ensuing consequences, can be illustrated by surveying various events in the Lake District which were important both to the general campaign for national parks and to the specific campaign to preserve the Lake District area as a national park. The period 1931–36 has been chosen as it can be clearly distinguished from that period immediately after when the SCNP exerted a more central influence, the economic climate improved, and the limitations of the 1932 Town and Country Planning Act were more obvious. Before this time, the amenity groups struggled along more or less independently in their efforts to achieve national parks, hoping to secure State-owned national parks and to influence the development of rural planning. The potential national parks were divided into two types: there were those such as the New Forest, the Forest of Dean and parts of Dartmoor, which were largely State-owned and could be turned into national parks without local authority planning; and there were those regional areas including the Lake District, North Wales, the Northumberland Fells, and the East Yorkshire Wold where national parks could be achieved through planning under the 1932 Act [9]. This division of types was compatible with the Addison Committee's proposals to obtain national parks through a mixture of judicious land planning and acquisitions.

The Lake District region is chosen for study for four main reasons. In the first place, above all other places, it was recognized as being the most important in terms of national park objectives. Even the Ramblers' Organizations that had given evidence to the Addison Committee elevated the importance of the Lake District above that of the Peak District, the major battleground for the Ramblers in the 1930s and the main region supporting the Ramblers from the northern industrial conurbations [10]. Moreover, the main attempt to bring county councils together to establish regional planning on a national park basis took place in the Lake District. Of the voluntary agreements, none surpassed the importance of the Forestry Commission agreement in 1936 to preserve a central core area of the Lake District from afforestation by the Commission. This was a dramatic concession both to the natural beauty of the Lake District and to the national park ideal. It was the events leading up to this agreement that most clearly demonstrate the conflict between the various pressure groups involved, with formal communications between the CPRE and FLD virtually breaking down towards the end of 1935 over this issue. The second reason is that the Lake District attracted a high proportion of influential individuals concerned with advancing the national park ideal. It was in the Lake District, that K. Spence, H. H. Symonds, J. Dower, L. P. Abercrombie, R. S. T. Chorley and N. Birkett, to name but a few, became most involved. Thirdly, the National

Parks campaign, in the first five years after the Addison Committee Report, lacked a strong central organization. Under these circumstances the initiative of local societies was of great importance, none more so than in the Lake District [11].

Finally, it can be argued that the local amenity society, the FLD, which grew out of the Lake District National Reserve Committee (LDNRC), was the principal body exerting pressure for national parks. Tradition has it that the CPRE was principally responsible for the series of negotiations with the three county councils in the Lake District for the organization of the National Parks campaign before and after the creation of the SCNP towards the end of 1935 [12], and for the successful negotiations with the Forestry Commission [13]. What actually happened was, however, very different from this simple picture and much more credit should be given to the FLD.

### The Lake District Three Counties Joint Advisory Committee

Between May and July 1931, the LDNRC and CPRE decided to take joint action in an attempt to implement one of the few specific recommendations of the Addison Committee, namely that the Lake District should be considered as a planning unit for the purpose of safeguarding its amenities and providing for its development as a national park. The LDNRC accordingly proceeded to inform the three county councils of Lancashire, Westmorland and Cumberland that it intended holding an informal conference on the advisability of the proposals for a single regional executive planning committee for the Lake District. The date of the conference was delayed, however, as the secretaries of the CPRE and COSFPS, H. G. Griffin and L. Chubb respectively, both thought it important to arouse the interest and influence of the landowners. Their cooperation, it was argued, was needed for two reasons: the first was that without such cooperation rural planning would get nowhere as landowners could be obstructive with claims for compensation, and thus any scheme, although statutory, could in effect be stillborn; secondly, it was thought desirable to show the county councils that something could be gained by the development of a national park scheme.

K. Spence [14], secretary of the LDNRC and Lake District Safeguarding Society, was advised by Abercrombie and Griffin of the CPRE not to attend the meeting with the landowners on the grounds that, as his position as secretary to the two principal Lake District preservation societies brought him into conflict with owners of land, his presence might inhibit free discussion [15]. This irritated Spence and it is clear that even at this early stage in the National Parks campaign there was to be a difference in tactics. Spence wrote to Griffin expressing these differences:

> I am a little amused by your continual requests that I should not antagonize anyone. You must know that you and I both have our different methods and

what seems like antagonizing to you and Nigel Kennedy may only be getting on with the job to me, whereas what is getting on with the job to you may only seem like maintaining the status quo to a hard-bitten revolutionary like myself! [16]

Griffin, however, was less willing to accept Spence's more direct and less conciliatory approach; as far as he was concerned it was just as well Spence had been absent from the meeting as it had been an undoubted success and would lead to something really worthwhile in the future. It was apparent that the landowners were of the opinion that they had been insufficiently consulted in the past, and Griffin was convinced that the amenity movement needed every concession possible from them before going to the local authorities.

The time-consuming tactics of gaining the support of the landowners were probably a mistake for the delay allowed the county councils to consolidate their own separate positions: Lancashire County Council had already asked the Ministry of Health for an order to set up an executive joint town planning committee for North Lonsdale, and Westmorland County Council also lodged an application for an order setting up a committee covering the western half of South Westmorland Rural District Council, the Borough of Kendal, Grasmere, Ambleside and Windermere. G. L. Pepler, Chief Town Planning Inspector at the Ministry of Health, recognized the consequences of delay and advised Griffin to get the county councils together as soon as possible so as to decide upon a principle and a machinery for intercounty regional planning in the Lake District:

> That principle must be settled soon or otherwise you will have every keen county setting up an executive committee covering a portion of Lakeland and this would be very much better than no committee at all. The splendid work you have in hand in educating the land agents and landowners will be an enormous help when the committee or committees are formed, but the matter that it is so necessary to get agreement upon first is what is to be the machine; and what area it is to deal with. [17]

By the time the conference was held on 2nd February 1932, the local authorities, especially Lancashire, had become committed to their own plans, and the proposals put forward by three national amenity boards—the CPRE, National Trust, and COSFPS—for a joint executive planning committee were rejected. The amenity societies were obviously disappointed by this outcome but salvaged a little hope in the belief that some progression might be made from an advisory committee to the development of an executive committee once interauthority suspicions had died down and the advantages of cooperation were realized. However, any such progress was thwarted as a result of county boundary readjustments and the delay in setting up a statutory joint planning committee for North Lonsdale.

It was in fact almost a year before fresh initiatives came, following a meeting of the LDNRC in February 1933 when it was decided to send a resolution to the three county councils [18]. This urged them to set up a joint advisory committee whose task would be to comment on regional reports; to advise on the most economic and effective administration of planning; to comment on the implications arising from the 1932 Town and Country Planning Act; and finally to seek cooperation from the landowners. While the response from Cumberland and Westmorland County Councils was promising, the clerk of the Lancashire County Council did not deem the resolution worthy of consideration by his Council. It was still waiting for the North Lonsdale order, and, in any case, was under the impression that the preliminary steps in setting up the joint advisory committee would be taken by the CPRE. The favourable responses from two of the county councils spurred the CPRE on to try and convene the advisory committee [19], but no sooner had Lancashire County Council agreed to send representatives than Cumberland County Council turned tail, becoming more concerned with its own internal problems of coordinating town and country planning. So once again there was a long delay, this time from April 1933 to August 1934, before a further initiative could be taken.

In the meantime, the LDNRC was disbanded in favour of a new society (an 'association' rather than a 'committee') that was actively to seek membership and financial support. Previously, the committee was constrained by the fact that its membership was confined to representatives from local and national societies. Plans for the new society were begun in March 1934. The society was to promote the policy laid down in the National Park Committee Report of 1931 and in particular was to try and get the three county councils to form a joint executive regional planning committee; by having a membership, it would mobilize local and national support in order to secure good planning under the 1932 Act; and finally it would create a fund which would be available to assist local authorities to provide the compensation necessary to reserve land for agricultural use or as private or public open space. The society was to take the view that it was unreasonable to expect local authorities to pay any substantial sums of money in order to safeguard what should properly be regarded as a national interest [20].

The Lake District National Reserve Association (to be known informally as the Friends of the Lake District) was launched on 17th June 1934 at a meeting organized by the Cumberland and Lake District Ramblers Federation, the Youth Hostels Association and the LDNRC [21]. The FLD, unlike the CPRE, was much more closely associated with the ramblers and youth movement than landowning organizations [22]. This alignment emphasized the more radical position held by the FLD which, although a local organization, also sought national support; it was after all campaigning for a national park and so formed FLD branches in some of the large towns with an interested population such as Manchester, Liverpool, London, Leeds, and Cambridge [23].

Representatives of the three counties met again on 20th November 1934. However, little came of the meeting as they made little more than a gesture towards consultation, believing that any joint committee would have to have full statutory powers and not merely be advisory. Furthermore Cumberland County Council, while appreciating the work done by the amenity societies in convening the meeting, did not want landowner representatives to be on the committee as had been suggested. In fact, it insisted that all future meetings should be between representatives of the county councils alone. In any case, Cumberland County Council was still uncertain whether or not it wanted to take part in a joint advisory committee and so nominate members. The position of the county councils was so ambivalent that none was willing to take an initiative; in these circumstances they allowed J. W. Cropper (chairman of the FLD, and representative of Westmorland County Council) and Griffin to continue as chairman and secretary and to call the next meeting at their discretion. There seemed therefore little prospect of commitment to the policy of Lake District planning on a regional basis, let alone the involvement of a national interest as voiced by the amenity societies. The view of the amenity societies expressed at the meeting was that an advisory committee could perform either of two valuable functions. The less effective one would be to ask the planning bodies to submit their planning proposals when formulated but before adoption, and then to comment constructively upon such proposals. Alternatively, and perhaps more effectively, the Committee would examine the proposals already made or about to be made [24], and then decide on the general scheme which in their opinion was most suitable for the Lake District. After this all planning authorities would draw up their respective schemes accordingly.

Despite the disappointing meeting in November, the CPRE and FLD still felt that something might be gained from the Three Counties Joint Advisory Committee. They still believed that the amenity bodies could impose their advice and technical assistance upon a Joint Advisory Committee; they would suggest to the three county councils, the next time they met, that they should commission a survey plan for the Lake District funded in the main by the amenity societies [25]. They had in mind a blueprint that ought to be accepted by the three counties, and Dower and Abercrombie would be called in to draw up the scheme. This would be prepared in collaboration with the major authorities, already preparing or about to prepare statutory schemes, through a technical subcommittee. The landowning interests would also be brought in either by representatives to the Joint Advisory Committee or at least through a negotiating subcommittee to collaborate with Abercrombie. Even the detailed aims of the plan were discussed: it would broadly show (a) the areas which might be allowed to be developed under the terms of local planning schemes; (b) the areas which ought to be protected from building and safeguarded as private open spaces or agricultural lands; (c) the areas where afforestation might take place; (d) the uplands, fells and commons to which public access might be definitely secured; and perhaps (e) new main roads which might be absolutely necessary and existing roads which need improvement [26].

The amenity bodies spent much time thinking about this blueprint for national park planning in the vain hope that there would be a voluntary agreement by the three county councils to follow the plan. Their case rested not only on the integrity of their proposed scheme but also in a belief expressed to the county councils that if local authorities failed to take up the national park ideal then the Addison Committee proposal would be implemented by central government. This would mean that more formal national interference would prevail, something the local authorities would no doubt want to avoid. The only stumbling block foreseen by the amenity societies was one of finance. The FLD, in particular, recognized that the main constraint on realizing the Lake District National Park was that of the compensation which would have to be paid in order to prevent undesirable building and development. The most expedient way to establish a fund for this purpose would be to seek public aid for the Lake District, on a pound for a pound basis; this would ensure a large volume of private donations. It would be necessary to make a deputation to the Prime Minister with this policy in mind. If any Treasury money were forthcoming the FLD thought it should be administered through an 'intercounty compensation committee', constituted by the Ministry of Health with representatives from local authorities, central government and open-air interests. The CPRE, on the other hand, thought that any effort in this direction would be unfruitful as it did not think that government money would be forthcoming. Instead it would be more likely to secure financial assistance from the Carnegie Trustees or the Pilgrim Trust.

The extensive commitment and involvement of the FLD and CPRE in an attempt to promote the Joint Advisory Committee with some definite programme relating to a national park blueprint was to be a resounding failure. By February 1935, Cumberland County Council was grudgingly prepared to join the advisory committee but it was also clear that as it controlled two-thirds of the Lake District it wanted to have the major say and certainly did not want to be dictated to by Westmorland County Council. Even before the Three Councils Joint Advisory Committee meeting on 12th March, it was clear that Cumberland County Council would block any move to give the Committee any authority and it definitely did not want to have any truck with amenity societies or landowner representatives; the Committee was to be a talking shop between the three counties, but a dead letter as far as the National Park movement was concerned [27].

Despite last minute attempts to clear up any misconceived idea that a joint committee would have statutory power rather than be advisory, the policy put forward by the FLD and CPRE was largely rejected. Instead, the Advisory Committee was to be composed solely of local authority representatives;

there were to be no experts called in to create advisory schemes and the offer of financial assistance from the FLD and CPRE was rejected; however, an Advisory Technical Committee was to be formed with representatives from Lancashire, South Westmorland, Cumberland and Windermere; Griffin was to relinquish his post as honorary secretary and was replaced by G. W. A. Hodgson, Clerk to the Cumberland County Council; and finally, Cumberland County Council made it very clear that it was already committed to its own planning procedure and did not welcome outside interference. For the CPRE and FLD, the meeting saw the end of their last and abortive attempt to move the county councils towards the National Park goal [28]. As such it marks a turning point in the National Park campaign as thereafter attention was to focus increasingly upon trying to force some action from central government.

## THE FORESTRY COMMISSION AGREEMENT OF AUGUST 1936

That the amenity societies had little success, despite their cooperative actions in inducing a move towards national park planning from the local authorities, is fairly clear. But such failure was not carried over to negotiations with the Forestry Commission which was much more pre-disposed to the National Park movement; it had already been prepared to set up national forest parks on its large estates which had a considerable amount of unplantable land [29]. Concern for the amenity aspects of afforestation was precipitated towards the end of 1934 through the Forestry Commission's purchase of the Hardknott estate (figures 8.1 and 8.2) in the Upper-Eskdale and Dunnerdale region of the Lake District, an unspoilt area of particular beauty. The amenity societies' grounds for concern were based upon earlier afforestation, especially on the Whinlatter Pass and in Ennerdale; accordingly, they argued that less attractive areas should be used and a potential national park area should be safeguarded from the blight of coniferous plantations. At this time, the Forestry Commission had a reputation for planting trim rows geometrically organized in military style on rounded hillsides. Such intrusions threatened the bare hillsides and soft deciduous woodland of the Lake District, of the land that Wordsworth described as 'clothed in the sunshine of the withering fern' [30].

Opposition to the Forestry Commission was not uniform. Whereas the FLD was uncompromising in its opposition, the COSFPS took the view, at least during the first stages of the controversy, that the Forestry Commission was behind the Open Air movement; the public would gain access to the unplantable land of the new estate as the Forestry Commission had made it its policy to allow the public onto such land, which had by this time amounted to some quite considerable amount [31]. The Forestry Commission's policy of developing large tracts of unplantable land as

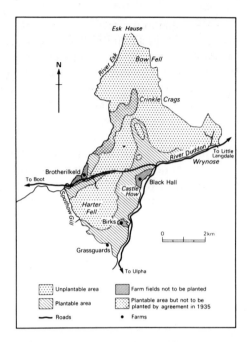

FIGURE 8.1. Map of Forestry Commission land in Eskdale and Dunnerdale, Cumberland.

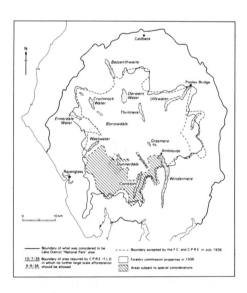

FIGURE 8.2. The 1936 afforestation agreement in the Lake District.

national forest parks also impressed the COSFPS. Nevertheless, more informed Lake District opinion on the access issue was, in this case, more to the point, namely that access to the hillsides was not a problem since most landowners freely granted this. The main effect of afforestation would, on the contrary, reduce both the possibilities and the desirability of access. Moreover, it was argued, further afforestation would threaten the Herdwick sheep of the area, a particular consideration for the Lake District and its fell farms.

The first reaction from the various amenity organizations, during the period December 1934 to February 1935, was to act independently. The FLD, through Symonds, had offered to buy back the Hardknott estate [32], an offer that was refused. G. M. Trevelyan and the National Trust were in private negotiation with the Forestry Commission in an attempt to agree some region in the 'central Lake District' which should be preserved. By the end of January 1935, Trevelyan had negotiated a gentleman's agreement by which the Forestry Commission would refrain from planting certain central areas of the Lake District amounting to some hundred square miles and including Borrowdale, Newlands, the Langdales, the head of Eskdale and the Roman camp in Eskdale. The Forestry Commission would also consult Trevelyan before planting in Wastdalehead or the woodland region between Ullswater and Windermere where the land might be suitable for afforestation if the woodland fell into decay [33]. The CPRE believed that it should negotiate with the Forestry Commission but on a wider basis than the National Trust which had been mainly concerned with its own concentration of properties in the central core of the Lake District and had not been willing to offer any assistance to the Forestry Commission outside this area. The CPRE, on the other hand, felt that a *quid pro quo* should be offered to the Forestry Commission: it would offer advice as to which areas should be preserved, but in exchange it would help the Forestry Commission's public relations elsewhere.

The Forestry Commission, for its part, saw the advantage of negotiating with the CPRE as a way of redirecting local conflict and also saw the shortcomings of negotiating with the National Trust alone. The Forestry Commission consequently agreed to set up a joint informal Advisory Committee with the CPRE which was to be represented by three persons involved in landscape planning, of whom only Abercrombie had a strong interest in the Lake District. The reasons for this were twofold: first, the CPRE responded to the Forestry Commission's request to deal with two or three landscape planners and architects with a good knowledge of the treatment of woodlands; secondly, the CPRE saw itself playing a national role and it was clear that the Lake District was just one of several areas where conflict existed between the Forestry Commission and local amenity interests [34]. Indeed during the following year conflicts arose in Dartmoor, Snowdonia, Breckland, the Peak District and the Furness area of

Lancashire, but none aroused the feeling of discontent which existed in the Lake District [35].

By the time of the first meeting between the Forestry Commission and CPRE on 30th April 1935 both the National Trust and COSFPS had recognized the importance of a joint approach through the representations of the CPRE. The Forestry Commission had also formulated its own position; it would discontinue communications with the FLD and would not resell the Hardknott estate (despite some disagreement amongst the commissioners) as the sale had been conducted on especially favourable terms by J. Ramsden,' the previous owner. It was argued that he could have obtained a higher price from the National Trust but had wanted the area to be afforested [36]. The Forestry Commission was willing to make some concessions: it would be prepared to reduce the plantable area by some 320–440 acres as long as compensation of some £2 per acre was forthcoming; it would also plant more than the normal proportions of beech, sycamore and alder where the soil was suitable. Although the CPRE representatives said they were only in a position to report back, they showed signs of acceptance and deference to the Commission and agreed to exclude the FLD from further negotiations. Abercrombie, who had not been at this first meeting, recognized that the CPRE had been outmanoeuvred, and regretted it had been drawn into the Hardknott estate affair, believing that CPRE's job was to draw up guidelines for future Forestry Commission acquisitions, and to warn it when opposition was likely to be great [37].

The FLD for its part, was concerned about the composition of the CPRE negotiating team and about the breakdown in its communications with the Forestry Commission, but nevertheless was willing to put its case through the CPRE and, at the same time, make as much noise as possible about the affair in public. The exclusion of the FLD from the Forestry Commission and the CPRE Joint Informal Committee went only so far as direct representation. The FLD was asked by the CPRE to prepare a report on its proposals. In the event, this report was totally uncompromising. If the Forestry Commission was unwilling to withdraw from Eskdale, it would issue a petition and raise the matter in the House of Lords. Such tactics were anathema to the CPRE whose preferred strategy was through committees, using the weapons of reason, tact and persuasion; it thrived on bringing organizations together, was a past master at accommodating conflicting parties, but would not be a party to active campaigns that might threaten one or other of its constituent organizations. Nevertheless, the CPRE expressed the FLD's position at the next meeting with the Forestry Commission on 28th May. The Forestry Commission had not told the CPRE about the special agreement with Ramsden, but at this meeting it played this trump card and the CPRE was more or less willing to accept the situation and was keen to discuss what seemed to be the more important question of a map indicating a sacrosanct area to be preserved in the Lake District, originally drawn up by Trevelyan and now open for wider negotiation. The CPRE also wanted to make a national survey to assess the likely opposition to Forestry Commission acquisitions in the so-called national park areas, but the Forestry Commission's response to this was lukewarm and it was anxious to settle the Eskdale business before August, when R. Robinson, Chairman of the Forestry Commission, was going on a visit to South Africa. In any event, it intended to start planting in the Duddon valley immediately.

The position of the CPRE and the other national societies, the National Trust and COSFPS, was difficult, as they felt that all-out opposition to planting in Eskdale would endanger a wider agreement in the Lake District and elsewhere. The FLD, on the other hand, disagreed and was determined to do all it could to influence the situation. Lord Howard of Penrith, President of the FLD, tried unsuccessfully to negotiate with Ramsden [38]. The FLD also persuaded the CPRE representatives, at a conference of the societies involved, to tell the Forestry Commission in no uncertain terms that they were against afforestation of the Hardknott estate. This the CPRE proceeded to do at the next meeting on 12th July 1935. At the same time the first of several maps of the Lake District, drawn up by Dower for the FLD, with a boundary in red demarcating the desirable area to be preserved from afforestation was lodged with the Forestry Commission (see figure 8.2). As far as the Forestry Commission was concerned it had offered its final compromise on the Hardknott estate and was not willing to make further concessions beyond those already made at previous meetings or indeed those decided upon in March [39]. The CPRE, with the National Trust and COSFPS support, decided to accept this, and the agreement was announced in the press in August 1935 as was also its intention to seek a more general agreement for the Lake District as a whole.

The FLD refused to give in and, after the unsuccessful negotiations with Ramsden, carried out its threat to launch a petition, which it did on 18th July 1935. This petition urged the Forestry Commission to reconsider its decision to proceed with the afforestation of the Hardknott estate. It also expressed the view that further extension of afforestation within the heart of the Lake District was undesirable. The CPRE, National Trust and COSFPS now refused to support the FLD campaign and its petition. This situation, together with the joint Forestry Commission and CPRE statement to the press, precipitated a crisis in communications between the FLD and CPRE. The two organizations purposefully restricted the flow of information between them, and the relationship between the two secretaries became quite bitter. Griffin constantly mentioned to his colleagues the lack of cooperation from the FLD, its misuse of confidential information and the mishandling of the petition despite the fact that he had given it support from May to July. He also tried to revive the old Lake District Safeguarding Society with the intention that it should exert a moderating influence on the FLD. Griffin resigned from the FLD executive on the pretext of not being able to attend enough meetings. Members of the FLD likewise distrusted any further move by the CPRE in this affair as they felt that it had already compromised itself beyond redemption [40]. The polarization was not complete though. While there was failure to communicate via the secretaries in the normal way, others with significant influence such as Abercrombie, Dower and Chorley had a firm foot in the FLD, CPRE and other amenity societies; it was through these people that information passed between the societies and it was they who tended to mediate between the more entrenched views within the CPRE and FLD [41].

The FLD petition secured some 12,000 signatures, including a large number of notable persons in high office. Amongst the amenity societies it was widely recognized as a formidable petition. However, the Forestry Commission was not so impressed, claiming that the wording of the petition had made exaggerated claims concerning the effects of afforestation, that the FLD had not received local support in the two valleys concerned, and had not referred to the Forestry Commission's concessions announced after the distribution of the petition. Once again the Commissioners were unwilling to make any further concessions except that they would refrain from planting in Eskdale for at least five years, when a more balanced view could be taken after the conflict had died down [42]. The FLD was not satisfied but its executive committee decided that if concessions were to be made, they should be in the following order: first, the Duddon from Grassguards to Birks; secondly, the Duddon from Birks to Castle How; thirdly, the Esk from Spothigh Gill to Hardknott Gill (see figure 8.1) [43]. In fact the Forestry Commission was not to make any further concessions on the Hardknott estate until 1938 when it agreed not to plant the remaining 300 acres in Eskdale in return for a compensation fee of £600 [44]. The petition and the FLD's later decision to raise the issue in the House of Lords were, however, important in influencing the series of negotiations over afforestation policy in the Lake District.

On 3rd March 1936 the Forestry Commission and CPRE Joint Informal Committee met for the fourth time. The red-line map submitted by Dower on behalf of the FLD had indicated an area of some 520 square miles which it wanted to be kept free from further afforestation. At this meeting the Forestry Commission proposed that it should refrain from planting within a much smaller core area of approximately 220–240 square miles [45] and also try to refrain from acquiring property within the red line so long as other properties were forthcoming. This offer was a considerable improvement on the hundred or so square miles that were to have been the basis of an agreement between Trevelyan and the Forestry Commission one year earlier. Moreover, the Forestry Commission was in a very strong bargaining position. Afforestation was seen by the government as an important means of reducing unemployment. As early as 20th February 1935, the Chancellor of the Exchequer announced that the annual grant to the Commission for the next five years would be increased to £500,000 instead of £450,000, which had been the annual grant during the previous three years. One year later, in February 1936, the Chancellor of the Exchequer announced that the Forestry Commission's annual grant was to be raised to £700,000 with the additional funds to be used specifically for afforestation and the creation of forest workers' holdings in or within fifteen miles of the special areas. In effect this meant that the whole of the Lake District was covered by the Special Areas' Afforestation Scheme [46].

Other arguments of the amenity lobby had not been entirely convincing. The Forestry Commission prided itself on its contribution to the access movement and had already persuaded the Treasury to sanction the expenditure of £5000 to establish the first national forest park of 500,000 acres in Argyll. Its record in the Lake District was also respectable as it had, in 1927, given the National Trust a 500-year lease of the unplantable land at Ennerdale at a peppercorn rent. Consequently it did not feel that the accusation of hindering access was well founded. It was also clear that the Herdwick sheep were in decline for reasons of agricultural depression and that those sold due to afforestation were insignificant in comparison [47]. In such circumstances, it was claimed that employment of locals in forestry work would help to alleviate distress. Indeed the Divisional Officer of the Forestry Commission claimed that local farmers were in favour of the Hardknott estate acquisition for this very reason.

The CPRE members of the Committee recognized that the Forestry Commission's offer was a good one in these circumstances. Even Dower wrote to Howard, suggesting to him that it would be unwise to go ahead with the debate in the House of Lords as this might damage the negotiations. The FLD rejected this advice, which led to an emergency meeting of the Forestry Commission and CPRE Joint Informal Committee on 18th March 1936 to discuss any further possible concessions that could be made. The COSFPS, influenced by Spence who had recently joined its executive, was also by this time less happy with the offer, and was in no hurry to reach an agreement since Howard's motion in the House of Lords had already been tabled. The CPRE and National Trust were consistent, as they had been in the past, in considering the Forestry Commission's proposals reasonable. Indeed Lord Crawford, Chairman of the CPRE, spoke against the motion and for the Forestry Commission in the House of Lords Debate on 1st April 1936 [48]. This debate was aimed at influencing the government to intervene in the Eskdale affair and also to set up a Parliamentary Select Committee to assess the planting policy of the Forestry Commission. In the end, the debate was an amiable enough affair, although Abercrombie felt that Crawford had given the impression that the CPRE was with the Forestry Commission and against the country. The debate itself brought no immediate reward, but did give further publicity to the Lake District conflict and the FLD was able to make use of this to arrange a deputation, from those who had signed the petition the previous year, to the Forestry Commission on 16th June 1936. This extended activity continued to embitter Griffin, but nevertheless continuance of the conflict ensured further important concessions.

Between the debate in the House of Lords and the deputation there were more negotiations based on Dower's map. At the seventh meeting with the Forestry Commission on 12th May 1936, the area requested by the FLD had been reduced to 420 square miles and the Forestry Commission conceded the following additions to the sacrosanct areas: (1) the southern slopes of Skiddaw; (2) Loweswater; (3) an addition north of Ullswater; (4) Martindale; and (5) Troutbeck. The FLD reduced its demand again to 390 square miles at the deputation and the Forestry Commission had raised theirs to 275 square miles. The main areas of controversy remaining were Kentmere, Esthwaite, Coniston and the Eskdale/Dunnerdale region [49]. By July, the Forestry Commission finally agreed to concede 300 square miles of the central Lake District. This still left the southern part of the Lake District in dispute, but the Commission agreed that if it acquired any land in this area it would afforest with special consideration to amenity. In such instances, the Forestry Commission and CPRE Joint Informal Committee would be consulted. In the final report published in August 1936 [50], the CPRE representatives, as a matter of course, regretted the failure to include these southern areas, but nevertheless were satisfied in general with the outcome.

## FORMATION OF THE STANDING COMMITTEE ON NATIONAL PARKS

The Forestry Commission agreement was an important achievement for the National Park movement, and much of this success can be attributed to the perseverance of the FLD. The influence of the FLD was also to be felt in the creation of the SCNP which was to spearhead the National Parks campaign from 1936 onwards. As early as 1931, Spence had expressed the view that there should be a central organization to campaign for national parks and press for the implementation of the Addison Committee proposals. However, his suggestion that all those societies that had given evidence to the Addison Committee should call upon the government to press for legislation was rejected at the CPRE Executive Committee on 24th June 1931. During the summer of 1933, Spence made another move towards this end by enlisting the support of the Bowland-Malhamdale, Cannock Chase and Dovedale National Reserve Committees in requesting the formation of a national committee under the auspices of the CPRE. However, the CPRE did not take up the challenge as it felt there was little chance that the government would implement the Addison Committee proposals at that time [51]. However, the CPRE did call upon the British Association to set up a correlating Committee to deal with the national parks issue. As this was unsuccessful, it was thought the annual CPRE conference would provide an adequate forum. Spence then tried unsuccessfully to get the other local societies who were campaigning for national parks to form a national organization when they met at Buxton immediately after the CPRE annual conference in 1933 [52]. Spence took the view that because the government was unwilling to act on the national park issue, the interested societies should strengthen their campaign rather than take little or no action, but at this time he was unable to get sufficient support.

In the early part of 1934 Spence tried to stimulate the press into a debate on national parks and got a question asked by G. Mander in the House of Commons. But after a disappointing response from the Minister of Health, he suggested that the LDNRC should reconstitute itself so as to press the National Parks campaign and so it was decided to launch the FLD with as much public support as possible. The initiative for a national body pressing solely for the national parks finally bore fruit on 30th November 1935 when the Joint Committee of Open-Air Organizations held a conference to consider what action could be taken to further the establishment of national parks. The initiative had not come from the CPRE, whose secretary and chairman were decidedly against its creation. Griffin wrote with great feeling to Abercrombie, who gave one of the addresses at the conference, in the belief that the setting up of a new committee would lead to the break-up of the CPRE. Griffin argued, as he had done before, that the CPRE was dealing with the national park issue and that to have another organization doing so would be fatuous [53]. Griffin was clearly concerned to ensure that the National Parks campaign should not slip out of the CPRE's grasp, and it was only when the formation committee met to work out the machinery of the SCNP that the CPRE was actually made responsible for its administration. Symonds and Spence had tried to resist the CPRE control, having been estranged by the Forestry Commission affair, but in vain [54]. The impetus for the National Parks campaign had once again come from the FLD but was absorbed and modified by the CPRE. The membership of the SCNP was to be confined to national societies and up to eight co-opted members. Consequently the FLD was not directly represented; but despite this, the FLD continued to exert a significant influence on the SCNP. At a meeting of the SCNP on 26th May 1936 it was resolved to co-opt Birkett, Spence, Dower and E. J. Salisbury, the first three of whom all held key posts within FLD at one time or another. Moreover, Birkett was to be Chairman of the SCNP [55]. It was also resolved to form a small preparatory subcommittee to help formulate policy, and to this body were appointed Abercrombie, J. Huxley, Dower, J. A. Southern, Symonds and Spence. Four out of these six also held key posts within the FLD [56].

## CONCLUSIONS

This study has described the complex interplay of personalities, organizations and events which affected the development of the National Park movement in the Lake District. Certain personalities such as Spence and Griffin, who were secretaries of the FLD and CPRE respectively, played a crucial part in influencing the course of events. Within the constraints of the organizations they represented, they were in a strong position to organize the timing, structure and control of meetings and events. Griffin sought and reflected advice from such persons as Chubb and Lord Crawford, whereas Spence operated more closely with Symonds and Chorley. Others, like Dower and Abercrombie, mediated in the middle so that when formal communications broke down there was an alternative channel for the exchange of rather more limited information. The study also illustrates the advantage of looking at the use, management and appreciation of land resources during the interwar period. Access to the archives containing letters and memoranda of the organizations in conflict over these resources allows one to reveal more fully the tactics and strategies of the parties in question, and so lead to a greater understanding of the mechanics of decision-making.

With hindsight it is possible to see that the activities of the CPRE and FLD were in striking contrast. The CPRE, as a constituent organization acting in close cooperation with the Department of Health and other central and local government organizations, acted not so much as a campaigning organization but more as a body that mediated between groups with conflicting interests. It accepted the ideals of the amenity movement but believed that education, not aggressive publicity, was the tactic to be employed. The Forestry Commission and the local authorities were informed of the preservationist ideals but, in deference to their authority, their very limited concessions were accepted by the CPRE in good faith. Although the CPRE claimed to be the organization mainly responsible for the National Parks campaign it would be fairer to say that it played a conciliatory rather than campaigning role. In contrast to the CPRE, the FLD progressively adopted much more aggressive tactics and by sheer tenacity in the face of opposition or obstruction from more powerful bodies, did succeed in achieving a significant part of its objectives. It is to be noticed that in the last analysis, the National Parks campaign and the development of a central organization (the SCNP) to press the case were largely influenced by those who had strong links with the Friends of the Lake District.

## NOTES

1. This paper was originally written as a contribution to the First International Conference on the History of Urban and Regional Planning, Bedford College, London, 14th–18th September 1977. It was published as an article in the *Transactions of the Institute of British Geographers,* **3** (4), pp. 498–514. Research for this paper was mainly based upon files held at the Council for the Protection of Rural England (CPRE), the Friends of the Lake District (FLD) and the Public Record Office. The research forms part of a project, financed by the Nuffield Foundation, on the history of the CPRE. The assistance given by the CPRE and FLD is gratefully acknowledged.

2. See for example, Sheail, J. (1975) The Concept of National Parks in Great Britain 1900–1950. *Transactions of the Institute of British Geographers* **52,** pp. 41–56.

3. Sheail, J. (1976) *Nature in Trust: The History of Nature Conservation in Britain.* Glasgow: Blackie.

4. Rickwood, P. W. (1973) Public Enjoyment of the Open Countryside in England and Wales 1919–1939. Unpublished Ph.D. thesis, University of Leicester.

5. While Lord Bledisloe is commonly held to have initiated the demand for national parks, Bledisloe himself regarded Major General Robb as the originator of the idea in 1923. See letter from Bledisloe to Hinds (1938), Public Record Office, F19, 33.

6. Addison, C. (1931) *Report of the National Park Committee,* Cmnd. 3851. London: HMSO.

7. For events leading up to the National Parks Act of 1949 see Cherry, G. E. (1975) *Environmental Planning, Volume 2. National Parks and Recreation in the Countryside: an official peacetime history.* London: HMSO.

8. This policy was formulated at the Standing Committee on National Parks (SCNP) meeting of 26th May and 18th June 1936. The committee decided to co-opt up to eight additional members who did not represent a society but whose contributions were deemed important.

9. In October 1935, all the societies formed in 1929–30 to promote national parks in specific areas, with the exception of the Forest of Dean National Park Committee, were attempting to influence statutory schemes under the 1932 Town and Country Planning Act. These societies included the Bowland-Malhamdale, Dovedale and Cannock Chase National Reserve Committees, the Peak District Regional Reserve Committee and the FLD.

10. The mass trespasses by ramblers in the Peak District were extremely important, but here restrictions on access resulting from nineteenth-century enclosures and game shooting interests provided a tension and hostility of a different kind, a conflict based more overtly on class and a mass movement. Such tensions were absent from the Lake District where access to the fells was easier and the distance from major industrial conurbations was greater.

11. It was not until March 1933 that a deputation to the Treasury was organized by the amenity societies and the Parliamentary Amenity Group. They asked the Government to implement the Addison Committee proposals, but this request met with an outright rejection. The only times that consideration was given to governmental financial aid for the establishment of national parks in the interwar period were immediately after the Addison Committee reported in 1931 and then again in 1938. On the former occasion financial aid was rejected after delay due to the passing of the 1932 Act, change in government, and a reaction against any form of additional public expenditure (despite the fact that there was no fall in government expenditure in real terms). In 1938, it was decided that coastal preservation was more urgent than the establishment of national parks and in any case local authority plans in the national park areas had been completed, or were near to completion, so a change in policy would mean abandoning these plans and another long delay. See Public Record Office, HLG 52, 723 and HLG 68, 56.

12. Rickwood throws a little light on this myth, but does not go far enough. See

Rickwood, P. W. (1973) Public Enjoyment of the Open Countryside in England and Wales 1919–1939. Unpublished Ph.D. thesis, University of Leicester.

13. Even H. M. Symonds, who was the Forestry Commission's *bête noire* and a leading member of the FLD, officially played down the conflict between the CPRE and FLD which was crucial to the negotiations with the Commissioners. See Symonds, H. H. (1936) *Afforestation in the Lake District—A Reply to the Forestry Commission's White Paper on 26 August 1936.* London: Dent.

14. K. Spence was also secretary of the Lake District Advisory Architectural Panel, later became Chairman of the Ramblers' Association and was one of its first Vice-Presidents. He was also on the executive of the Youth Hostels Association, CPRE and COSFPS.

15. The Lake District National Reserve Committee was formed in October 1929 and its membership was composed of representatives from fourteen interested local and national bodies. The Lake District Safeguarding Society was founded in 1919 by Canon Rawnsley (cofounder of the National Trust in 1895). It was confined almost entirely to property owners in the Lake District and its membership was by invitation and not by subscription. See letter from Griffin, H. G. to Matheson, D. M., 22nd June 1935, Council for the Protection of Rural England file 181/11, and McCarthy, M. (1976) The Politics of Influence—An Analysis of the Methodology of an Environmental Pressure Group. Unpublished M.A. thesis, University of Keele.

16. Letter from Spence, K. to Griffin, H. G. on 8th March 1932. Spence regarded himself as a long-haired aesthete, a Bolshevik and a busybody! Letter from Spence, K. to Griffin, H. G. on 28th October 1931. Council for the Protection of Rural England file 232/2.

17. Letter from Pepler, G. L. to Griffin, H. G., 23rd December 1931. Council for the Protection of Rural England file 232/2.

18. This move was in fact proposed by Griffin who had recently joined the LDNRC. See the *Lake District Herald,* 25th February 1933.

19. Council for the Protection of Rural England Executive Committee meeting, 28th March 1933.

20. The proposal to form the FLD was made by Spence at the LDNRC meeting on 9th March 1934, Council for the Protection of Rural England, *Monthly Report,* April 1934, p. 18. See also *The Times,* 16 June 1934; and Spence, K. (1934) The Future of the Lake District. *The Listener,* 24th August.

21. Addresses were given by T. A. Leonard, Chairman of the National Ramblers' Federation; C. Trevelyan, radical campaigner for ramblers' rights; L. P. Abercrombie, Honorary Secretary and principal founder of the CPRE, who was to become the first technical adviser to the FLD; and H. H. Symonds, who was later to become Secretary of the FLD and drafting adviser to the SCNP.

22. Griffin was very concerned about the creation of the FLD because of its backing by the youth movement and the lack of landowner representation. See Council for the Protection of Rural England file 232/2.

23. These branches were soon found to be cumbersome and now no longer exist.

24. For example, the Lake District (south) Report by Mattocks; the Cumbria Report by Abercrombie; and the North Lonsdale Report which Spence and Dower were about to produce.

25. At the FLD Executive Committee meeting on 11th January 1935, it was agreed

to allocate £75 from the funds for this purpose and raise more money if necessary. The CPRE, after consideration of the resolutions passed by the FLD at this meeting, decided also to offer financial assistance and skilled advice. The CPRE Executive Committee meeting of 29th January 1935, reported in the Council for the Protection of Rural England, *Monthly Report,* March 1935, p. 26.

26. Letter from Chubb, L. to Griffin, H. G., 1st January 1935, Council for the Protection of Rural England file 232/2.

27. Griffin wryly wrote to Spence on 19th February 1935: 'Nine out of ten authorities would jump at the chance to have the skilled advice which representatives of the CPRE can provide, as well as financial assistance. But not Cumberland, who administer two thirds of a national possession! They consider the planning of it as a job for the County Surveyor in his spare time! The other one third think it important enough to employ two fully qualified planners. It would be incredible if it were not true'. Council for the Protection of Rural England file 232/2.

28. The Clerk of the Westmorland County Council was rather more optimistic and wrote to Griffin on 19th March congratulating him on getting the matter as far as he had: 'the birth has been a long and painful one, but some children who are born feeble grow to be strong men'. Council for the Protection of Rural England file 232/2.

29. The Forestry Commission had recognized that in other countries, such as Canada and Australia, national parks were controlled by the government forest authority. Consequently, they had shown considerable interest in creating national forest parks. When giving evidence to the Addison Committee they proposed the creation of a national park on the unplantable land in Glenmore Forest. They argued that such a park could be created at a capital cost of £8900 and an annual cost of £1190. *Report of the National Park Committee,* Cmnd. 3851. London: HMSO, pp. 126–8.

30. For economic reasons, the Forestry Commission planted mainly coniferous forests, as the major home demand was for soft wood rather than hard wood which had been so important to the economy in the mid-nineteenth century when it was still an important structural material for shipbuilding. Since then the demand for hard woods had fallen off while the demand for soft wood for house-building, paper, pitprops, etc. had escalated. See Miles, R. (1967) *Forestry in the English Landscape.* London: Faber.

31. The unplantable land amounted to 335,000 acres or 35 per cent of the total land held by the Forestry Commission on 30th September 1936. See the *Second Report from the Select Committee on Estimates.* London: HMSO, 1936, pp. xxiii–xxiv.

32. Letter from Symonds, H. H. to Robinson, R. 15th February 1935 in Council for the Protection of Rural England file 181/11.

33. Symonds calendar of events noted on 2nd October 1935 in the Friends of the Lake District box file on afforestation.

34. Originally the CPRE representatives were to include a much stronger Lake District contingent. At the beginning of February 1935 Abercrombie, J. Scott, Spence and Chorley had been suggested. Letter from Griffin, H. G. to Trevelyan, G. M., 4th February 1935, CPRE file 181/11. However, due to the Forestry Commission's request, the CPRE began its negotiations with W. Harding-Thompson, G. A. Jellicoe and Abercrombie. Later Chubb and E. N.

Buxton were added, representing the COSFPS and National Trust respectively. Griffin attended as Secretary of the CPRE and J. D. K. Lloyd represented the Council for the Preservation of Rural Wales when matters concerning Wales arose. In 1936 Trevelyan also attended the meetings and H. J. Tozer attended *vice* Chubb on several occasions.

35. There had already been a significant controversy with the Forestry Commission as early as 1930 over its afforestation policy on Dartmoor which was to lead to another long-standing controversy in the Bellever Tor District. The Dartmoor Preservation Association had brought this matter to the attention of the CPRE whose executive committee decided on 26th November 1930 not to support the Association's protest. CPRE Executive Committee Minutes, 26 November 1930, p. 2. See also Harding-Thompson, W. (1932) *Devon, a survey of its coast, moors and rivers with some suggestions for their preservation.* London: Council for the Protection of Rural England.

36. 131st meeting of the Forestry Commissioners on 28th March 1935, Public Record Office, F19, 21.

37. Letter from Abercrombie, L. P. to Griffin, H. G., 16th May 1935, Council for the Protection of Rural England file 181/11.

38. F. Acland, from the Forestry Commission, had told Lord Crawford, Chairman of CPRE, that the Commission might accept an alternative area of land if Ramsden was willing to agree. Friends of the Lake District box file on afforestation.

39. However it was now definitely decided that 440 acres and not just 320–440 acres of plantable land should be preserved at a compensation of £2 per acre to be paid by the amenity societies. Much of this plantable land was in fact fairly inaccessible and was of dubious economic value for planting. Public Record Office, F19, 21.

40. Symonds resigned from the Lancashire branch of the CPRE over this issue, and Spence lost his job as Secretary to the Lake District Safeguarding Society. Griffin confided with the Secretary of the Lancashire branch that he was keeping information from the FLD because of its past behaviour, and also wrote to Dower on 21st October 1935 expressing his regret about the strong-arm tactics of the FLD. Council for the Protection of Rural England file 181/11.

41. Abercrombie, for example, was not in agreement with Griffin over the way they had failed to give the FLD more support. He wrote to Griffin on 1st November 1935: 'for the first time in 10 years we have not seen eye to eye over this wretched Eskdale affair'. Council for the Protection of Rural England file 181/11.

42. At the 12th July 1935 meeting of the Forestry Commission and CPRE Joint Informal Committee the Forestry Commission had announced that it would not begin to plant in Eskdale for some years, but no firm commitment to a period of time was given.

43. The order of concessions was decided at the FLD Executive Committee meeting of 16th December 1935.

44. The Hardknott estate affair was not, however, settled in 1939. Controversy over the form of covenant to the National Trust raged throughout the early part of the Second World War and a temporary settlement was reached in 1943 only by designating the land a national forest park. Public pressure against afforestation

continued after the war, resulting in a further agreement not to plant in the upper part of the Duddon Valley. Eventually the national forest park was closed in 1959 as the remaining forest area was insufficient to justify the title. See Miles, R. (1967) *Forestry in the English Landscape.* London: Faber.

45. The report of the Forestry Commission and CPRE Joint Informal Committee meeting states a figure of 240 square miles, the 141st meeting of the Forestry Commissioners on 26th March 1973 reported a figure of 220 square miles, and the minutes of the CPRE Executive Committee meeting of 31st March 1936 quoted a figure of 225 square miles.

46. The unemployment issue was obviously an important one, but not everybody was in agreement with the government over the value of afforestation in reducing it in the Lake District. W. Beveridge, for one, found little strength in the argument and took the side of the petitioners at the deputation to the Forestry Commission on 16th June 1936, CPRE file 181/11. The advantages to the relief of unemployment by afforestation in the southern part of the Lake District in general and in Eskdale and Dunnerdale in particular was also questioned by Symonds: 'It is on the north-west of the Lake District that the commissioners should look: there, in the iron-ore and coal district, unemployment is, and for years and years has been, black and pitiable, and there is no man but would wish God speed to any true relief of it. But the new Hardknott estate is for this purpose a relief *pour rire:* the estate is peculiarly inaccessible, eventual transport for the grown timber is at a prohibitive distance, there is an unusually high proportion of unplantable land, unusually little scope for small holdings, and so a minimum of relief for unemployment'. Symonds, H. H. (1936) *Afforestation in the Lake District—A Reply to the Forestry Commission's White Paper on 26th August 1936.* London: Dent, p. 74.

47. There was inevitably some loss of sheep from afforestation. In the Lake District for example, on the Ennerdale estate, the Forestry Commission disposed of 819 sheep out of 1132; the remaining sheep grazed the unplanted land. On the Whinlatter estate the number of sheep had been reduced from 805 in 1927 to 384 in 1935. Public Record Office, F19, 22.

48. Griffin wrote to Abercrombie on 18th May 1936 justifying the position the CPRE had taken throughout this affair stating that the CPRE should not 'dictate procedure in circumstances where by courtesy we have been invited by a Government Department to consult with them and assist them if possible'. Council for the Protection of Rural England file 181/11.

49. The Forestry Commission was particularly concerned about these areas as there was a lot of potentially good plantable land. Public Record Office file 19/22.

50. *Afforestation in the Lake District, Report by the Joint Informal Committee of the Forestry Commission and the Council for the Preservation of Rural England.* Forestry Commission, London: HMSO, 1936.

51. CPRE Executive Committee meeting, 26th September 1933.

52. Spence suggested that this committee would probably only have to meet once a year, but Griffin expressed the view that the CPRE should carry on co-ordinating the National Park campaign. It was this view that held the day. Minutes of the Co-ordinating Conference of National Park Committees and other interested bodies on 14th October 1933, Council for the Protection of Rural England file 232.

53. On 31st December 1935, Griffin confided with Miss B. Ashford, of the Women's Institute: 'If the "Access" group like to set up a National Park committee of their own, that is their affair and there is no reason whatever why they should not be invited to nominate their representatives on to the CPRE Committee. All the bodies concerned are either constituent bodies or affiliated bodies of the CPRE ... What I did not like about the meeting at Central Hall was the apparent suggestion to set up new machinery for this purpose when the proper machinery was already in existence'. Council for the Protection of Rural England file 232.
54. This view was expressed at the FLD Executive Committee on 10 January 1936.
55. Other SCNP members who had been on the FLD Executive Committee included Abercrombie (CPRE), Chorley (National Trust), Symonds (Youth Hostels Association), and Griffin (CPRE, and Secretary of the SCNP).
56. Abercrombie had been technical adviser to the FLD; Dower replaced Abercrombie as technical adviser in 1937; Spence was secretary; Symonds was treasurer, then secretary and finally chairman; and Birkett was later President of the FLD. The resolutions and appointments to the SCNP are referred to in the CPRE *Monthly Report* for July 1936, p. 31. The influence of the FLD between 1936 and 1938 is also reflected in its membership statistics. In November 1936 there were 2000 members. One year later there were 2400 members, and in November 1938 the membership had risen to a peak of 2680. This figure was not to be exceeded until mid-1971. In comparison, the CPRE's membership (including donations) for the years 1936, 1937 and 1938 was 1082, 1201, 1245, respectively.

# 9

# Changing perceptions of land-use controls in interwar Britain

JOHN   SHEAIL

Some years ago, Professor Dyos introduced a conference on urban history by reviewing the objects and content of that comparatively young field of research. In doing so, he expressed regret that the study of the urban past and urban present were often treated quite separately. Research policies and programmes were usually drawn up to deal with present-day problems with little reference to the past. For their part, many historians had little interest in recent and modern urban developments. As if to underline his point, none of the speakers at that conference ranged beyond the First World War [1].

A hiatus has tended to develop, not only in urban history, but across the entire spectrum of historical studies of the British environment. During the last ten years, two major studies in the historical geography of England have been published—neither has penetrated the years beyond 1900 [2]. Such neglect has prevented trends in the eighteenth and nineteenth centuries from being seen in wider perspective. It may also have caused many observers to exaggerate the novelty of much that has been perceived and achieved since the Second World War.

One of the deterrents to 'penetrating' the twentieth century was the lack of documentary evidence due to the fact that much of the relevant material was still treated as highly confidential. The student of the period was so dependent on published sources that it was felt that this partial view would be inadequate as a basis for a detailed and comprehensive appraisal. With the opening up of most of the archives of central government that are over thirty years of age, a lack of documentary data has been replaced by a deluge and,

141

in the view of some commentators, the historian has responded by becoming almost obsessed with the papers of the Cabinet and central departments of government. This has led not only to an excessive concentration on the processes of policy-making and the neglect of the causes and effects of policy, but it may have also led to an exaggerated view of the role of central government in the domestic affairs of the nation during, say, the interwar period [3].

One way of complementing and extending the still very necessary reference to the archives of central government may be to investigate more thoroughly those of local government. Parish, district and borough councils were created or restructured in the late nineteenth century and, in the eyes of many, they represented the nub of democracy. It was these local organs of government that were the first to experience the consequences of demographic, economic and social change. The population of Haslemere in Surrey rose from 2000 to 3000 between 1901 and 1905, and its historian has recounted how the consequent 'problems of housing, roads, sanitation, organizations, water and other public service supplies, all tested the temper, patience and ingenuity of all residents', and in particular the parish council. A councillor must have spoken for all his colleagues in 1907, when he recalled 'many a long evening spent in the back parlour of Peter Aylwin (the Chemist) trying in a primitive way to keep the village sweet and clean, trying too to interpret long letters of criticism which seldom failed to be a prelude to proceedings' [4].

By means of three case studies, it is the purpose of this paper to identify some of the ways in which environmental problems were perceived in the interwar period, as indicated by the archives of local and central government.

## EASTBOURNE

The penalties of neglecting the period of the 1920s and 1930s may be illustrated by reference to the south-coast resort of Eastbourne. Numerous writers have described how the character of the resort was largely determined by the principal landowner, the Duke of Devonshire, in the second half of the nineteenth century [5]. He not only planned the Grand Parade along the seafront, but he concerned himself with such matters as the provision of roads, mains drainage and street-lighting. The Minister, John Burns, cited the experience of Eastbourne when he introduced the first general legislation on town planning in 1909 [6]. Statutory planning could be justified not only as a means of tackling the evils of industrial towns but as a method of sustaining the amenity of any town experiencing growth and change. Through legislation, it was hoped to apply more widely some of the lessons learned in Eastbourne and other centres where public-spiritedness had been given its head in the nineteenth century.

FIGURE 9.1. An air photograph, taken in August 1938, illustrates how the chalk downland provided a 'backdrop' to the resort of Eastbourne. It was in order to prevent building spreading onto the Downs that the Eastbourne Borough Corporation promoted a Bill in 1926.

The retention of Eastbourne's distinctive charm could not be taken for granted. A major battle was still to be fought, namely over the permanent preservation of its unspoilt downland setting. With the advent of the motor-bus, motor-cycle and private car, there was an unprecedented desire to live in the countryside, and the Town Clerk recalled in later years how the Council was worried lest the Downs might become 'a developed housing area'. A 'harassed landowner with heavy taxes and high rates of wages to pay' might easily be persuaded to sell his land to a speculative builder. A new initiative was urgently needed for protecting the downlands around Eastbourne. This time it was the Corporation that took the initiative and, in doing so, Eastbourne helped to identify a further role for local government [7].

Perhaps the first man to perceive this new role was a recently-elected member of the Council, John Woolnough. As a surveyor, builder and architect, he had participated in the expansion of the resort for over forty-five years. During 1923, he submitted a document to the Council which began by stressing how the combination of the sea and downs made Eastbourne a 'unique watering place and health resort'. Whilst the sea was inalienable, the downs were in private hands and therefore 'liable to all sorts of violation'. Not only was there a danger of building development, but the erection of fences was making it more difficult for the public to wander at will over the downland for recreation and exercise [8].

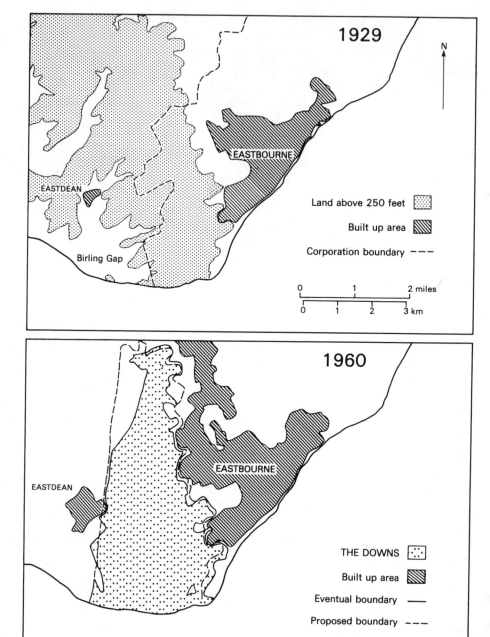

FIGURE 9.2. Top: the setting of Eastbourne in relation to the Downs, as indicated by the Ordnance Survey in 1929. Bottom: the proposed and eventual extent of the Corporation's downland estate, in relation to the development of Eastbourne as indicated by the Ordnance Survey of 1960.

Woolnough proposed a simple way of preserving the Downs for the public at little expense to the ratepayer. The Corporation should purchase the whole of the crest of the Downs above 270 feet. The protected area would include land both in the Borough and in the neighbouring parishes, comprising up to 3600 acres of downland. Most was still owned by a few large landowners, who would probably sell on reasonable terms, perhaps for as little as £36,000. The land would continue to be let to farmers, who would pay an annual rent of ten shillings per acre. The interest and repayment of the loan over thirty years would cost about £2800, making a half-penny rate.

After an initial setback, Woolnough succeeded in securing the Council's support in July 1924. There were no precedents for acquiring extensive tracts of land purely for amenity purposes, although the Hastings Corporation had recently been given powers by Parliament for the purchase of land outside the borough and, in 1925, Scarborough Corporation had obtained powers to lend money to a group of people wishing to preserve woodlands near the resort. Encouraged by these precedents, the Council resolved by a majority of 30 to 4 to promote a Local Bill in December 1925 to enable 'the Council to acquire by purchase or otherwise such parts of the Downs and Downland as may be necessary and to hold the same for the preservation of the amenities of Eastbourne' [9]. As usual, both Houses of Parliament referred the Bill, without debate, to Select Committees, whose recommendations were accepted automatically by members.

The Town Clerk told the Select Committees of the Council's desire to preserve the Downs, particularly the turf, so as to ensure public access and prevent building. They were willing to pay the fair market value for the land, and the farms would be let in the normal manner. A number of provisional agreements with landowners were attached to the Bill, which was given the Royal Assent in August 1926 [10]. About 4000 acres of downland were eventually secured by the Corporation for £87,510 (figure 9.2). The limits of the County Borough were extended to incorporate the new downland estate in 1937.

The Council became one of the first local authorities to recognize the difficulties of managing extensive, open spaces. A firm of land agents took over the supervision of the farms, and a management committee was appointed to regulate public access and usage; a ranger was appointed in 1929. The public were asked not to drop litter, pick the wild flowers, or drive their cars over the downland. There were soon reports of people trespassing on the farmland and, when asked to desist, asserting their supposed rights to go where they pleased. In a letter to the local newspapers, Woolnough, as chairman of the management committee, stressed that the farmers should be helped, and not hindered, in their work. He reminded readers that 'the land must be farmed and grazed or the turf would be spoilt and lose all its beauty' [11].

The progress made by the Council in safeguarding the Downs was by no means inevitable, as was demonstrated by the council elections of 1930. The unexpectedly high cost of acquiring the Downs, and the costs of management in relation to the disappointingly low income from farming, appeared to many voters to be another example of extravagance on the part of the Council. As the keenest advocate of downland preservation, improved visitor facilities and road-access to the resort, Woolnough became the natural target for hostility from those demanding thrift and frugality. For the first time, he was opposed at an election. In vain did he plead the need to spend 'wisely and generously' on those objects which would help to keep Eastbourne ahead of its rivals as a resort. In the election Woolnough suffered the humiliation of being defeated as the sitting member by the large margin of 700 to 153 votes [12].

Clearly, the story of the development of Eastbourne as a distinctive and attractive resort is not complete without the inclusion of a reference to the interwar years when it fell to the Council to take up the role of promoter and custodian of the public interest, and when the Council used the opportunities provided by Private Bill legislation to safeguard the unique downland-setting of the town. The stimulus came from one man, Woolnough, who was described as 'outspoken and fearless ... too keenly interested in the cause he espouses to trouble whether they are popular or not'. Such men demonstrated both the potential and constraints of local government in this field of corporate land-use planning.

## THE WOODBRIDGE BY-PASS

The comparative neglect of the interwar years is particularly striking when seen in the context of the fast-growing literature on the earlier growth of towns and cities, and the numerous studies of turnpikes, canals and railways. One usually looks in vain for similarly detailed studies of the circumstances in which the interwar by-pass was built and of its repercussions on neighbouring land use and settlement. The immediate and wider significance of a by-pass scheme may be illustrated by the comparatively modest scheme for the Suffolk town of Woodbridge.

Traffic through the market town was especially heavy in summer, when buses of holidaymakers scraped between the walls of the narrow streets. The Ministry of Transport supported a proposal of the County Council in 1923 to build a by-pass, but there was so much opposition from landowners that no further progress was made until 1925 when a modified form of the Council's scheme was accepted. By this time, the County Council, as the highway authority, was extremely concerned lest building development might occur across the line of the intended by-pass. Construction of the road could not begin until the Ministry offered grant-aid from the Road Fund, and this was contingent on the Minister of Labour agreeing that the work would help to

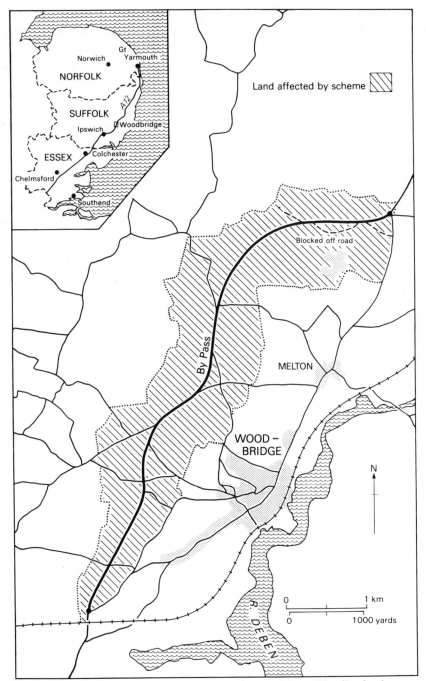

FIGURE 9.3. The area affected by the planning scheme for the Woodbridge by-pass in relation to Woodbridge and that part of East Anglia.

relieve unemployment. In the event, work did not begin until 1930. But even when completed, the County Council could not prevent building development along the road. Under the Town Planning Act of 1925, it was the smaller district and borough councils that had discretionary powers to draw up planning schemes: the county councils could only participate in an advisory capacity [13].

The Clerk of the East Suffolk County Council, Cecil Oakes, later recalled how the Council was worried lest the comparatively unspoiled countryside through which the road would pass would suffer the same fate as had befallen other parts of the country and 'deteriorate into a closely developed built-up area, transforming the road into a street rather than a traffic by-pass' [14]. The Ipswich by-pass had already suffered this kind of fate. With the encouragement of the Ministry of Transport, the County Council succeeded in persuading the Woodbridge Urban and Rural District Councils, through whose districts the road would pass, to form a joint town planning committee, made up of three members of each council, with Oakes and the County Surveyor acting as secretary and surveyor respectively to the joint committee. At its first meeting in 1927, the joint committee agreed to prepare a planning scheme to cover 1554 acres, namely an area large enough to regulate land use on both sides of the by-pass (figure 9.3) [15]. Once the formal approval of the Ministry of Health had been obtained, it became possible under the Town Planning Act of 1925 to control building development under what was called a general interim development order. This required builders to obtain planning consent, otherwise they risked having their buildings demolished or altered without compensation in the event of their not conforming with the eventual planning scheme.

Although the Woodbridge scheme was one of the simplest and smallest of any to be devised by a local authority in England and Wales, the drafting of the proposals took many years, largely because the County Council could relinquish so few staff from other duties to undertake the necessary work. The eventual scheme envisaged the widening of some feeder roads on to the by-pass, the stopping-up of others, and the designation of 80 acres as private open space. About 280 acres were scheduled for immediate building purposes, and temporary restrictions were placed on a further 833 acres in order to encourage grouped development. Oakes emphasized that 'we particularly want to preserve as much land fronting on the By-pass Road from development as is compatible with fairness to landowners'. Virtually no opposition was encountered, and the scheme was eventually submitted to the Minister for approval in 1934. After a public enquiry, the Minister's Inspector reported favourably, commending the scheme for being 'free from fussiness' and 'gratifyingly free from criticism by the landowners, &c' [16].

Encouraged by the County Council, the two district councils took the unprecedented step of proposing that the scheme should be administered by a joint committee. The Ministry retorted that this was quite unjustified: it would be far simpler to follow the normal practice of making the district councils individually responsible for their own areas. At the public inquiry, Oakes stressed the need to administer the scheme in a uniform manner, especially as so much land was subject to temporary building restrictions. The Inspector supported this view, writing in his report that 'if planning is to assume the position which it should rightly occupy there will eventually need to be special bodies set up for the entire control and administration of planning matters and in this small scheme one may perhaps see an opportunity for an experiment and a chance of learning some valuable lessons in this form of administration'. Although quite capable of fulfilling their normal administrative functions, the district councils had serious misgivings about taking on the 'novel and complex matters which planning involves'. They felt that the task was 'better placed in specialist hands'. On receipt of this report, the Ministry agreed to approve 'in the special circumstances' the setting up of what became the first executive joint planning board in England and Wales. The scheme became operative in July 1937 [17].

The success of the initiatives may be judged from the absence of ribbon-development along the by-pass. There were also wider implications. Under the Local Government Act of 1929, the county councils became the highway authority for all roads in rural districts and, at the invitation of the district and borough councils, they could also play a direct and executive part in statutory planning. In the light of these changes, and encouraged by the progress with the by-pass scheme, the County Council convened a conference of all local authorities in 1931, with a view to establishing an advisory joint planning committee, covering the entire county. The *East Anglian Daily Times* welcomed the move. The 'mushroom bungalow village' of Kesgrave, near Ipswich, was a warning of what could happen elsewhere unless preventative action was taken quickly. A beauty spot had been almost obliterated. The local authorities were conscious of the danger, but had been previously deterred from taking action by the legal complexities and costs of planning schemes. The newspaper believed the County Council had 'done a profound service ... by associating itself, as a partner, with all the district councils in its area in the movement to ensure the ordered evolution of the county, industrially, commercially and residentially' [18].

The conference of local authorities was addressed by Oakes, and the Chief Town Planning Inspector of the Ministry of Health. Perhaps the most significant encouragement came from the fact that Lord Ullswater, a county alderman and very distinguished public figure, gave his wholehearted support to the concept of a joint planning committee by agreeing to act as chairman of the conference. It was he who urged Oakes to keep 'the pot boiling' in the following months and, when the country was thrown into a severe financial crisis of 1931, Ullswater continued to give the Clerk vital encouragement. Although he conceded in private that 'we shall be met with the Economy objection as a ground for doing nothing', Ullswater added that he was 'a great supporter of economy but I think in this case it might be argued that the whole scheme is designed in the interests of economy in future development'.

Nearly every local authority agreed to participate on the joint committee. The distinguished planner, Patrick Abercrombie, was commissioned to draw up a regional report and plan, which would provide a framework for the statutory schemes which the individual councils would later promote. By the time the report and plan were completed in 1934, statutory schemes were already being drawn up by three councils for areas where large-scale development was taking place or was contemplated. In order to prevent the awakening interest in planning from being dissipated by piecemeal effort, the report successfully advocated the appointment of six executive joint planning committees, made up of local authorities and the county council. They would draw up statutory schemes for their respective parts of the county and absorb those already being drafted. The costs would be met by the County Council, which would set up a county planning office to provide the necessary expertise and services [19].

The logic of this joint approach to the preparation of schemes was set out by Oakes, when he wrote to the only district council that refused to join one of the area committees. He pointed to the considerable savings in cost and effort by appointing a county planning officer, as opposed to each council appointing its own expert in the form of an outside consultant. Not only would a centralized approach, funded by the county precept, expedite the preparation of schemes, but a full-time county planning officer would have a much better appreciation of local needs than a consultant working from London [20]. It was highly significant that the councils that had participated in the Woodbridge by-pass scheme, and which formed the joint board, were the most eager to form an area committee for the planning of the remainder of their districts. By the outbreak of war, a further three schemes in East Suffolk had become operative, and considerable progress was made with the others. The main impediment continued to be a lack of staff and resources in the county planning office [21].

The effects of events in East Suffolk were felt further afield. There was a considerable traffic in ideas and experiences between the officers of the various county councils. Abercrombie found his experience in East Suffolk very relevant when he was commissioned in 1933 to prepare a report and plan for the North Riding of Yorkshire, another predominantly rural county. Soon there were proposals for statutory schemes, each covering a different part of the Riding. Once completed and approved, they would be administered by joint boards made up of the relevant local authorities and the county council [22].

Although guidelines were being established as to how statutory planning in rural areas might be promoted and achieved, the progress made by such counties as East Suffolk and the North Riding also highlighted important differences in approach and emphasis. In East Suffolk, the tasks remained in the hands of the district and borough councils; they merely delegated their statutory powers to joint committees made up of themselves, and serviced by the county planning office. In the North Riding, the County Council succeeded in persuading nearly all the local authorities to delegate their rights to draw up schemes to the County Council which would, through the planning office, be entirely responsible for preparing the statutory schemes. Abercrombie believed this would prove the more efficient and effective method, but Oakes opposed it on the point of principle. He asserted that 'some of us who take what I might call a philosophical interest in local government are of the opinion that now the rural district councils have been shorn of so many of their functions (under the Local Government Act of 1929 and other legislation), it is important to keep alive those they are still charged with otherwise the personnel of these bodies which has been of high quality in the past is likely to suffer'. Clearly, a conflict was developing between the need for more effective planning, as achieved through an enhanced role for the county councils, and the wider interests of the existing patterns of local government, as based on the district and borough councils [23].

## THE LINCOLNSHIRE COAST

Because of the lack of attention given to the interwar years, there is a tendency to exaggerate the novelty of many of the problems and concepts associated with the postwar period. There is, for example, a tendency to overlook the precedents for what Michael Dower has called the Fourth Wave, namely the impact of recreation on the countryside and coast in the 1950s and 1960s [24]. A closer investigation of the experiences of such areas as the Lincolnshire coast indicates how recreation was having a marked effect on the appearance of the coastline, even before the war. Ways were already being sought of reconciling recreation with other forms of land use.

Until the 1930s, most holidaymakers were confined to those resorts served by a railway but, with the increasing availability of the motor-bus, motor-cycle and private car, increasing numbers could penetrate the entire length of the coastline. In a letter of 1935, the Clerk of the Lindsey County Council, which was responsible for the greater part of the Lincolnshire coast, described how considerable numbers of visitors drove their cars and caravans into fields as near as possible to the sea, and remained there for any time up to a month. Others made an arrangement with the landowner to leave their caravans, or an old bus or railway carriage, either as weekend-homes or for hiring out to other holidaymakers. In view of the growing demand for relatively cheap, self-catering holidays, the owners of fields near the sea were themselves beginning to hire out caravans and erect holiday huts and shacks. In many cases, there was no proper layout nor provision for piped-water or the disposal of sewage and refuse [25].

The first action to be taken to regulate the recreational use of land was in 1932, when the Lindsey County Council promoted a Local Bill to control the use of and, if appropriate, to purchase the sand dunes of the Lincolnshire coast for the purposes of a public open space. Anarchy was arrested: it was no longer possible to establish squatters' rights on the dunes, public access was assured, and steps could be taken to prevent further offensive structures and to remove those already erected [26]. Within a year of the Bill's Royal Assent, it was obvious to the County Council that this expensive, piecemeal solution would not suffice. The new Act was 'driving' the problem further inland and, to make matters worse, the urban district councils for Skegness and Mablethorpe had decided to mount 'furious campaigns' against caravans in order to preserve the amenities and, therefore, the prosperity of the two major resorts. As a result, the caravans were 'settling like a cloud of locusts' on the neighbouring rural districts. In the words of the Chief Town Planning Inspector of the Ministry of Health, 'all kinds of shacks, caravans, old motor-buses and trams, are being dumped about and are causing a nuisance both from the point of view of amenity and a danger to health' [27].

A more comprehensive solution had to be found with minimal delay. It was recognized that several years must elapse before a statutory planning scheme could be implemented and that the kind of development controls that would normally have regulated building development during the interim period were unlikely to deter the shack and caravan dwellers. The rural district councils and County Council saw no alternative but to draft an outline scheme that would deal primarily with the shack and caravan menace, and leave all the other aspects of planning to supplementary schemes of a later date. The simple scheme might then become operative in time for the next holiday-season of 1936. The Ministry of Health agreed to this in principle, and officials were instructed to treat the scheme with the utmost urgency, when submitted for the Minister's approval. As soon as work began on preparing the scheme the councils discovered that it was impracticable to treat the recreational use of land separately from such aspects as communications and normal residential and industrial development. Despite its apparent simplicity, the scheme could not be implemented before the next season. It was reluctantly concluded that any benefits would be so slight that a more orthodox scheme, covering all aspects of planning, should be promoted instead.

Drawing on the experiences of East Suffolk, the County Council and rural district councils formed a joint advisory committee, with the intention of drawing up proposals for an area of up to six miles from the sea. Abercrombie and Kelly were commissioned to prepare a report and plan, which stressed the scale of holiday-development that was likely to occur. The trans-

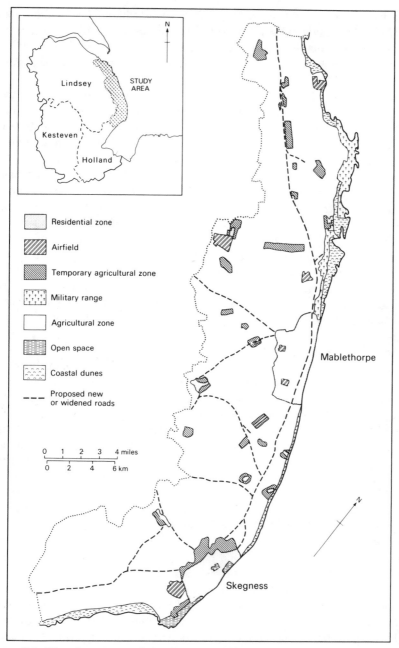

FIGURE 9.4. The plan proposed for East Lindsey by L. P. Abercrombie and S. A. Kelly, which included an agricultural zone where building would be limited to low-density development, and a temporary agricultural zone, which would be converted to residential use when no further building land was available in the existing settlements.

formation of the coast into a form of 'coastal ribbon development' was regarded as inevitable in the longer term. There was only 'a limited amount of first rate coast available', and it was useless to try to persuade people to take their holidays inland. In any case, prohibition would involve heavy sums in compensation [28].

Abercrombie and Kelly, in the report of 1936, outlined two alternative courses of action. One was the *laissez-faire* approach, but they warned that 'though it may sound far fetched, there is a real danger of this Coastal hinterland becoming dotted with houses which in the future may demand water supply and other services, causing unnecessary expense' and damage to amenity. The other course of action was to exploit statutory planning as a means of reserving public open spaces, such as golf courses. Full use should be made of controls which would temporarily ban development from large parts of the area, so as to encourage grouped development. This would maintain the open appearance of the area for as long as possible and help to minimize the cost of providing public services and utilities (figure 9.4). Under a planning scheme, it should be possible to prohibit the use of land for any tent, caravan, shed or other structure for a period of more than three months, without the previous consent of the planning authority, which had to be satisfied that the site was well laid out and furnished with adequate roads, water-supply, and sewerage and refuse disposal facilities.

The report encouraged the councils to form an executive joint planning committee, which formally resolved to prepare a regional planning scheme in February 1938. The County Council had paid half the fees of the report by Abercrombie and Kelly, and it similarly met over half the costs of the executive committee. Because of its highway responsibilities, the County Council had a direct interest in planning and, in the words of the Clerk, the Council felt it was 'very desirable to have the advice of experts before any work was undertaken by the individual Councils, otherwise there might have been a lack of co-ordination which would have been regrettable' [29]. It was also realized that the rateable income of the rural district councils was so low that they were unable to contemplate meeting the legitimate claims for compensation that might be lodged by landowners adversely affected by the eventual scheme. In giving financial support, the County Council was criticized by those few councils that had begun to draw up planning schemes, financed entirely out of their own resources. These councils contended that it was unfair that they should be called upon to finance planning elsewhere in the county through the county precept. In Lindsey and elsewhere, the county councils were finding themselves in an increasing dilemma as to how they might support individual councils, faced with the preservation of a more vulnerable or attractive part of the environment, and, at the same time, treat the remainder of the administrative county in an equitable manner.

War prevented further progress in Lindsey, but not before the lineaments of the postwar debate as to the optimal response to the pressures of outdoor recreation and holidaymaking had emerged. The difficulties of finding a sufficiently effective and flexible method of reconciling the different kinds of outdoor recreation with other forms of land use were already becoming apparent.

## CONCLUSIONS

It may be argued that the three examples of local initiatives, cited in this paper, were not typical of the lethargic response of most authorities to the changes taking place in the contemporary use and management of land. But it was their uniqueness that made them so important as examples for the future of environmental planning. The success of local government was not judged on the degree to which a council conformed with some master plan laid down by a government department. There was no such plan, and none was sought. Parliament saw the role of central government as that of providing a framework within which the local authorities could adopt permissive powers to secure the optimal degree of regulation within their respective areas. The initiative lay with those with the most intimate knowledge, namely the local councillors, their officers and electorate. They were thought to be the best qualified to perceive new trends and the most appropriate form of response. It was only when the local authorities alighted on some concept or procedure of potential value to other authorities that central government had a part to play. It was the duty of Parliament to adjust the criteria by which its Select Committees scrutinized Local Bills, and it was the responsibility of the Ministry of Health to decide whether the statutory framework might be revised.

The interwar period might be described as an innovative and transitional period in land-use management. Previously land-use policies had been largely the prerogative of the individual landowner, but economic circumstances were thought to be making it increasingly difficult for even the most responsive landowner to reconcile his personal interests with those of the wider, public interest. Faced with the erosion of private wealth, and the repercussions of unprecedented building activity, the increasing volume of road traffic, and the growing popularity of outdoor recreation, certain local authorities were obliged, by default, to take up some of the responsibilities previously borne by the public-spirited individual. The devices of the Local Bill and planning schemes were adapted for the purpose, but it was soon clear that any local solution would not suffice. Such was the scale of change taking place in the landscape that a number of districts and larger tracts of land might be affected by a single development. There was, consequently, a resort to joint planning committees and boards, and the role of the largest unit in local government, the county council, became increasingly conspicuous. By the outbreak of war, it was clear that some of the regional problems were taking on a national dimension. The terms of reference given to the new Ministry of Town and Country Planning and local authorities in 1943 represented the next logical step, namely a responsibility to secure 'consistency and continuity in the framing and execution of a national policy with respect to the use and development of land throughout England and Wales'. By then, the issue had become confused with another, namely the concept of a national plan, formulated by a national planning authority and delegated to the local authorities. The reconciliation of the two approaches was to become a major preoccupation of postwar planning.

Whilst many local authority archives are uncatalogued and there are serious lacunae in the archival data, the student of the interwar years can usually visit the county record office with an assurance that he will find some of the documentation he seeks. In doing so, he will not only be quarrying in a massive archive that has hardly been touched, but he will be among the first to investigate in any depth one of the most formative periods in landscape history.

NOTES

1. Dyos, H. J. (ed.) (1968) *The Study of Urban History.* London: Arnold, pp. 4–5.
2. Darby, H. C. (ed.) (1973) *A New Historical Geography of England.* Cambridge: University Press; Dodgshon, R. A. and Butlin, R. A. (eds.) (1979) *An Historical Geography of England and Wales.* London: Academic Press.
3. Booth, A. and Glynn, S. (1979) The public records and recent British economic historiography. *Economic History Review,* 32, pp. 303–15.
4. Rolston, G. R. (1964) *Haslemere, 1850–1950.* Farnham: the Author, pp. 45 and 47.
5. Enser, A. G. S. (1976) *A Brief History of Eastbourne.* Eastbourne: Local History Society; Elleray, D. R. (1978) *Eastbourne.* London: Phillimore.
6. Ashworth, W. (1954) *The Genesis of Modern British Town Planning.* London: Routledge and Kegan Paul, pp. 186–7.
7. Fovargue, H. W. (1933) *Municipal Eastbourne, 1883–1933.* Eastbourne: Town Council; The papers of the Council relevant to downland preservation have been gathered into a number of parcels and preserved in the offices of the Eastbourne Borough Council (EBC). EBC has kindly granted permission to quote from these.
8. EBC, Miscellaneous parcel: scheme for the purchase of downlands.
9. EBC, Minutes of Council, 1923–4, pp. 600, 1044, 1184–5 and 1341; 1925–6, p. 176; Correspondence with Parliamentary Agents.
10. House of Lords, Session 1926, Minutes of Evidence on the Eastbourne Corporation Bill, 15–17 June 1926; House of Commons, Session 1926, Minutes of Evidence before Local Legislation Committee (Section B), 15–16 July 1926; Eastbourne Corporation Act, 1926, 16 and 17 George V, c 95.
11. *Eastbourne Gazette,* 19 February 1930.
12. *Ibid.,* 15, 22 and 29 October; 5 and 11 November 1930.
13. East Suffolk Record Office (ESRO), 1874/10 and 17.

14. ESRO, 1874/13.
15. Public Record Office (PRO), HLG 4, 3661.
16. PRO, HLG 4, 3662; ESRO, 57/1.
17. PRO, HLG 4, 3663–4.
18. ESRO, A 300, P.01/1/1.
19. ESRO, A 300, P. 01/1/2; Abercrombie, L. P. and Kelly, S. A. (1935) *East Suffolk Regional Planning Scheme.* Liverpool: University Press and Hodder and Stoughton.
20. ESRO, A 300, P.01/6/1.
21. ESRO, 44/1; PRO, HLG 4, 3666–9 and 3789–91.
22. Sheail, J. (1979) The introduction of statutory planning in rural areas: the example of the North Riding of Yorkshire. *Town Planning Review,* 50, pp. 71–83.
23. ESRO, A 300, P.01/1/3–4.
24. Dower, M. (1965) *Fourth Wave: the Challenge of Leisure.* London: Civic Trust..
25. Lincolnshire Record Office (LRO), Lindsey County Council (LCC) parcels, 1518.
26. Sheail, J. (1977) The impact of recreation on the coast; the Lindsey County Council (Sandhills) Act, 1932. *Landscape Planning,* 4, pp. 53–72.
27. LRO, LCC parcels, 1518; PRO, HLG 4, 3290.
28. LRO, LCC parcels, 1389–91; PRO, HLG 4, 3852.
29. LRO, LCC parcels, 1517–18; PRO, HLG 4, 3851.

# 10

# An American way to conservation: comments on Federal river basin development

## J. B. SMALLWOOD

Governmental concern for preservation and proper utilization of the natural resources of the United States reaches back to the nation's earliest days when groups and leaders, concerned with maintaining agriculture as the basis of American life, decried the accelerating destruction and waste of the nation's forests and soils [1]. They, as well as latter-day planners and ecologists, presented not only practical, but also aesthetic and philosophic, reasons to encourage increased concern for more careful use of the nation's natural resources [2]. From among the many concepts that have emerged to deal with proper use and rehabilitation of the nation's natural and human resources none has perhaps been more controversial or innovative in its conception than the experiment begun in the Tennessee valley in the early 1930s. The product of an evolution of ideas reaching far back into American experience and European social philosophy [3], this experiment became a reality only after a decade of effort on the part of the Senator from Nebraska, George W. Norris. It was an experiment in planning unique in American history, which has been admired by many foreign leaders as one of the American experiences most applicable to the needs of the developing parts of the world.

In the United States, concepts of planning have developed not so much from philosophic sources as from practical attempts to solve immediate problems. Prior to the Civil War it had been technically impossible to consume the nation's resources at an alarmingly exploitive rate, but after 1865 such exploitation seemed unlimited. With increasing frequency groups of insistent reformers, humanitarians, and progressive-minded individuals demanded that profits from the country's resources be distributed more equitably and be used with greater benefit to society as a whole. From this rather heterogenous group of often contentious individualists came the impetus for increased public control over economic activities in the United States. In the years after Reconstruction they began to formulate their varied answers to the nation's problems and attempted to institute their diverse and sometimes conflicting programmes. Inherent in all these programmes was the belief that traditional attitudes toward individualism and property rights would have to be modified to attain the human and social benefits offered by industrialization.

Although each group of reformers manifested its concern in different ways, all attempted to resolve the social and economic problems caused by the new technology. City planning, conservation, scientific management, public regulation of corporations, and social legislation were all part of this same movement. Among these, however, conservation gave a peculiarly American orientation to activities in the United States. From the Republic's earliest days many Americans had been concerned with maintaining agriculture as the basis of life in the new nation. Not surprisingly, then, early groups decried the accelerating destruction and waste of the nation's forests and soils, not only for practical reasons but also for aesthetic and philosophic ones.

Land-use planning began in the United States with the Ordinance of 1785, and thereafter, repeated attempts were made to improve the use of the country's agricultural resources. As inhabitants of the early Republic deserted the worn out lands of the Atlantic coastal plain and pressed toward the fertile virgin areas across the mountains, men like George Washington and Thomas Jefferson noted the spoilation they left behind. In their letters and diaries these American leaders recorded their concern over the profligate ways of their fellow countrymen. Directing their attention to the problems of soil and forest conservation, they, along with men like Edmund Ruffin, John Taylor of Caroline, and others, anticipated the approach of scientific farming.

During the period of westward expansion an abundance of land submerged any general concern for preservation of the nation's resources. By the time of the Civil War, however, demands for a more systematic approach to agricultural problems resulted in the passage of the Morrill Act, establishment of the Department of Agriculture, and creation of agricultural experiment stations under the Hatch Act of 1887. These Acts represented a dichotomy when contrasted with the profligate land policy then sanctioned by the federal government. With little concern for the future, Congress transferred to private control, under very favourable terms, ownership of vast areas of the nation's most valuable resources. Waste and a concern for immediate private gain characterized the use of the nation's natural resources. Various conservation groups cried out against this age of exploitation and great fortunes. With ever increasing insistency they placed their ideas before the American people.

## THE EMERGENCE OF 'SCIENTIFIC PLANNING'

Chief among the critics of America's exploitive methods was a group of scholars and government employees who emphasized the need for improved scientific knowledge of the nation's resources and the systematic application of such information to the problems confronting the country. These technicians rested their concepts in the belief that long-range planning could be successfully accomplished only through scientific management. Implicit in their theories was a need to reverse traditional methods of resource exploitation. They insisted that scientific survey to determine best uses of resources should precede private exploitation. To some the solution meant planning for a large area with control by a governing unit sufficiently powerful to redirect economic developments as well as capable of awaiting returns on its investments [4]. Many of the supporters of scientific planning refined their concepts while working in government bureaux charged with finding solutions to the problems technology had thrust upon the nation after 1865. Geographers like Charles Marsh and Richard Van Hise provided much of the information needed for solving conservation problems; they acted also as advocates for positive action. Government bureaucrats like John Wesley Powell, W. J. McGee, and Gifford Pinchot became the backbone of the new movement. Casting off the traditional concept of individualism, they determined to use the power of the central government to improve human welfare. The increased control from Washington expected by these advocates of scientific planning implied concepts of the welfare state and national paternalism as part of their programme; thus, they subtly questioned traditional American ideals of individualism [5].

As conservationists, planners, and regional geographers attacked the problems of natural resource wastage they became increasingly aware of the interrelated nature of all such problems. Most agreed, however, on the crucial role of forests and the critical situation deriving from the waste of forest reserves, while they recognized that reafforestation was tied to the preservation of water for irrigation, navigation, and flood control. Forests, some argued, provided an ecological balance favourable to the harmonious existence of all creatures and plants. Reformers quickly called on the central government to develop a comprehensive forest control programme. Even before 1900 Congress demonstrated in its legislation an awareness of the connection between forest and water conservation problems. Once Congress accepted the concept of the interrelated nature of physical resources, the navigation clause of the Constitution provided considerable latitude for federal legislation [6]. The conservationists' claim that soil erosion was an integral part of forest and water conservation was amply demonstrated in the southern Appalachian region. By 1933, despite efforts by the conservationists to reorient American attitudes and practices, areas such as the Tennessee valley were rapidly becoming monuments to the waste of soil, forest, and water resources [7].

In their struggle for water conservation, reformers were aided by those interested in promoting use of the nation's navigable streams for transportation purposes [8] as well as those advocating intelligent use of water resources in the arid areas of the American West. John Wesley Powell was one of the first to define the main problem facing agriculture west of the Mississippi River. He pointed out that potentially good agricultural land in the West far exceeded the water available to make it productive. To him the answer lay in some form of communal water rights, although this did violence to the traditional concepts of independent, small farmers so dear to the heart of Jeffersonian America. Powell noted, however, that under circumstances of abiding aridity the Indian, the Spaniard, and the Norman had all ultimately turned to a communal approach to satisfy their agricultural needs. To Powell, proper use of water resources in the West required planning on a massive scale. Within the system, Powell implied, the only agent both capable of designating the lands best suited for cultivation and powerful enough to close the rest to settlement was the central government [9].

Many of Powell's concepts easily fitted into the emergent populist thinking which was reshaping politics throughout the American Middle and Far West. The forces of nature in this area had served notice that man could not continue on a present path which ignored the balance of nature and the interests of his fellow man [10]. The lessons learned in the West found receptive students in many of the region's politicians, especially Senators Francis G. Newlands of Nevada and George W. Norris of Nebraska. Powell, like many other of the scientists and bureaucrats of that day, viewed a river system as an ecological whole connected integrally into an entire watershed. They stressed the multiple-purpose approach to solving water resource problems, recognizing the interrelation of irrigation, forestry, water power, domestic water supply drainage, and navigation. Hydrographers realized too that because of the interstate character of most river systems the multiple-use approach of water development meant federal control and development [11]. With dissemination of these ideas more national political figures called for control and development of all water resources by the national government. President Theodore Roosevelt, supporting the right of private development where feasible, nevertheless, believed that public lands should be reserved for the homemaker. It would be undesirable, he stated, 'to let our land policy be shaped so as to create a big class of proprietors who rent to others' [12]. Certainly a new social philosophy began to emerge in the United States with the scientific approach to conservation.

## RIVER BASIN PLANNING

The tendency of conservationists to view a river valley as a unit often brought the planner into direct conflict with the special interests of particular states or local communities. As has often been true in attempts to solve problems of ecological balance, ideas were generally supported until their application necessitated personal and community sacrifices in the interest of the larger society. Frequently, for example, the water stored in one state could best be used to irrigate more fertile land in another state downstream, yet the state of origin insisted on reserving the waters for its own use [13]. This difficulty became more acute after 1900 and still remains one of the main deterrents to effective, unified water resource development, as typified by the controversy that still exists concerning use of waters from the Colorado River.

Among the most debated issues in the discussion of river basin development was the use of water for hydroelectric power production. Few denied that the development of water power was a necessity for American technological growth, but a bitter debate developed over which agencies, public or private, would supervise that development [14]. The tendency toward monopoly control in the water power industry quickly became the concern of those interested in unified river basin development [15]. By 1912 the question of monopoly in water power had become so urgent that Congress instructed the Bureau of Corporations to investigate the problem. Although the conclusions of that report tended to be somewhat hostile to public control of power production, the authors did recognize the benefits of developing as a unit the power potential of a whole river system. Production of electricity in such a fashion would allow for 'coupling-up' the various units to supplement and reinforce each other [16].

One section of the Bureau of Corporation report claimed that a unified system of storage reservoirs on the same waterway would offer the greatest economic advantage. Waters gathered at the source could contribute to the steady flow at every power site downstream. This concept provided the rationale for those who advocated unified development of power potential by a government agency. In addition, the report concluded that concentration of control in the power industry required, at least, rigid supervision by both state and federal governments to prevent abuse of public interests [17]. Some reformers argued that the public interest could be protected only through public control. Although few went so far as to call for outright public ownership, most envisaged a control that would leave no doubt of the government's power to dictate the best course for power development [18].

It was in the area of power development that the greatest demand for government action was sounded. Production and distribution of electricity encouraged a monopoly, since only one power company could profitably operate in any given area. Because electricity offered a way to revolutionize the lives of the people, reformers insisted that its benefits could not be left to the caprices and profit-making motives of a private monopoly. Since the most efficient method of conserving water power was through concentration and coupling of adjacent power units, conservation of power resources actually required encouragement of concentration. The utilities problem, then, encouraged the movement for river basin planning since a system of intimately related power plants in the same watershed merged naturally with the growing tendency to view each river system as a unit. Even those suspicious of governmental control or competition with private enterprise spoke strongly for multipurpose development of water resources as the only sensible way effectively to develop hydroelectric potential. They generally recognized that power, water supply, irrigation, flood control and navigation were inseparably connected and argued that development for any one purpose must be consistent with the development of others [19].

Gradually there developed an attitude toward conservation which centred around water control as the key to all other problems. New ideas challenged traditional solutions that had been used for decades in dealing with flood control, navigation, soil erosion, and reafforestation. By the turn of the century electric power was becoming essential, flood control on the Mississippi had gained widespread attention, and increasing urbanization had brought new water supply demands. There was an interrelationship among all these needs, and frequently they all demanded the use of water from the same stream. At the same time improvements in engineering techniques and advances in scientific knowledge made possible the construction of large reservoir dams which opened up new possibilities for the solution of the increasingly serious water problems of America's industrial society [20].

The most difficult problem in achieving maximum utilization of water resources was that of maintaining a regular flow of water from season to season. Of major importance in solving the problem of uniform flow was acceptance of the reservoir concept, which projected the establishment of an interconnected system of dams throughout an entire river system. Storage dams in the headwaters could catch heavy rainfall in the upper reaches to prevent flooding on the main stream, thus retaining water which could later be released in drought periods to maintain an even flow for navigation and power production throughout the year. By 1896 the concept of multiple-use reservoirs, combined into a unified interconnected system, had become an important part of the official debate on water resource development. As the concept of multipurpose reservoir control gained popularity, advocates of traditional methods of water control increasingly attacked it, especially members of the United States Corps of Engineers. The Corps' official opposition to the validity of multipurpose reservoirs as late as 1916 demonstrated the tendency of established institutions to resist experimentation with new and creative solutions to pressing problems [21].

Much of the support for the multipurpose reservoir system came from men in the arid regions of the West who saw a justification for the increased expenditure of federal monies in providing reservoirs to store the precious water so vital to their livelihood. The multipurpose theory greatly appealed to the populist and progressive congressmen from those areas in search of solutions to their constituents' water problems. By stressing the desirable effect on flood control for the lower Mississippi they could justify the expenditure of funds for irrigation reservoirs on the Missouri and its multitude of vital but capricious tributaries.

According to the public-control advocates, many factors also necessitated government intervention and supervision of water resource development. The concept that a stream be treated as a whole implied that from the humblest rivulet to the mightiest river the same agency needed full control in order to achieve maximum results [22]. Reformers agreed that public control would guarantee the greatest benefit to the people as a whole and provide for the fullest utilization of a river's potential. Public leaders, including President Theodore Roosevelt, contended that the problems of industrialization required new uses of governmental power in order to protect the public interest [23]. By the end of the first two decades of the twentieth century most conservationists recognized more fully the interrelated nature of all water uses and water problems. In the debates which ensued among men of every shade of political opinion there was a slow working out of an adjustment between the American private enterprise system and the realities of modern problems of water resource planning.

## FORMULATION OF NEW PLANNING PHILOSOPHIES IN THE 1920S

The decade from 1920 to 1930 was the incubation period for new concepts of planning. The very prosperity of the 1920s stimulated the development of techniques which undermined the spontaneous individualism of earlier days. Herbert Hoover, the great apostle of rugged individualism, recognized the changes that were occurring in America's social system when he called for economic and social planning, always, of course, within the context of traditional individual values [24].

Attitudes toward planning during the 1920s tended to separate into three divisions: business planning, socialistic planning, and social-progressive planning. Supporters of all these approaches wanted some central guidance and coordination of the various aspects of American life, but they differed widely on specific policies, methods, and ultimate goals. Most in keeping with native liberal political movements in the United States was the liberal-progressive approach, which essentially envisaged the distribution of the benefits of industrial progress without resorting to the alien concepts of socialism [25].

In the campaign of 1920 some political leaders indicated they were no longer afraid to proclaim the benefits of planning. The Democratic vice-presidential candidate, Franklin Delano Roosevelt, of New York, declared that the former waste of natural resources dictated a coordinated plan for the use and development of the nation's resources. In his speech accepting nomination by his party, Roosevelt revealed his affinity for the social concepts of progressive reformers such as John Wesley Powell.

During the campaign Roosevelt returned time and again in his speeches to the need for conservation of water which would allow the fullest use of that valuable resource. His interest in the subject during the campaign had so stimulated him that afterwards he wrote a long letter on the subject of reclamation in which he expressed abhorrence of the fact that the government's hit or miss approach resulted from lack of definite policy. Since he believed that all water was interstate in nature, the central government, he felt, should develop a programme that continued from year to year. In this way 'all expenditures would be made in accordance with a far-reaching plan looking ahead . . . twenty years . . .' [26]. F.D.R.'s attitude toward integrated water planning was the natural outgrowth of his interest in the conservation of forest and human resources, and was the logical extension of a social philosophy developed over many years. He differed in some ways from other supporters of integrated water planning such as Norris and Newlands, whose attitudes came from the grim realities of the arid West, with its improper use of limited water resources. Whatever the origin of their attitudes all three men developed a belief in coordinated and planned use of all natural resources.

During the 1920s the most spectacular struggle between the traditional concepts of individualism and the new ideology of planning emerged from the debate over conservation of the nation's water resources. By 1920 the argument over what agent, public or private, should develop this potentially revolutionary form of power was no longer academic. Private entrepreneurs, fully aware of the value of hydroelectric power, determined to control its development. Reformers, however, feared entrusting development of water power, so important in the daily lives of the people, to an economic unit which they felt had failed in the past to exhibit responsibility for the people's heritage.

George W. Norris urged the government to assume the lead in developing water power. He, and like-minded leaders, were determined that the benefits of cheap power would be distributed to the mass of people rather than being used to swell corporate profits. Norris challenged politically-conservative conservationists with his concepts of increased government competition in traditional areas of private business activity; he opposed as well a large group of Wilsonian reformers who believed that the main duty of the government was to keep all economic and political units as small as possible [27]. Norris's position on water power development led him into a loose alliance with those who advocated using a river system as the basic unit in regional planning. His continued association with these thinkers during the first two decades of the twentieth century led him to incorporate many of their ideas into his basic social and political philosophy. At first primarily interested in power development, the Nebraska senator emerged as the foremost crusader for development of all potential power units within one watershed under supervision of a government-owned agency. He argued that every stream in the country, 'no matter how small, should be developed and linked up with the larger developments for power development and transmission' [28]. Essentially that statement summed up what became Norris's position on the conservation and use of the nation's water power resources. To be effective, such a plan necessitated considerable prior investigation and planning of the kind advocated by the technocrats.

Norris's support of integrated development of water resources stemmed particularly from his desire to provide a way for the farmer to acquire needed aid for reclamation projects. By demonstrating that storage of water for irrigation benefited flood control, navigation, soil conservation, and power development, he justified the distribution of costs for water development among the various uses to be made of the water [29].

## The Tennessee Valley Authority

Norris, and others concerned with scientific multipurpose development of water resources, centred their attention on the public development of hydroelectric power on the Tennessee River, at Muscle Shoals, Alabama. Federal control over the water power site at Muscle Shoals had been preserved when Theodore Roosevelt vetoed a bill leasing the area to a private power company. President Woodrow Wilson's Secretary of War, Newton D. Baker, chose that site for construction of a hydroelectric dam intended to expedite the manufacture of nitrates for explosive purposes during World War I. On Armistice Day the dam stood partially complete, leaving to Congress the question of disposing of the property. Private industrial representatives quickly demanded its sale as war surplus, but conservationists and reformers objected. Reformers recognized Muscle Shoals as the key to the Tennessee River and insisted that the government develop the navigation and power potential of the river as a basis for general conservation of the valley's resources [30].

In his struggle to provide for development of the Tennessee valley under the control of a publicly-owned corporation, Senator Norris had to wage his battle within limits compatible with basic American philosophic attitudes [31]. In analysing the difficulties of obtaining support for planning in the United States the historian, Charles A. Beard, noted in 1926 that Americans responded more quickly to a practical demonstration than to abstract theory. They could readily understand the concrete, dollars-and-cents logic of

FIGURE 10.1. Barge traffic on the Tennessee Valley Authority lakes.

FIGURE 10.2. Fontana dam high in the Appalachian mountains.

FIGURE 10.3. Reafforestation by the TVA.

practical conservation or water power development, but grand theoretical schemes for revolutionizing society through planning did not often stir their enthusiasm. Beard exposed also the tendency of businessmen to support only those elements of planning and conservation that benefited them, while resisting anything that would lessen individual profit. Basically, the problem was to convince the individual in concrete terms that he had more to gain through comprehensive planning than through maintenance of the *status quo* [32].

After a decade of exhausting, often discouraging, political struggle the Nebraska senator achieved success [33]. On 18th May 1933, President Franklin D. Roosevelt affixed his signature to Public Law No. 17 of the Seventy-third Congress, which authorized the establishment of the Tennessee Valley Authority. The bill called for a project in the Tennessee valley to demonstrate to the American people the benefits gained from a multipurpose, unified approach to water resource development [34]. This Act embodied ideas from many sources—the conservation movement, the planning movement, and agrarian radicalism.

The Act attempted to find the proper balance between the need for centralization and localism. Regionalists had always contended that only through such a balance could the needs of modern society be met. Certainly the diversity of American culture precluded any attempt at complete centralization, yet some unity was necessary to provide for long-range goals and plans as well as for a satisfactory tax base. As one planner stated in 1929:

'There is a human problem in regional government, and a proper solution will recognize the need of centralized authority in matters of common concern, with preservation of local freedom of action in purely local affairs' [35]. The board of the Tennessee Valley Authority was assigned the task of making that concept a reality under practical conditions.

Nearly five decades have passed since Congress charged the TVA with the task of planning for the development of all the natural and human resources of an entire river valley. In that period TVA has provided for full development of the regions's power resources [36]. Reafforestation, soil conservation, water control, and a 500 mile navigation channel from Knoxville, Tennessee, to the Ohio River are also monuments to the Authority's success [37]. Nevertheless, the Tennessee Valley Authority has yet to fulfil its promise as an agency of broad social planning for full resource development.

The Tennessee Valley Authority remains little more than a highly efficient power-producing agency. Stress on power production has blunted the broader planning activities envisaged in the original Act. In addition, with the return of prosperity after the Great Depression, support for the novel ideas of social planning waned among political leaders. Traditional commitment to individual exploitation also helped reduce support for experimentation with new methods of directing resource development. Once basic prosperity began to return to the American economy Americans shied away from more unfamiliar forms and methods. After 1938, an increasingly conservative Congress responded to pressures from private business and narrow local interests to curtail the planning impulse so vigorously supported by President Roosevelt. Congress refused to extend to other river systems in the United States the concept of using a river valley as the basis for social planning on the broadest scale [38].

## NOTES

1. Gustafson, A. F., Guise, C. H., Hamilton, W. J., Jr., and Ries, H. (1949) *Conservation in the United States,* 3rd ed. Ithaca: Comstock Publishing Co., pp. 15–16; Gray, L. C. (1933) *History of Agriculture in the Southern United States to 1860,* vol. 1. Washington: Carnegie Institution of Washington, pp. 301, 303, 446, 460–1, 799–800; Ford, W. C. (ed.) (1904–37) *Journals of the Continental Congress,* 4, p. 224; Jefferson, T. (1955) *Notes on the State of Virginia,* Peden, W. (ed.). Chapel Hill: University of North Carolina Press, pp. 77, 85; see correspondence of George Washington on this subject in Brooke, W. E. (ed.) (1919) *The Agricultural Papers of George Washington.* Boston: R. G. Badger, pp. 22–3, 27–52, 92–3, 100–5, 128; Jefferson, T. (1903–07) *The Writings of Thomas Jefferson,* vol. 9, A. A. Lipscomb and others (eds.). Washington: Government Printing Office, p. 141; Jefferson, T. (1944) *Thomas Jefferson's Garden Book, 1766–1824, with Relevant Extracts from his Other Writings,* W. M. Betts (ed.). Philadelphia: The American Philosophical Society, pp. 220–3; Jefferson, T. (194–?) *Jefferson's Letters,* W. Whitman (ed.). Eau Claire: E. M. Hal and Co., pp.

283–4; Richardson, J. D. (compiler) (1896–99) *A Compilation of the Messages and Papers of the Presidents, 1789–1897,* vol. 1. Washington: Government Printing Office, pp. 66–9, 201; Washington, G. (1931–44) *Writings of George Washington,* J. C. Fitzpatrick, (ed.). Washington: Government Printing Office, 31, p. 23; Barnett, C. R. (1928–58) Martin Wilson Philips, in Johnson, A. and Malone, D. (eds.), *Dictionary of American Biography,* vol. 14. New York: Charles Scribner's Sons, p. 537; U.S. Congress, House, 51st Congress, 1st Session (1891) *Agriculture* part V of *Reports of the United States Commissioners to the Universal Exposition 1889 at Paris,* C. V. Riley (ed.). House Executive Document no. 410, part 5, p. 810; Pinchot, G. (1899) *Suggestions to Southern Farmers,* in U.S. Department of Agriculture, Farmers' Bulletin no. 98. Washington: Government Printing Office.

2. For some examples of concern for a planned approach to resource development among America's pre-Civil War leaders see Southeastern Planning Conference (1935) Proceedings of Southeastern Planning Conference, Savannah, Georgia, 4–5 December; Alabama, Georgia, Florida, South Carolina. Unpublished, Albany, Georgia, National Resources Committee, Fourth District, p. 4; Rodgers, C. (1947) *American Planning, Past—Present—Future.* New York: Harper and Brothers, pp. 42, 101–7, 114–17, 126, 137, 147, 156–9, 173; Merriam, C. E. (1940) Planning in a Democracy, speech delivered at National Conference on Planning, San Francisco, California, July, 1940, in National Conference on Planning (1940) *Proceedings of the Conference.* Chicago: American Society of Planning Officials, p. 173; Davidson, D. (1938) *The Attack on Leviathan, Regionalism and Nationalism in the United States.* Chapel Hill: The University of North Carolina Press, p. 182; Lorwin, L. L. (1945) *Time for Planning, A Social–Economic Theory and Program for the Twentieth Century.* New York: Harper and Brothers, pp. 100–1; U.S. Congress, Senate, 60th Congress, 1st Session (1908) *Preliminary Report of the Inland Waterways Commission,* Senate Document no. 325, pp. 536–8, 554.

3. For material concerning European social philosophy which affected concepts of resource planning see National Resources Committee (1935) *Regional Factors in National Planning and Development.* Washington: Government Printing Office, pp. 142–3; Abercrombie, P. (1945) *Town and Country Planning,* 2nd ed. Oxford: Oxford University Press, pp. 28ff.; Zimmerman, C. C. and Frampton, M. E. (1935) *Family and Society.* New York: D. Van Nostrand Co., p. 74; Brown, A. J. and Sherrard, H. M. (1951) *Town and Country Planning.* Carlton: Melbourne University Press, pp. 279–80; Mumford, L. (1938) *The Culture of Cities.* New York: Harcourt Brace and Co., pp. 222, 392; Guittard, F. G. (1930) Roosevelt and Conservation. Unpublished Ph.D. thesis, Stanford University; for a full discussion of California utopian movements see Hine, R. V. (1953) *California's Utopian Colonies.* San Marino: The Huntington Library; Hilberseimer, L. (1949) *The New Regional Pattern, Industries and Gardens, Workshops and Farms.* Chicago: Paul Theobald, pp. 52–3; Boardman, P. (1944) *Patrick Geddes, Maker of the Future.* Chapel Hill: The University of North Carolina Press, pp. 41–2, 99–100, 102–37, 183–4, 200–6, 209–18, 251, 278, 280, 365, 369, 374, 408, 460, 477; White, G. F. (1957) A perspective of river basin development. *River Basin Development,* vol. 22 of *Law and Contemporary Problems, School of Law, Duke University,* p. 168; Odum, H. W. (1944) Patrick Geddes' heritage to 'the making

of the future'. *Social Forces,* **22** (3), p. 280; MacKaye, B. (1928) *The New Exploration, A Philosophy of Regional Planning.* New York: Harcourt, Brace and Co., p. 27.

4. Lorwin, L. L. (1945) *Time for Planning, A Social–Economic Theory and Program for the Twentieth Century.* New York: Harper and Brothers, pp. 104, 108–9.

5. Swain, G. F. (1915) *Conservation of Water by Storage.* New Haven: Yale University Press, p. 2; National Resources Planning Board (1936–43) *Regional Planning.* Washington: Government Printing Office, part 11, p. 42; Hays, S. P. (1959) *Conservation and the Gospel of Efficiency, The Progressive Conservation Movement, 1890–1920.* Cambridge: Harvard University Press, pp. 2–3; Stegner, W. (1954) *Beyond the Hundredth Meridian: John Wesley Powell and the Second Opening of the West.* Boston: Houghton Mifflin, pp. 118, 270–2, 334, 347; McGee, W. J. (1909) Water as a resource. *The Annals of the American Academy of Political and Social Science,* **33** (3), p. 37; Van Hise, C. R. (1910) *The Conservation of Natural Resources in the United States.* New York: The Macmillan Co., pp. v–vi, 1–16, 362; the preceding work was revised and republished in 1930 as Van Hise, C. R. (1930) *Conservation of Our Natural Resources, Based on Van Hise's The Conservation of Natural Resources in the United States,* L. Havemeyer, G. A. Roush, F. H. Newell, H. S. Graves, G. S. Wehrwein, P. G. Redington, and E. Higgins (eds.). New York: The Macmillan Co.; Pinchot, G. (1908) *The Conservation of Natural Resources,* in U.S. Department of Agriculture, Farmer's Bulletin no. 327. Washington: Government Printing Office, p. 11.

6. Guittard, F. G. (1930) Roosevelt and Conservation. Unpublished Ph.D. thesis, Stanford University, pp. 199ff, 236; Humphreys, A. A. and Abbot, H. L. (1876) *Report upon the Physics and Hydraulics of the Mississippi River; upon the Protection of the Alluvial Regions Against Overflow; and upon Deepening of the Mouths; based upon Surveys and Investigations. . . . Submitted to the Bureau of Topographical Engineers, War Department, 1861,* no. 13 of the *Professional Papers of the Corps of Engineers, U.S. Army, 1861.* Washington: Government Printing Office, p. 198; Marsh, G. P. (1885) *The Earth as Modified by Man's Action. A Last Revision of 'Man and Nature'.* New York: Charles Scribner's Sons, pp. 188–308, 318, 382–3; Van Hise, C. R. (1910) *The Conservation of Natural Resources in the United States.* New York: The Macmillan Co., pp. 113, 129, 218, 245–7, 251; Swain, G. F. (1915)*Conservation of Water by Storage.* New Haven: Yale University Press, pp. 245ff., 280–1; Roosevelt, F. D. (1957) *Franklin D. Roosevelt and Conservation, 1911–1945,* vol. 1, E. B. Nixon (ed.). Washington: Government Printing Office, p. 32; the preceding letter primarily discussed Col. C. Townsend's (1914) *Flood Control on the Mississippi River,* U.S. Congress, Senate, 63rd Congress, 2nd Session, Senate Document no. 1094, which criticized reafforestation and reservoirs as a method of flood control; Vance, R. B. (1934) What of submarginal areas in regional planning? *Social Forces,* **12** (3), p. 318; U.S. Congress, House, 60th Congress, 1st Session (1908) *Power of Federal Government to Acquire Lands for National Forest Purposes,* House Report no. 1514, p. 14; U.S. Code, Section 471, Title 16; U.S. National Resources Committee (1938) *Drainage Basin Problems and Programs, 1937 Revision.* Washington: Government Printing Office, p. 106; Gustafson, A. F., Guise, C. H., Hamilton, W. J. Jr., and Ries, H. (1949) *Conservation in the United States,* 3rd ed. Ithaca: Comstock Publishing Co., p. 18.

7. Van Hise, C. R. (1910) *The Conservation of Natural Resources in the United States.* New York: The Macmillan Co., pp. 253, 279–92, 310; U.S. Congress, 60th Congress, 1st Session (1909) *Congressional Record,* vol. 42. Washington: Government Printing Office, pp. 6520, 6687, 6526; U.S. Congress, Senate, 60th Congress, 1st Session (1908) *Preliminary Report of the Inland Waterways Commission,* Senate Document no. 325, pp. 512–14; Shaler, N. S. (1906) *Man and the Earth.* New York: Fox, Duffield and Co., pp. 1–20; Gustafson *et al., ibid.,* pp. 109–11; *Agriculture,* part V of *Reports of the United States Commissioners to the Universal Exposition 1889 at Paris,* Riley, C. V. (ed.), House Executive Document no. 410, p. 809; King, F. H. (1911) *Farmers of Forty Centuries of Permanent Agriculture in China, Korea and Japan.* Madison: Democrat Printing Co., pp. 274–6; United States Department of Agriculture (1928) Bennett says erosion menacing agriculture in *The Official Record,* 7, p. 3.
8. Davidson, D. (1948) *The New River: Civil War to TVA,* vol. 2 of *The Tennessee* in Allen, H. and Carmer, C. (eds.) *Rivers in America.* New York: Rinehart and Co., p. 163; *Preliminary Report of the Inland Waterways Commission, ibid.,* pp. 15–16, 314–76, 387, 585–7; McGee, W. J. (1907) Our great river. *The World's Work,* 13 (4), pp. 8576–84; Hays, S. P. (1959) *Conservation and the Gospel of Efficiency, The Progressive Conservation Movement.* Cambridge: Harvard University Press, pp. 91–4, 98, 102–5, 112–14, 220–2, 226; Van Hise, C. R. (1910) *ibid.,* pp. 165–70; see also Van Hise, C. R. (1930) *Conservation of Our Natural Resources, Based on Van Hise's The Conservation of Our Natural Resources in the United States,* L. Havemeyer *et al.* (eds.). New York: The Macmillan Co., pp. 217–21.
9. Stegner, W. (1954) *Beyond the Hundredth Meridian: John Wesley Powell and the Second Opening of the West.* Boston: Houghton Mifflin, pp. 223ff, 229, 301, 307–8.
10. *Ibid.,* pp. 230–1, 351.
11. Newell, F. H. (1909) What may be accomplished by reclamation. *The Annals of the American Academy of Political and Social Science,* 33 (3), pp. 177–8; Hays, S. P. (1959) *Conservation and the Gospel of Efficiency, The Progressive Conservation Movement.* Cambridge: Harvard University Press, pp. 22–6, 100–2; Van Hise, C. R. (1910) *The Conservation of Natural Resources in the United States.* New York: The Macmillan Co., p. 194.
12. Roosevelt, T. (1971) *Addresses and Presidential Messages of Theodore Roosevelt, 1902–1904.* New York: Kraus Reprints, pp. 196–8.
13. Hays, S. P. (1959) *Conservation and the Gospel of Efficiency, The Progressive Conservation Movement.* Cambridge: Harvard University Press, pp. 240–5, 248–52.
14. U.S. Congress, Senate, 60th Congress, 1st Session (1908) *Preliminary Report of the Inland Waterways Commission,* Senate Document 325, p. 447; Van Hise, C. R. (1910) *The Conservation of Natural Resources in the United States.* New York: The Macmillan Co., pp. 25, 34, 121–4, 131–2; Shaler, N. S. (1906) *Man and Earth.* New York: Fox, Duffield and Co., pp. 21–8, 121–38; Pinchot, G. (1908) *The Conservation of Natural Resources,* in U.S. Department of Agriculture, Farmers' Bulletin no. 327. Washington: Government Printing Office, pp. 10ff; Miller, M. M. (ed.) (1937) *Great Debates in American History From The Debates in the British Parliament on the Colonial Stamp Act (1764–1765) to the Debates in Congress at the Close of the Taft Administration (1912–1913),* vol. 10. New York:

Current Literature Publishing Co., p. 111. In May, 1909, *The Annals of the American Academy of Political and Social Science* devoted an entire issue to the conservation question, reserving section II for consideration of water resources.

15. Baldwin, E. F. (1913) The fight for the nation. *Outlook,* 105, p. 693; *Preliminary Report of the Inland Waterways Commission, ibid.,* p. 448.

16. U.S. Bureau of Corporation (1912) *Report of the Commissioner of Corporations on Water Power Development in the United States.* Washington: Government Printing Office, pp. xix, 16–29, 85ff.

17. *Ibid.,* pp. xvi–xx, 7–34, 90–2, 156–7, 185, 199–200, 205; Lepawsky, A. (1953) Dams and democracy. *The Virginia Quarterly Review,* 29 (4), p. 543.

18. Barber, O. C. (1913) Popular control of natural wealth. *Outlook,* 104, p. 613; G. Pinchot to F. D. Roosevelt, Harrisburg, January 20, 1933 in Roosevelt, F. D. (1957) *Franklin D. Roosevelt and Conservation, 1911–1945,* vol. 1, E. B. Nixon (ed.). Washington: Government Printing Office, p. 130; U.S. Congress, 63rd Congress, 2nd Session (1914) *Congressional Record,* vol. 51. Washington: Government Printing Office, pp. 13675, 13692–3; Van Hise, C. R. (1910) *The Conservation of Natural Resources in the United States.* New York: The Macmillan Co., pp. 35, 134–6.

19. Baker, C. W. (1909) The necessity for state or federal regulation of water power development. *The Annals of the American Academy of Political and Social Science,* 33 (3), pp. 99–112; Powelson, W. V. N. (1913) *Conservation of Natural Resources in the United States,* U.S. Congress, Senate, 63rd Congress, 1st Session, Senate Document no. 243, pp. 3–4; National Conservation (1910) *Outlook,* 96, p. 14; U.S. Congress, House, 55th Congress, 2nd Session (1898) *Preliminary Examination of Reservoir Sites in Wyoming and Colorado,* House Document no. 141, pp. 30, 54–5, 58–9; Van Hise, *ibid.,* p. 394; Wright, C. E. (1909) The scope of state and federal legislation concerning the use of water. *The Annals of the American Academy of Political and Social Science,* 33 (3), pp. 88–90, 97–8; *Power of the Federal Government over the Development and Use of Water Power* [Report of the Subcommittee of the Judiciary, United States Senate, on Senate Resolution, no. 44 . . .] 62nd Congress, 2nd Session (1912) *Congressional Record,* vol. 48. Washington: Government Printing Office, pp. 11568, 11572; U.S. National Resources Board (1934) *A Report on National Planning and Public Works in Relation to Natural Resources and Including Land Use and Water Resources with Findings and Recommendations, December 1, 1934.* Washington: Government Printing Office, pp. 378–9; Swain, G. F. (1915) *Conservation of Water by Storage.* New Haven: Yale University Press, pp. 29–33, 41ff, 98, 110.

20. Wengert, N. (1957) The politics of river basin development, in *River Basin Development,* vol. 22 of *Law and Contemporary Problems, School of Law, Duke University,* p. 267.

21. McGee, W. J. (1909) Water as a resource. *The Annals of the American Academy of Political and Social Science,* 33 (3), pp. 44–50; Van Hise, C. R. (1910) *The Conservation of Natural Resources in the United States.* New York: The Macmillan Co., pp. 125–9, 395; Mitchell, G. E. (1908) Checking the waste of our natural resources. *Review of Reviews,* 37 (5), pp. 589–90; White, G. F. (1957) A perspective of river basin development, in *River Basin Development,* vol. 22 of *Law and Contemporary Problems, School of Law, Duke University,* pp. 163, 165–7; U.S. Congress, House, 55th Congress, 2nd Session (1898) *Preliminary*

*Examination of Reservoir Sites in Wyoming and Colorado,* House Document no. 141, pp. 3, 31–2, 50, 79–80; U.S. Congress, Senate, 60th Congress, 1st Session (1908) *Preliminary Report of the Inland Waterways Commission,* Senate Document no. 325, pp. 451–6, 478–90; Kerwin, J. G. (1926) *Federal Water-Power Legislation.* New York: Columbia University Press, p. 167; King, J. (1959) *The Conservation Fight from Theodore Roosevelt to the Tennessee Valley Authority.* Washington: Public Affairs Press, p. 32; Hays, S. P. (1959) *Conservation and the Gospel of Efficiency, The Progressive Conservation Movement.* Cambridge: Harvard University Press, pp. 107–8; Leighton, M. O. (1909) Water power in the United States. *The Annals of the American Academy of Political and Social Science,* 33 (3), pp. 53–63, 75–6.

22. Van Hise, C. R. (1910) *ibid.,* pp. 138–44.

23. Baker, C. W. (1909) The necessity for state or federal regulation of water power development. *The Annals of the American Academy of Political and Social Science,* 33 (3), pp. 99–112.

24. Lorwin, L. L. (1945) *Time for Planning, a Social-Economic Theory and Program for the Twentieth Century.* New York: Harper Brothers, pp. 130–7.

25. *Ibid.,* pp. 115–28, 173.

26. F. D. Roosevelt's speech accepting the Democratic vice-presidential nomination, Hyde Park, New York, September 9, 1920; speech by Roosevelt, Spokane, Washington, August 19, 1920; F.D.R. to Egerton Brown, Hyde Park, November 17, 1920 in Roosevelt, F. D. (1957) *Franklin D. Roosevelt and Conservation, 1911–1945,* vol. 1, E. B. Nixon (ed.). Washington: Government Printing Office, pp. 38, 41, 43–4.

27. Article enclosed in a letter from G. W. Norris to W. H. Savery, Washington, November 23, 1923, entitled Brief history of the proposed water power development at Great Falls, in Norris Papers. Washington: Manuscript Division, Library of Congress; U.S. Congress, Senate, 66th Congress, 3rd Session (1921) *Development of Great Falls for Water Power and Increase of Water Supply for the District of Columbia,* Senate Document no. 403, pp. 4–6.

28. *New York Times,* January 17, 1924, p. 20; Zucker, N. L. (1966) *George W. Norris, Gentle Knight of American Democracy.* Urbana: University of Illinois Press, pp. 75–7, 114–26; for the most thorough treatment of Norris's career see the three volumes by Lowitt, R. (1963) *George W. Norris: the Making of a Progressive, 1861–1912.* Syracuse: Syracuse University Press; (1971) *The Persistence of a Progressive, 1913–1933.* Urbana: University of Illinois Press; (1978) *The Triumph of a Progressive, 1933–1944.* Urbana: University of Illinois Press.

29. Norris to F. R. Kingsley, Washington, March 3, 1930 in Norris Papers. Washington: Manuscript Division, Library of Congress; see also an unpublished essay by Grubbs, R. M., Senator George W. Norris, a Study in Statesmanship, in *ibid.*

30. Clipping, Chattanooga *Times,* August 25, 1940, in Norris Papers, *ibid.;* King, J. (1959) *The Conservation Fight from Theodore Roosevelt to the Tennessee Valley Authority.* Washington: Public Affairs Press, pp. 78–9; Van Hise, C. R. (1910) *The Conservation of Natural Resources in the United States.* New York: The Macmillan Co., pp. 132–3.

31. The most thorough examination of the ten year long debate over the fate of the government's property is found in Hubbard, P. J. (1961) *Origins of the TVA: The*

*Muscle Shoals Controversy, 1920–1932.* Nashville: Vanderbilt University Press.

32. Beard, C. A. (1926) Some aspects of regional planning. *The American Political Science Review,* 20 (2), pp. 276–82.

33. Copies of S. 1272 and H. R. 4883 (73rd Congress, 1st Session) which became the basis for the TVA bill can be found in the Norris Papers. Washington: Manuscript Division, Library of Congress; see also U.S. Congress, 73rd Congress, 1st Session (1933) *Congressional Record, op. cit.,* 77, pp. 1460, 2055, 2186–205, 2247–97, 2341, 2623–39, 2661–72, 2676–91, 2777–809, 3084–5, 3125, 3374–81, 3423, 3474, 3554–603, 3681–2, 3703, 3764, 3775; U.S. Congress, House, 73rd Congress, 1st Session (1933) *Muscle Shoals Development,* House Document no. 15, pp. 1–2; King, J. (1959) *The Conservation Fight from Theodore Roosevelt to the Tennessee Valley Authority.* Washington: Public Affairs Press, pp. 268–74; *New York Times,* April 12, 1933, p. 1; April 13, 1933, p. 2; April 15, 1933, p. 22; April 26, 1933, p. 4; May 4, 1933, p. 1; May 17, 1933, p. 8; May 18, 1933, p. 18; G. F. Milton to John Dickinson, May 19, 1933, in G. F. Milton Papers. Washington: Manuscript Division, Library of Congress.

34. *New York Times,* April 16, 1933, Section VIII, p. 3; May 19, 1933, p. 1; *U.S. Statutes at Large,* vol. 48, pp. 58–72; Norris to F. Brenckman, Washington, December 20, 1935; clipping of an article written by F.D.R. in Washington *Daily News,* April 4, 1938; clipping of a statement by Norris in [Louisville] *Courier-Journal,* March 12, 1933; E. C. Stallings to Norris, Paris, Texas, May 20, 1933; B. B. Peete to Norris, Montevallo, Alabama, February 7, 1933; A. T. Grayson to Norris, New Market, Alabama, May 21, 1933; T. Coombs to Norris, Los Angeles, May 19, 1933; Norris to J. E. Mills, Jr., Washington, May 10, 1933; Norris to A. J. Weaver, McCook, Nebraska, September 22, 1933, in Norris Papers. Washington: Manuscript Department, Library of Congress; Davidson, D. (1948) *The New River: Civil War to TVA,* vol. 2 of *The Tennessee* in H. Allen and C. Carmer (eds.) *The Rivers of America.* New York: Rinehart and Co., pp. 218–19; Lief, A. (1938) *Democracy's Norris.* New York: Stackpole Sons, p. 411.

35. Keyserling, H. (1929) Genius loci, the civilization of these United States. *The Atlantic Monthly,* 144, pp. 302–3; Lorwin, L. L. (1945) *Time for Planning, a Social-Economic Theory and Program for the Twentieth Century.* New York: Harper Brothers, p. 61; Knowles, M. (1929) Governmental organizations to make regional plans effective, in *Housing Problems in America,* vol. 10 of the *Proceedings of the Tenth National Conference on Housing, Philadelphia, January 28, 29, 30, 1929,* p. 124.

36. See McCraw, T. (1971) *TVA and the Power Fight, 1933–1939.* Philadelphia: J. B. Lippincott Co., for the most recent study of power development by the Tennessee Valley Authority.

37. See Droze, W. H. (1965) *High Dams and Slack Waters: TVA Rebuilds a River.* Baton Rouge: Louisiana State University Press, for the most thorough study of navigation developments by the Tennessee Valley Authority.

38. McGraw, T. K. (1971) *TVA and the Power Fight, 1933–1939.* Philadelphia: J. B. Lippincott Co., pp. 140–61.

# 11

# The city as an artifact: building control in modern Paris

## NORMA EVENSON

A member of the French Chamber of Deputies once observed that, 'A work of art doesn't always involve a canvas or a block of marble. A great city can be a work of art, a collective and complex art, but a superior art' [1]. In any city, the human fabric constantly changes. It is the relatively stable architectural environment which gives the city its physical identity. Paris is Paris because it looks like Paris, and although it is frequently observed that a vital city cannot be a museum, architectural innovation in the French capital has often been met with an instinctive opposition. Paris has been regarded by some critics not merely as a city containing artifacts, but as a single artifact which must be preserved intact.

The maintenance of unity and harmony within the city has been in part the result of regulations governing building height, roof profiles and façade projections. The artistic freedom of the architect has thus been limited by law. At the same time, the law has been responsive to changing architectural concepts.

Included among the most long-lived building regulations in Paris have been controls over projections on building façades. Such controls initially reflected the introduction of classical ideals, and a reaction against the medieval heritage of multiple overhangs. From the seventeenth century onward, Parisian building façades were strictly regulated.

The continuance of such controls into the nineteenth century was conspicuously evident in the large volume of building accompanying the renovations of Haussmann between 1853 and 1870. At this time pilasters

FIGURE 11.1. Building of the Haussmann era on the Avenue George V.

could be no more than nine to ten centimetres in depth. Balconies could be constructed only with permission, and could not project more than eighty centimetres. They were restricted, moreover, to the façade area beginning six metres above ground level. Encorbelment was forbidden. Even on streets where façades did not follow prescribed government designs, such as the Avenue de l'Opéra, a relative uniformity was maintained through application of existing building controls. Although these regulations assured a prevailing orderliness in the urban fabric, some observers deplored the lack of architectural variety in Paris, maintaining that the rigour of the façade regulations produced an architecture of monotony and frigidity, hampering to architectural imagination and detrimental to urban richness.

Commenting on the Parisian avenues, the Baedeker guide of 1888 noted that, 'most of them . . . exhibit an almost wearisome uniformity of style' [2]. Another observer expressed the opinion that 'our great Parisian streets, like the Boulevard Magenta, produce a fatiguing impression of monotony, with their building façades strictly uniform and rigorously aligned, with a frigid and self-effacing decoration, without improvization or movement' [3].

FIGURE 11.2. The Rue de Rennes, created by Haussmann.

Although a new regulation with regard to façade design was put into effect in 1882, it made no radical changes in existing restrictions. Encorbelment remained prohibited. The allowable dimensions of balconies remained the same, although they were permitted at a height of 5.75 metres above ground instead of six metres. Exact dimensions were fixed for every decorative element, including columns and pilasters, friezes, cornices, consoles, and capitals. It was required, moreover, that each façade be aligned with that of the adjoining building. Increasingly, such restrictions conflicted with the new ideals of artistic freedom and the growing predilection for picturesque form.

In 1898 the architect Louis Charles Boileau pointed out that 'artists and men of taste complain of the lack of variety in the buildings erected in our new streets, and of their decorative insignificance'. He went on to praise the superior picturesqueness of such cities as Brussels, London, and Vienna. The 'narrow and timid' regulations of 1882, in the view of a municipal councillor, 'have led to a dryness and virtual absence of decoration, and this rigid rectilinearity has ended in a flat uniformity, and what one could call an architectural militarism'. Urging a greater freedom of design, the supervising architect of the Paris government, Louis Bonnier, maintained the 'the French artistic spirit, which sleeps sometimes, but awakens always, makes us see that after all aesthetics are for people, not a luxury, but a need and a right, as important as hygiene' [4].

Responding at last to pressures for a modification of building controls, the Parisian Municipal Council instituted a series of studies during the 1890s resulting in a new set of regulations, which became law in 1902. From the many reports and discussions relating to the creation of the new regulations, it was evident that aesthetic considerations were the motivating factor. The Director of Works, reporting to the Prefect in 1896, had stressed a desire for 'projections more accentuated, more plastic, which could give to our buildings a less banal physiognomy, and thus contribute to the beautification of the city' [5].

Among the innovations of the new law was a regulation of building façades based, not on specific dimensions for each element of design, but on an overall spatial envelope, or *gabarit*. Within this *gabarit*, the architect was to have a new freedom in composing the façade, with the permissible degree of overhang related to the width of the street.

In comparison with the law of 1882, the 1902 law permitted an increase in the maximum projection on the upper façades from eighty centimetres to 1.20 metres. Such overhangs could also descend from 5.75 metres to three metres above ground on large streets. The overall amount of projecting surface could now cover one-third of the upper façade. Alignment with adjacent façades was no longer necessary, although a separation of fifty centimetres between overhangs on adjacent buildings was required. In addition to the increased plasticity permitted on the façade, the upper silhouette of a building could now be dramatized through vertical extensions of decorative elements past the line of the cornice.

The supervising architect of Paris, explaining the new regulations in a speech at the Ecole Nationale des Beaux-Arts, maintained that a new freedom had been given to 'the fantasy of architects', and 'would permit an extreme diversity of composition'. He was sure that a more creative design would develop, for 'one would no longer be able to employ the clichés that have been used continually in Parisian building, ready-made plans, ready-made façades, ready-made studies! It will be necessary to study, to work, to take pains, to do the work of an architect!' [6].

The modifications in building regulations, effected in 1902, also involved the question of height. In 1783, a royal ordinance had stated that, 'the excessive height of buildings is prejudicial to the wholesomeness of the air in a city as large and as heavily populated as Paris' [7]. At this time, an attempt was made to regulate building height according to street width, fixing the maximum height of new stone buildings at twenty metres. Although modifications were later made in height regulations, this maximum was to be incorporated in many subsequent laws.

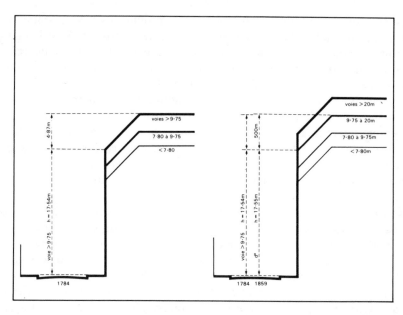

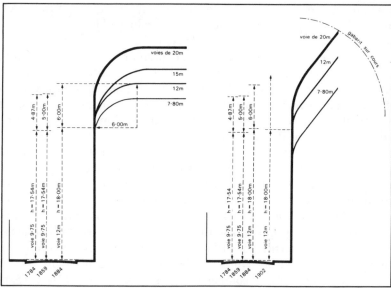

FIGURE 11.3. The evolution of Parisian building profiles. 1784: The attic storey is contained within a sloping wall of forty-five degrees. Regulations as modified in 1859 maintain the same building profile as before, although maximum heights are increased. Following the 1884 regulations, the profile of the attic storey is determined by the arc of a circle, permitting a greater total height. Following the 1902 regulations, the profile of the attic storey is established by the arc of a circle extended by a roof inclined at an angle of forty-five degrees. The result is an increase in height.

A change in building profile, however, produced an augmentation in overall height, following a modification of regulations in 1884. Although the maximum height from ground to cornice line remained at twenty metres, the form of the attic storey was altered. Previously, this storey was contained within the envelope of a wall sloping away from the street at a forty-five degree angle, plus a horizontal roof, adding four to five metres to the height above the cornice. The new regulations specified that the profile of the attic storey be determined by the arc of a circle, of which the radius would be equal to one half of the street, with the maximum radius of such a circle established at 8.50 metres. The effect on building of the new code was to increase the overall possible height on wide streets from twenty-five to twenty-eight metres.

In 1902, the regulation was further modified. At this time, a detailed table of maximum cornice heights was drawn up, comprising twenty categories of street width ranging from one metre to twenty and over. The new limits provided for a lowering of heights on narrow streets, in comparison with previous laws. For major streets, however, although the maximum height from ground to cornice remained at twenty metres, a new profile for the attic storey permitted a greater upward extension than before. The arc of the circle determining the form of the attic could now have a maximum radius of ten metres, and this curving plane could then be prolonged by an inclined roof at an angle of forty-five degrees. As a result, buildings conforming to the twenty-metre height limit could, with the addition of a high attic, attain a total height of over thirty metres. Instead of a single attic level, two, or even three floors could be constructed above the cornice line. It was observed that, 'in this new zone which is conceded to him, the architect can execute a high monumental crown in the form he prefers. An undefined field is open to his spirit of invention' [8] (figure 11.3).

Although the intent of the 1902 regulation had been to enhance design freedom and thus, presumably, embellish the Parisian street, the results were highly controversial. A critic was soon to denounce, 'the horrors which shock us today in the streets of Paris, resulting, for the most part, from this misguided decree of 1902, which has permitted the most abusive elevations and bizarre designs' [9]. The additional height permitted to buildings had been welcomed by speculators wishing to add the last possible centimetre of profitable area to their structures, while the increased plasticity of surface had, in the view of many, encouraged ugliness and vulgarity. By 1913 it was observed:

> To the eyes of the stroller in Paris, buildings can be classed in two categories: old buildings, characterized by a great uniformity of type, a perfect sobriety of lines and of decoration, by the measured proportions of their attics, which shelter only one floor; and new buildings, startling in their whiteness, which clash with the first through the discordance of their appearance, the profusion of their decorative motifs, the protuberance of certain parts of their façades,

FIGURE 11.4. The Hôtel Lutètia, designed by Louis-Charles Boileau and Henri-Alexis Tauzin.

the immoderate height of their attics, which give refuge to two and three floors—in short, by their character of bad taste, and the enormity of their disproportion. [10]

Although the Second Empire building of Haussmann had previously been deplored for its monotony, it was now seen to exemplify an admirable simplicity, unity and harmony, when compared with some of the new construction following the 1902 decree. It was noted that building façades had become, 'vast undulating surfaces', which could no longer be said to possess architectural lines, and, 'architectural decoration, strictly speaking, has almost disappeared'. Particularly derided was the Hôtel Lutètia, completed in 1910, which, 'with its decorative pastry, resembles an enormous soft cheese with bizarre blisters' [11]. Included in the offensive decoration of the new buildings was 'a profusion of flowers and vaguely allegorical figures, a heap of sculptural details which clash strangely with the sober elegance of older façades' [12].

While objecting to the amount and type of decoration permitted by the new regulations, many observers found it illogical that such projections should be concentrated on the upper part of the building. 'Some of these structures', it was pointed out, 'give the impression of being built upside down All the important decorative work overflows on the upper parts, while toward the ground the façade empties and simplifies. It looks as though we wanted to express defiance not only of good taste and good sense, but also of the laws of equilibrium' [13].

FIGURE 11.5. Apartment houses on the Avenue Rapp. Their decorative work is concentrated in the upper part of the structure.

All in all, the greatest criticism resulted from the new increase in building height, for the conspicuous profiles of many new buildings were seen to create disharmonious street façades throughout the city, and to threaten the appearance of historic sites. Increases in height were found, not only in new buildings, but also in additions to existing building. It was observed that, 'on the façade of stone was superimposed a second building of zinc, containing no less than three storeys and surmounted by a terrace' [14]. New attic storeys were added to buildings on the Rue de la Paix, the Rue Royale, the Avenue de l'Opéra and the Rue de Castiglione. The Rue de Rivoli, which maintained rigid architectural controls on the lower portions, was reconstructed above the cornice line. It was noted that, 'One still doesn't dare touch the arcades, but the roofs have had two or three floors added. . . . We are in the process of changing all the architectural lines in inflating these buildings with unbelievable coiffures' [15].

Architectural perspectives were suddenly changed as new buildings emerged above existing roof lines. Critics seemed particularly incensed by developments in the vicinity of the Arc de Triomphe, where the upper storeys of two new *hôtels* were visible above the uniform houses surrounding the Arc. For some, the unity, harmony and equilibrium of the monumental plaza had been irrevocably destroyed by, 'these great buildings *à l'américaine,* these sky-scrapers which insolently stretch up to dominate a *place* which isn't made for them' [16].

If such buildings could be erected near the Arc de Triomphe, there was

FIGURE 11.6. The Rue de Rivoli.

nothing to prevent them from springing up to mar urban harmony elsewhere. One could, for example, erect a 'skyscraper' behind the façades of Gabriel to loom over the Place de la Concorde. According to a pessimistic prophesy published in 1913

> before twenty years, enormous structures will be built along the Rue de Rivoli, on the Place de l'Étoile, on the Place de l'Hôtel de Ville, the Luxembourg Palace, Notre Dame . . . and nothing will remain of the formerly famous beauty of Paris. [17]

Strong pressures arose to have the 1902 regulations abolished, and government studies for revision began in 1907. Involved in the lively controversy over the law had been an examination of the whole question of artistic freedom. A lawyer, actively opposed to the law, had argued that in a city like Paris, special aesthetic controls were needed. He insisted that,

> in Paris, the city of beauty, which is to say of order and harmony, in Paris, the city of good taste, elegance and distinction, we cannot allow to be constructed, absolutely by chance and whim, the fantasies, perhaps fortunate and perhaps also monstrous, of architects and owners. It involves more than the interest of Paris. It involves the interest of France, and I would say even of the civilized world. [18]

The thirty-metre 'skyscrapers' which so alarmed conservative Parisian critics were, of course, modest in terms of what was technically possible and in comparison with the towering structures which had already transformed the centres of many American cities. A visitor from the United States would have found it difficult to understand what all the fuss was about. Many architects were coming to believe that tall building was the normal building form for a modern city, and it was perhaps inevitable that French architects interested in advanced technology, and concerned with the scale of modern urbanism would envision skyscrapers for Paris. One of the earliest of these was the pioneer of concrete construction, Auguste Perret, who outlined his ideas to a journalist in 1905. His recently-completed apartment house on the Rue Franklin had ten storeys, and was a relatively tall structure for the Paris of its day. He dreamed, however, of constructing, 'a building of twenty storeys'. 'As in the United States?', he was asked. 'Exactly', he responded, 'and be persuaded that the aesthetic of Paris would not suffer from it' [19]. Perret had wished to surround Paris with a belt of tall building and, in addition, to place a skyscraper *hôtel* of twenty storeys at the Porte Maillot.

One of the most persistent advocates of high-rise building in Paris was, of course, the architect, Le Corbusier. In 1925, he was to create an exposition project, the Voisin Plan, in which he proposed the demolition of a large area in the centre of Paris and its reconstruction as a complex of skyscraper office towers. Far from detracting from the image of Paris, the new high-rise ensemble would be, according to Le Corbusier, a contemporary embodiment of the grand scale of French tradition. Included in his many representations of the project was a series of drawings showing the evolution of major additions to the urban fabric of Paris. The city had received Notre Dame, the Louvre, the Invalides, Sacré Coeur and the Eiffel Tower, and had remained Paris. 'Paris was transformed on its own ground, without evasion. Each current of thought is inscribed in its stones, throughout the centuries. In this way the living image of Paris was formed. Paris must continue' [20].

The virtue of the skyscraper, according to such enthusiasts as Le Corbusier, lay in its ability to concentrate activity on a small ground area. Through wide spacing, such building could presumably provide for a large population, while leaving ample ground available for parks. High-rise building was continually justified as a device for opening up the urban fabric, and Le Corbusier once illustrated his skyscrapers with the caption, 'How to have air, light and greenery all around us again' [21].

While Le Corbusier was the most persistent and energetic advocate of high-rise building for Paris, other architects during the 1920s shared his conviction that this form of building could appropriately be employed in the French capital.

Although city officials examining the problem of building controls were not unaware of pressures for change inspired by the modern movement in design, no substantial modifications were made in regulations before the Second World War. Studies for a revision of building codes had begun in 1907, prompted by criticism of the 1902 law, and resulting in the adoption of a slightly modified text in 1914. Following the First World War, in 1923, a

FIGURE 11.7. Changing taste. Apartment houses in the Sixteenth Arrondissement.

municipal commission resumed study of the regulations, submitting a report in 1930. The two major questions still involved overhangs and height. The permissiveness of the 1902 regulations had reflected a contemporary predilection for ornamentation and plasticity, and had been blamed by many critics for encouraging deplorable excesses. By the 1920s, taste had changed and modernists energetically rejected both ornate eclecticism and the Art Nouveau. It was observed that, 'the triumph of moulded pastry has been succeeded by a Jansenist passion for walls of unbroken nakedness' [22]. Although the problem of excessive ornamentation had more or less solved itself, the commission believed that control was still necessary, 'even though today the ornamentation of façades is almost abandoned, even despised, which is, without doubt, only a passing fashion' [23].

A more pressing question involved building height. Basing its decision on urban aesthetics, the commission reported that,

> In its general physiognomy, the city of Paris must conserve its own character, its discipline, its quality of order and measure. And so, without exception, buildings of excessive height, like those which provide the attraction of certain foreign cities, should be forbidden.... Reason dictates that Paris should be held to the same order of height as before.[24]

Thus, although the Modern Movement embodied a change in style, new additions to the urban fabric were required to accord with existing regulations, and skyscrapers were momentarily restricted to the visionary

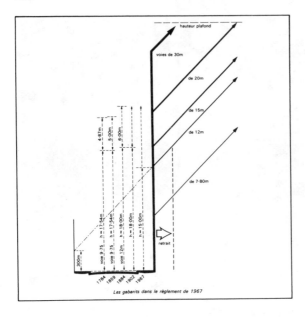

FIGURE 11.8. The building profile established by the 1967 regulations.

schemes of *avant-garde* architects. The more ambitious proposals of the modernists, of course, went far beyond the advocacy of tall buildings; many envisaged a total reordering of the urban environment. Le Corbusier, for example, had urged the separation of building lines from the street pattern to achieve the abolition of the 'corridor street'. In his new urban vision, the city was to be characterized by widely-separated slabs and towers freely disposed in open areas of greenery. Although building regulations before the Second World War remained largely uninfluenced by the propaganda of the modern movement, the postwar period reflected a decided change in the thinking of municipal planners.

In Paris, a new comprehensive building code was put into effect in 1961, and was subsequently incorporated in the Plan d'Urbanisme Directeur of 1967. The presentation report of this plan adopted much of the terminology of the Modern Movement, making specific reference to, 'the doctrines known as the Athens Charter, which introduced *urbanisme of the ensemble,* where individual works form part of large development plans', and where projects are oriented toward, 'structures of great height, with deliberately simple lines, with a concern for orientation and unity of composition.... Such compositions deliberately break with the conformity of neighbouring areas'. It was pointed out that, 'the urban fabric is no longer defined by streets, but by an ordering of structures, itself guided by functional considerations'. In its conclusion the report stated that,

> the aspect of the city will change. One will no longer go about between parallel walls, in these corridors, the streets, but in spaces alternating with buildings and greenery. Outside of certain streets, where a controlled architecture

FIGURE 11.9. Building on the Avenue d'Iéna reflecting the 1967 regulations.

remains valuable for its high quality or historic aspect, façades will present a variety of views. Housing will be separated from noise, commercial centres will be grouped in low buildings easily accessible to pedestrians . . . [25]

The new building regulations embodied a departure from previous codes, which had presupposed an alignment of buildings along the street, and had regulated height according to street width. The 1967 regulations embodied a control based on a *coefficient d'utilisation du sol* (CUS), which determined building volume in relation to the occupation of the plot. Restrictions remained with regard to height, although the maximum limits were increased to thirty metres in the central districts defined by the exterior boulevards, and thirty-seven metres in the outlying arrondissements. Outside the city, heights might meet a maximum of forty-five to fifty metres, with certain areas virtually free of control. The profile of the upper levels was also modified with regard to the 1902 regulations. The employment of a segment of a circle to define part of the roof line was abandoned in favour of a terraced set-back with a forty-five degree angle [26] (figure 11.8).

Building height continued to be related to street width, and for narrow streets, maximum heights were reduced. As street widths were measured from building line to building line, however, owners could attain increases in height by setting buildings back from the street. The overall result was an increase in new building which not only ruptured the existing urban fabric in terms of height, but which also destroyed the existing street alignment. In consequence, the same complaints which had arisen following the 1902 regulations were heard again, and the same arguments marshalled with regard to preserving the urban harmony of the city.

The question of regulation was again subject to discussion, and a revised code adopted by the Municipal Council in 1974. A government publication, analysing the faults of the 1967 law, observed that the aim of its creators had been,

> to aerate the city, to increase the importance of the spaces opened up. The preference of the authors went naturally to the free placement of buildings away from the street, that is to say in the heart of the block or in the centre of re-aligned plots. [27]

One of the major flaws in this regulation was considered to be a uniformity of control which did not take into consideration the existing character of many districts. The new regulations were embodied in Paris' *plan d'occupation des sols,* which attempted to prevent the destruction of the established townscape. Control was attempted not only of building form, but of building type. The increased construction of offices in the city centre was discouraged, and the construction of housing encouraged. Rules of ground coverage were framed to maintain the existing character of many districts, and also to discourage speculation in the vicinity of public projects.

With regard to height, it was noted that, 'This question of building height has been at the centre of the reconsideration of urbanism in the capital, in the press as in public opinion. It has too often been reduced to the problem of towers'. With regard to the overall fabric of Paris, it was opined that the effect of the existing towers was, 'probably less serious than destruction of the Parisian fabric, not in the form of a clean break, but by a multitude of blows and dents which it has been given, in the greatest disorder, by buildings of twelve to fifteen storeys' [28].

New construction was to be much more strictly controlled in an effort to maintain the traditional Parisian texture. Regulations reflected the principle that, 'every building to be built along a public street must be built according to the alignment' [29]. Set-backs might be authorized in certain cases, but would not permit an increase in height. It was observed that a continuity of street façade was characteristic of most of Paris and thus important to the image of the city.

Building heights under the new regulations were lowered to conform to prevailing patterns in different parts of the city. In the historic centre, the cornice height limit was placed at twenty-five metres, six metres, or two storeys below the 1967 maximum. This district was defined to extend as far south as the Boulevard Montparnasse and west to the Champs de Mars. To the east it included the Saint Antoine district and the canal Saint Martin, and to the north it extended to surround Montmartre. Certain outlying quarters with a characteristically low-rise character were also included within the twenty-five-metre maximum limit. For districts beyond the centre, a maximum height of thirty-one metres was imposed, with a limit of thirty-seven metres permitted only in outlying arrondissements where many twelve- to fifteen-storey buildings already existed. Some quarters, such as Montmartre,

FIGURE 11.10. Old and new building on the Avenue d'Iéna. While departing notably in style from its neighbour, the new building maintains the same façade line and cornice height.

the historic quarter of the Marais, and certain neighbourhoods, were to be subject to special regulations, reducing the maximum height in some cases to twelve metres, or four storeys. As a result of the new regulations, two-thirds of the city could not receive new construction notably above existing levels. Construction above the cornice line was to be restricted to one habitable floor, with the total height of the attic limited by a horizontal roof six metres above the cornice. In addition to the general building regulations, special controls were to be instituted in order to protect important views, architectural perspectives and the surroundings of monuments.

Although the evolution of building regulation embodied a growing measure of conservatism, with regard to the overall townscape it could be observed that there were large parts of the city which were totally exempted

FIGURE 11.11. High-rise apartments in the Place d'Italie redevelopment area.

FIGURE 11.12. The Front de Seine redevelopment area.

FIGURE 11.13. The Maine-Montparnasse tower as seen from the Avenue du Maine.

from any controls. The postwar development of Paris embodied a series of large-scale urban renewal projects, in which entire quarters were razed and rebuilt. Such districts included the Hauts de Belleville, Montparnasse, Saint Blaise, la Chapelle, Riquet, the Place d'Italie and the Front de Seine. These sizable areas of renovation were regarded as 'new sites', to be developed freely, independent of prevailing restrictions. Characterized by high-rise building, and often forming a sharp and discordant contrast with their surroundings, the renewal districts became the focus of extensive criticism.

Although the centres of redevelopment were generally located outside the historic core of Paris, it became increasingly evident that a tall building could have a visual impact far beyond its immediate surroundings. With the creation of a new commercial centre near the Montparnasse station, the Parisian skyline was broken by a 210-metre office tower, the tallest building in Europe. Although government planners presented assurance that, 'the architectural composition of modern inspiration has been minutely studied so that it can be inserted without any fault of taste into the Parisian landscape', the tower was frequently invoked as dismaying evidence of the increasing 'Americanization' of the city [30]. Critics were reminded, of course, that the beloved Eiffel tower had been initially opposed for its anticipated blighting effects on the visual harmony of Paris, and had subsequently become an admired landmark. The promoters of the Montparnasse tower insisted that once Parisians became accustomed to the looming presence of the new building, they would regard it with similar affection and pride.

FIGURE 11.14. La Défense viewed near the Pont de Neuilly.

The greatest controversy over height in recent years concerned a new commercial complex at La Défense. This district, just beyond the boundaries of Paris, had been designed in 1964 to embody an ensemble of office towers twenty-five storeys in height. With construction under way, however, government officials attempted to augment potential revenues by permitting variances of the initial plan, resulting in larger buildings. An overall increase in height was allowed, expanding the previous limit to forty-five storeys and over, and by summer 1972, the Parisian press was filled with criticism of La Défense. The emplacement of the complex culminated the monumental axis of Paris, and apprehension was growing that the existing perspective from the Louvre toward the Arc de Triomphe would soon be marred by the bulky profiles of the rising office towers.

Not all, of course, agreed on the blighting effect of the towers. The former prefect of the Paris region, Paul Delouvrier announced, 'let the sky show behind the Étoile a new quarter of Paris, a modern Paris of big business . . . I myself find nothing to criticize'. To those with doubts, he offered the comfort that 'it is eight kilometres from Carrousel to La Défense, and five kilometres from the Étoile to the new quarter. With the sky of Paris often murky even in good weather, the towers will frequently blur in the distance' [31].

At the height of the controversy, the President of France, Georges

FIGURE 11.15. La Défense pedestrian plaza.

Pompidou, entered the fray with a lengthy interview published in *Le Monde* on 17 October 1972. To Pompidou, the physical transformation of modern Paris was a sign of progress and economic vitality, and he was a strong supporter of La Défense. As to the derogation of building controls, he observed that French regulations were 'extraordinarily strict and compli- cated', and that, 'practically nothing of importance can be built without some derogation of one or another of these codes' [32].

Considering the question of architectural perspective, Pompidou main- tained that there had never been, 'a perspective from Carrousel and the Tuileries to La Défense. There was a perspective from Carrousel to the Arc de Triomphe. Beyond this there was a void, an avenue, very wide but without either architectural or aesthetic finality'. As to La Défense, the nature of the project led inevitably to tall buildings. Although some had suggested that future towers should be constructed farther to either side of the monumental axis, Pompidou did not believe that this would help. He insisted that there was 'a good chance that the result obtained would be better if the Arc de Triomphe detaches itself from a *forest of towers*. Nothing is worse than five or six towers trying unsuccessfully to conceal themselves. Either one renounces towers, and there will no longer be any architecture in an ensemble of such importance ... or one multiplies them'.

Pompidou concluded that it was 'a fact that the modern architecture of the big city leads to the tower. The French prejudice, and particularly that of Parisians, against height is, to my eyes, completely retrograde.' He reminded his compatriots that, 'one can't stay mired in the past. Paris is not a dead city, it's not a museum to maintain. . . . We are the guardians of civilization. The difficulty is to be at the same time the creators'.

In 1972, *Time* magazine reported a young American tourist, viewing Paris from atop the Arc de Triomphe, to remark, 'this isn't quite what I expected, but I guess you can't stop progress' [33]. And yet, it appeared, following the election of President Giscard d'Estaing in 1974, that 'progress' could be stopped, or at least slowed down for a while. In contrast to his predecessor, who viewed vast new building complexes and motor expressways as tangible evidence of power and prosperity, Giscard d'Estaing took a far more conservative view of the physical fabric of Paris. He halted extension of the left-bank motor route, and announced his support for public transport. Expressing a desire that all planning operations respect the character of existing quarters, he also stressed the need for increased park space within the city. As to tall building, his policies produced exultant headlines on the front page of *France Soir: 'Les Tours à Paris: c'est Fini'* [34]. Although nothing could be done to abolish the large complexes of high-rise building already in existence in Paris, new construction could be halted. 'The city must remain familiar to all', stated the President, declaring a moratorium on office construction in the city, and subjecting all current planning projects to reconsideration with regard to design [35]. Several skyscraper projects, such as a 176-metre tower at the Place d'Italie, were reportedly abandoned.

Giscard d'Estaing's new policies appeared generally popular, judging from reactions in the press. His intention to restrict untrammelled growth in Paris coincided, moreover, with a downward shift in the economy, and what promised to be a chronic energy shortage. A growing disenchantment with the physical results of postwar growth gave increasing support to the concept of a Paris in which the physical form, at least, would still provide a measure of stability and permanence.

Public conservatism, however, has never daunted the visionary architect, and as opinion was coalescing against radical change, the more ambitious proposals of certain designers continued to encompass structures of ever-greater scale.

Although the visionaries' more far-fetched conceptions seem unlikely to be realized, it is equally unlikely that the desires of the most ardent conservatives will be satisfied in modern Paris. For if the city be considered a 'collective and complex art', it is a fluid art form, destined to evolve through time. The control of architecture cannot provide a permanent mould, but embodies rather an attempt to guide the speed and character of change.

The effects of regulation are frequently negative, in that controls are designed to prevent certain things, presumed undesirable, from occurring.

No amount of control, apparently, can assure good design. But then, beauty has never been easy to define. The 'ugly' may survive to become 'interesting' or 'significant'. What was once deemed 'monotonous and mechanical', may later be seen as 'harmonious and orderly', and the 'excessive and vulgar' become 'imaginative and vital'. Every building was once new, and the initially radical form may eventually be regarded as an exemplar of tradition. The buildings which prompted such critical outcry following the enactment of the 1902 building code, often appear to our eyes as both charming in decoration and modest in scale. Yet most lovers of Paris would probably agree that the beauty of this city is unique, fragile, and threatened. Although a permanent set of building controls is unlikely to be produced, and pressures for growth and change are likely to continue, the desire to maintain a sense of continuity and consistency in Paris seems widespread, not only among Parisians, but among all who cherish this city as a vital part of the heritage of Western civilization.

## NOTES

1. The Deputy Chastenet, quoted in Magny, Charles (1911) *Les moyens juridiques de sauvegarder les aspects esthétiques de la ville de Paris.* Paris: Bernard Tignol, p. 3.
2. Baedeker, Karl (1888) *Paris and Environs,* 9th ed. Leipzig: Baedeker, p. 48.
3. Lortsch, Charles (1913) *La beauté de Paris et la loi.* Paris: Recuel Sirey, p. 97.
4. Magny, Charles (1911) *Les moyens juridiques de sauvegarder les aspects esthétiques de la ville de Paris.* Paris: Bernard Tignol, pp. 65, 83–4, 62–3.
5. *Ibid.,* p. 65.
6. Bonnier, Louis (1903) *Les règlements de voirie.* Paris: Schmid, p. 82.
7. Léon, Paul (1910) Maisons et rues de Paris. *Revue de Paris,* August 15, p. 854.
8. *Ibid.,* p. 858.
9. Lortsch, Charles (1913) *La beauté de Paris et la loi.* Paris: Recuel Sirey, p. x.
10. *Ibid.,* p. 33.
11. *Ibid.,* p. 92.
12. *Ibid.,* p. 88.
13. *Ibid.*
14. Léon Paul (1910) Maisons et rues de Paris. *Revue de Paris,* August 15, p. 299.
15. Lortsch, Charles (1913) *La beauté de Paris et la loi.* Paris: Recuel Sirey, p. 130.
16. *Ibid.,* p. 108.
17. *Ibid.,* p. 104.
18. *Ibid.,* p. 202.
19. Une Maison de Dix Étages. *La Patrie,* June 20, 1905.
20. Corbusier, Le (1967) *The Radiant City.* New York: Grossman, The Orion Press, p. 103. First published in France in 1935 as *La ville radieuse.* Boulogne, Seine: Éditions de l'Architecture d'Aujourd'hui.
21. *Ibid.,* p. 101.
22. Warnod, André (1930) *Visages de Paris.* Paris: Firmin-Didot, p. 336.
23. Commission des Perspectives Monumentales (1930) *Rapport de la sous-commission chargée de la révision du décret du 13 août, 1902,* p. 79.

24. *Ibid.,* p. 44.
25. Atelier Parisien d'Urbanisme (APUR) (1975) Une volonté de remodelage du cadre urbain de Paris: le règlement de 1967. *Paris Projet,* **13/14,** p. 37.
26. Although building regulations had remained essentially unchanged since 1902, modifications had begun in 1948. At this time, a series of exceptions to the law were enacted, permitting an increase in the height of buildings along unusually wide streets or facing open space. On 20th December 1958, a ruling allowed buildings on streets over twenty-seven metres to reach a height of thirty-one metres including the mansard roof. In the outer arrondissements, a limit of thirty-seven metres was permitted. In addition, exceptions to regulations were often given for individual buildings, such as the Cité Morland, built to house the Préfecture of Paris, and the Science Faculty of the University, constructed in 1965.
27. *Paris Projet,* Atelier Parisien d'Urbanisme (APUR) (1975) Une volonté de remodelage du cadre urbain de Paris: le règlement de 1967, **13/14,** p. 45.
28. *Ibid.,* p. 69.
29. *Ibid.,* p. 79.
30. Préfecture de la Seine (1960) *Plan d'urbanisme directeur de Paris.* Paris: Imprimerie Municipal, p. 84.
31. Faut-il raser l'Arc de Triomphe?, *Le Monde,* September 16, 1972, p. 13.
32. Pompidou, Georges (1972) Le président de la République définit ses conceptions dans les domains de l'art et de l'architecture. *Le Monde,* October 17, pp. 1, 12-13.
33. Building a New Paris, *Time,* July 10, 1972, p. 60.
34. *France Soir,* October 11, 1975.
35. *Ibid.,* p. 4.

# 12

# Conservation planning in France: policy and practice in the Marais, Paris

ROGER KAIN

There are five events which can act as signposts to the history of postwar urbanism in France. The first of these is a pair of housing Acts, 1947–48, which paved the way for a massive expansion of State housing in the 1950s based on formulae of *Habitations à Loyer Modéré* (HLM) and introduced a system of controlled rents in the private sector. The year 1958 saw the beginnings of large-scale urban renewal and redevelopment employing the strategy of the *Sociétés d'Economie Mixte* (SEMs—companies financed by a combination of public and private money). Then, in 1962, when 'comprehensive redevelopment' was in full flood and city centre populations were being decanted to *grands ensembles* in the *banlieues,* the Malraux Act introduced *secteurs sauvegardés* (SSs—conservation areas) within which historic fabric was not only to be protected but positively enhanced. In 1967 the whole legal framework of town planning was changed when towns of more than 10,000 population were required to produce a *Schéma Directeur d'Aménagement et d'Urbanisme* (SDAU—structure plan) and a *Plan d'Occupation des Sols* (POS—land-use plan). Finally, in 1976, the government of President Giscard d'Estaing profoundly altered the laws governing architecture, finance of housing and general town planning statutes. This whole period is also one in which conservation ceased to be the sole concern of the small specialized branch of the Ministry of Cultural Affairs which had nurtured it and became instead a *sine qua non* of urban management.

There is not space in this paper to discuss French thinking on the general philosophy of conservation and its social and psychological importance, although there is probably now as large a literature on these topics in French as there is in English [1]. Nor is this paper concerned with the technical and constructional aspects of restoration where again there is a considerable French language literature [2]. The main object is to examine the general progress, achievements and problems of urban conservation in France and in the Marais area of Paris in particular. It begins with a brief survey of policy and legislation which focuses on the Malraux Act. This has been held up as one of the most important and influential pieces of European conservation legislation and it is one on which other countries have modelled their own policies. The Act embodies the radical ideas of the then Minister for Cultural Affairs, the late André Malraux, and gives the State powers not only to protect the architectual heritage of French cities, but also to designate areas for positive enhancement [3]. It laid down a 'grand design' for a renaissance of the historic quarters of French towns. This paper demonstrates that despite a number of individual beauties, no such general renaissance has in fact occurred and concludes with a discussion of recent legal changes resulting from an acceptance of this fact.

## THE DEVELOPMENT OF FRENCH CONSERVATION POLICIES AND LEGISLATION

In France the systematic protection of individual buildings in towns dates from the 1830s and early 1840s when the infant Department of Historic Monuments under the leadership of Prosper Mérimée published in 1840 one of the first European 'lists' of buildings [4]. All the various nineteenth-century listing procedures were codified by an Act of 31st December 1913, which though subsequently amended is still in force [5]. It authorized the arbitrary classification of private properties; and less valuable buildings could be provisionally listed on a supplementary inventory. A significant element of the 1913 Act was that 'protected perimeters' could be defined around classified monuments. As there can hardly be a town which does not have a listed church or *hôtel particulier* at its centre, this means in effect that the French government has negative control over virtually the whole of the country's architectural heritage. A department of the Ministry of Cultural Affairs administers the lists and also has some funds to assist owners with maintenance. But the value of this fund has hardly increased in real terms, although the number of buildings classified more than quadrupled over the period 1913 to 1970 [6]. By way of illustration, the budget for the arts complex of the Centre Pompidou on the Beaubourg plateau at 45m francs, and rising, is six times more than that allocated for the 18,000 monuments listed on the supplementary inventory [7]. The French government is also given negative control over groups of buildings under a law of 1930

FIGURE 12.1. Centre National d'Art et Culture Georges Pompidou.

concerned with the classification and protection of sites of artistic, historic or scientific interest. Most of these sites are in rural areas but some hundred small towns and villages and many of the old quarters of Paris are protected by this Act [8].

A major change in emphasis from negative protection to positive conservation came with the Malraux Act and its system of *secteurs sauvegardés.* The provisions of this Act have been extensively reported in the English literature and it is not intended to go through them in detail here [9]. Rather, attention will be focused upon some of the more crucial elements.

The basic aim of the Act and its implementing decree of 13th July 1963 was to conserve the old quarters of towns, to maintain their atmosphere, but to modernize living conditions, to regulate traffic, to reorganize the social and economic base, and to give the conservation area a specific role in accordance with structures determined in other town and regional planning documents (notably town development plans before 1967 and latterly structure plans and land-use plans). In short, a positive role was to be identified for there was never any question of SSs becoming architectural museums [10].

Implementation of the Act is the responsibility of the Ministries of Cultural Affairs and Equipment (coordinated by the new Ministry of Environment and Quality of Life) together with the Commission Nationale des Secteurs Sauvegardés (CNSS). *Secteurs sauvegardés* are designated after consultation with local mayors, councils, Prefects and Ministry representatives by a decree issued by the Minister of Cultural Affairs in cases where local authorities give their support, or by a decree of the Conseil d'Etat if municipalities oppose the idea. The latter clause has never been applied although the threat of it has [11]. An architect is appointed to produce a *Plan Permanent de Sauvegarde et de Mise en Valeur* (PPSMV—conservation plan). This is a set of building regulations and a cadastral plan at 1:500 which replaces all other land-use plans, i.e. the POS where applicable, and specifies buildings to be restored, demolitions and clearances to be carried out, new structures to be erected, the zoning of land use, the pattern and hierarchy of roads and pedestrian ways, and the layout of open spaces. Thereafter all work affecting the exterior of buildings is subject to a building permit which is issued only if proposals are in accord with the conservation plan. There were to be no *dérogations* or similar deals between developers and planning agencies which have made such a mockery of much French development control procedure [12].

The financing of works outlined in the PPSMVs was tied in large part to procedures established by the decree of 31st December 1958 relating to urban renewal. Special subsidized loans, outright grants and delegated powers of expropriation were available to public undertakings or groups (syndicates) of owners [13]. The public method involves the setting up of an SEM to work within a closely-defined perimeter [14]. This company works out a detailed restoration plan for an initial area, usually a few street blocks, and known as a *secteur operationnel* (SO) [15]. In the early years of the working of the Act, the SEM/SO approach was by far the most important in terms of work accomplished but future success will lie in persuading more owners to group together outside *secteurs operationnels* to restore their properties [16].

The specific preservation and conservation legislation has been grafted on to and subsequently modified by, the general town planning laws. These are reviewed briefly in relation to the architectural heritage.

## FRENCH TOWN PLANNING LAW AND URBAN CONSERVATION

In common with many aspects of French administration, town planning is under strong central control. The mechanisms are a vast set of written laws and decrees which have been added to over time and are continuously updated. From time to time a 'New Town Planning Code' is published which brings together these day to day adaptations and modifications [17]. The conservation and preservation legislation discussed above is but a tiny part of this code and is inextricably linked to it. Some of the complementary measures such as the laws of 1947 and 1948 defining standards of HLMs and controlling rents, and the law of 1958 instituting a set of financial arrangements have already been noted [18].

Since 1919, when development plans were first required for towns of more than 10,000 population, preservation has been included as part of the development plan process. These plans could be used to control building height, to protect amenity, open spaces, and buildings of historic and artistic interest. By 1939, for a variety of reasons, only 173 out of a total of 2300 possible development plans had been produced [19]. An Act of 1943 codified development plan procedure but added little that was new; the 1950s saw a closer liaison between local and national planning agencies via the Commissariat du Plan, while rapid urbanization in the 1950s showed up a number of defects with the 1919/1943 development plan system. In particular it was difficult to distinguish broad planning strategy from detailed land-use control [20].

The *Loi d'Orientation Foncière* of 30th December 1967 swept away this old system and substituted a suite of three planning documents for all towns of over 10,000 inhabitants. These are a written statement, a structure plan (SDAU) and a land-use plan (POS). The land-use plan in particular can be a very powerful tool for protecting historic areas as it defines land to be developed, zones land uses, establishes plot ratios *(coefficients d'occupation des sols,* COS) to govern density, and sets the alignment of roads [21]. Moreover, it is required to delimit areas, streets and buildings for protection and enhancement, and can specify regulations to govern the location, size, mass and external appearance of new constructions [22].

In addition to these plan specifications, the 1967 law provided for levying a local amenity tax on developers to enable local communities to finance infrastructure improvements [23]. It also redefined the type of proprietors' syndicate eligible for public financial backing. This has important consequences for work in *secteurs sauvegardés* outside the privileged *secteurs operationnels* [24]. These new syndicates are called Associations Foncières Urbaines (AFU) and can be constituted by a majority of property owners specifically for the purpose of conservation in a conservation area [25]. They are eligible for the whole range of loans and grants available to SEMs for restoration work; in fact they are in competition for the same funds [26].

A further measure passed in 1967 makes it easier to carry out 'holding' operations in historic quarters. An Act of 12th July 1967 encourages associations of owners to bring their properties up to certain minimum standards of amenity. Grants and loans can be obtained from the Agence Nationale d'Amélioration de l'Habitat Existant (ANAHE) [27]. These works are limited in scope, have no aesthetic pretensions but do help to prevent the total decay of ordinary buildings until full restoration can be effected [28].

ACHIEVEMENTS, PROGRESS AND PROBLEMS

This section makes some general assessment of the urban conservation movement in France over the past fifteen years and sets the subsequent

FIGURE 12.2. The pattern of *secteurs sauvegardés* in France.

Marais study into context. It is worth recalling at this point that the 1962 Act was born at precisely the time when urban renewal and *urbanisme périphérique* were drawing heavily on the resources of the State and local communities [29]. Conservation areas, scheduled for very thorough and expensive, high-quality architectural work over small areas, were the complete antithesis of work on city peripheries which was judged largely in terms of quantity.

By early 1977, some sixty conservation areas had been approved from the initial list of 400 towns (figure 12.2). The momentum of designation has not appreciably changed over the years; there were ten creations and two extensions between 1969 and 1972, and fifteen creations and one extension in the period 1972–76. But by the end of 1976, only seven conservation plans had received their final approval. The detailed surveys have taken much longer than expected [30]. Within the sixty SSs, thirty-four SOs had been defined by the end of 1976 totalling an area of just 37.6 ha. This one per cent of the 3387 ha of SSs has received grants to date of 136m francs, or about 3.6m francs/ha. There has been a tendency over time to reduce the size of each SO to match available finance. The average area has in fact halved from 1.86 ha in the period 1964–71, to 0.96 ha in 1972–76. It is unlikely that another SO will match the 4.78 ha of the first at Avignon. One of the latest at Chalon/Saône is also the smallest at only 0.26 ha [31]. In short, it is an expensive and relatively unproductive procedure which will restore in total just 6000 dwellings and construct 1000 new ones [32].

On grounds of both cost and slow progress, the implementation of the Malraux Act has been heavily criticized, not least by those intimately concerned with urban conservation. For example, Regis Neyret of Civitas Nostra calculated in 1970 that if the current rate of work continued, it would take 350 years to treat the forty SSs designated at that date [33]. François Bourguignon of the Ministry of Cultural Affairs extrapolated to a figure of 400 years which might be reduced as many of the first SOs were located where problems were most intransigent [34]. At the root of the cost/progress problem is the architectural perfectionism of the PPSMV [35].

Comments on the social injustice of the *secteur operationnel* method only just run second to those of costs and time [36]. It seems that properties are inevitably let at very much higher rents after restoration and improvement and tenants have to choose between paying a higher rent or taking their place in a rehousing queue. Usually this would be in flats in a *grand ensemble* on the city outskirts [37]. In this respect many of the early conservation plans were akin to the urban renewal philosophy of the 1930s. Street blocks were sucked empty like eggshells, the cadastral plan completely reshaped, and homes replaced by open spaces for a new generation of higher income occupants to enjoy [38]. In the SOs at Avignon and Colmar there has been a total replacement of the indigenous population; at Lyon less than a fifth of the original residents remain [39]. Public and government alike have, since 1974, been opposed to operations of this kind. There is now a firm resolve to rehabilitate central areas and curtail peripheral expansion [40].

It is important to distinguish between the effects of an SO scheme and operations effected by syndical groupings. The latter are much less likely to cause the social disruptions of the former. It is also necessary to distinguish between areas where really massive intervention is necessary and those where only light restoration work is needed to bring buildings up to standard. It is clearly a multivariate situation into which variables like the nature of architecture and characteristics of residents have also to be brought into account. A basic problem is that the desire to maintain social networks can run counter to the necessity to reduce living densities, usually a priority if the physical quality of life in a conservation area is to be raised. Room for manoeuvre is often very narrow. It is precisely upon this critical path that the Marais case study focuses [41].

## The Marais Townscape

The *secteur sauvegardé* of the Marais differs from most others in two ways. At 126 hectares it is one of the largest but it covers only a tiny fraction of the historic city of Paris (figure 12.3). The majority of provincial *secteurs sauvegardés* cover most of the historic cores of towns. Secondly, it is characterized by relatively homogeneous townscape at least as far as age and style are concerned. It is a veritable anthology of French classical architecture. More than seventy-five per cent of the buildings date from before 1871 (compared with twenty-seven per cent for Paris) and there are some 1893 buildings of high architectural quality dating from the sixteenth to eighteenth centuries [42].

The conservation area is bounded by three main routes. The western and northern edges are defined by the rue de Renard, rue Beaubourg, and rue Vieille du Temple; the eastern margin runs along the Boulevard Beaumarchais and the southern boundary is the right bank expressway along the quais of the Seine. The rue St. Antoine, used by Dickens as the setting of several grim scenes in his *Tale of Two Cities,* cuts through the area linking the Place de la Bastille in the east with the rue de Rivoli, the only really significant stretch of 'new road' in the area (figure 12.4). The other streets are narrow, forming a very dense, irregular grid with roughly north–south and

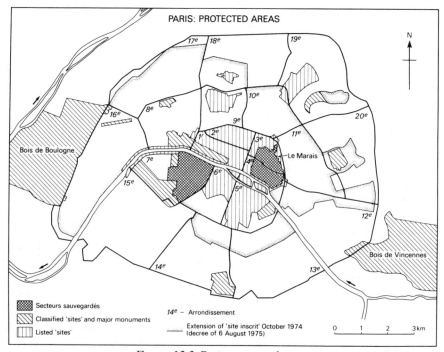

FIGURE 12.3. Paris: protected areas.

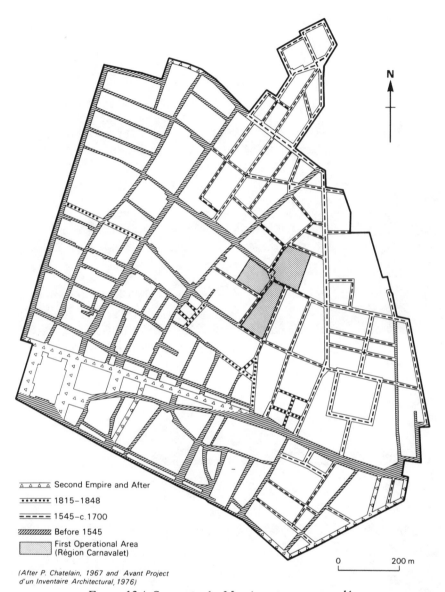

Second Empire and After
1815–1848
1545–c.1700
Before 1545
First Operational Area
(Région Carnavalet)

(After P. Chatelain, 1967 and Avant Project
d'un Inventaire Architectural, 1976)

FIGURE 12.4. Streets in the Marais *secteur sauvegardé*.

east–west axes. Streets account for as much as thirty per cent of the surface area (Paris average twenty-four per cent) and add to the visual quality of the Marais providing high ratios of enclosure to contrast with larger spaces, such as the rue St. Antoine and the Place des Vosges [43].

As its name implies, the Marais was originally an area of marshland on the flood plain of the Seine. By the later Middle Ages much of it had been drained and the whole area was brought within the Charles V wall of 1370. In

FIGURE 12.5. Hôtel de Sens, 1475–1507, which was bought and restored by the City of Paris in 1911.

FIGURE 12.6. Palais Soubise now the home of the French national archives.

FIGURE 12.7. Place des Vosges, an early seventeenth century *place royale.*

the fifteenth and sixteenth centuries, it was a popular recreation area for the monarchy and aristocracy and there was plenty of space to build houses and indulge in the new fashion for gardens [44]. In the course of the sixteenth century, the popularity of areas further west, to the north of the Louvre, began to rise but the Marais still retained its aristocratic flavour and this was reinforced by work on a *place royale* (now Place des Vosges) in 1604 [45]. The seventeenth-century townscape of the Marais was in many respects an exact reflection of the *ancien régime* which created it. The *hôtels particuliers* of the aristocracy were set amongst lesser buildings of their socially-inferior dependents—the whole ensemble formed an appropriately splendid setting for seventeenth-century life.

By the middle of the eighteenth century, this situation was quite definitely changing. The nobility was on the move to the west, attracted by the wide open spaces of areas like the Faubourg St. Germain where their architects could lay out a park, not just a garden as in the Marais. Then there was the Revolution. Great houses were appropriated by the State, subdivided, and the rot set in. All of this coincided with mass industrialization and the appearance of the low-paid artisan. Also, the extremely rapid population growth of Paris in the first half of the nineteenth century was not accompanied by a corresponding expansion of building activity [46]. The desperate housing shortage encouraged subdivisions, while workshop activities led to the construction of accretionary structures reducing the area

FIGURE 12.8. Nineteenth-century accretionary buildings infilling the courtyard of an *hôtel particulier*.

of open space. This whole process was compounded by the influx of workers engaged on the town planning projects of Napoléon I and then later of Haussmann. By the end of the nineteenth century, the Marais was as clearly a *quartier populaire* as it had earlier been the home of the aristocracy, the Paris of Madame de Sévigné and Dumas' Three Musketeers [47]. The nadir of the Marais' fortunes was probably reached around the time of World War I. From this time on the spirit began to rise but not before many buildings had been lost entirely and others stripped of their carved woodwork [48].

But the late nineteenth century was not all black. The City of Paris bought the Hôtel Carnavalet, restored it and opened it as a library and museum in 1875. Other buildings were converted to new uses such as schools. In December 1897, the Commission du Vieux Paris was established to foster concern for the city's historic fabric and in 1916 began serious listing of buildings worth saving. But destruction was still going on. Widening of streets was the greatest threat [49]. The 1920s and 1930s saw both destruction and piecemeal restorations [50]. The listing of buildings also went ahead, especially to the supplementary inventory after 1925 [51] (see figures 12.9 and 12.10). During World War II there was discussion of proposals for renovating the area around the St. Gervais church in the south-west of the Marais and these were put into effect under the guidance of Albert Laprade from 1945 [52]. The really important first step towards the preservation of the whole of the Marais came in 1951 when the draft Paris development plan was published. This envisaged its re-establishment as a middle-class residential area by restoring buildings, and clearing courtyards

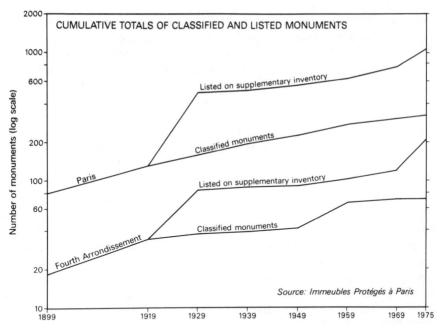

FIGURE 12.9. Cumulative totals of classified and listed buildings in Paris, 1899–1975.

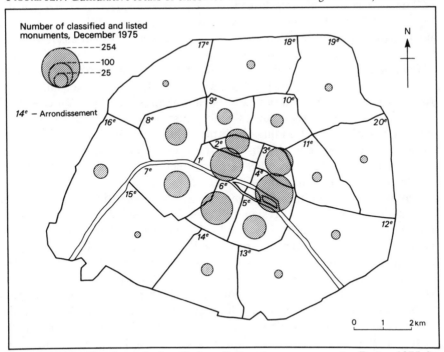

FIGURE 12.10. Number of classified and listed monuments in Paris, 1975 by *arrondissements*.

[53]. In 1961 a ten-year conservation scheme was presented to the city council at the same time as central government was considering the Malraux Act which in turn further strengthened the city's powers to restore the Marais [54]. Nor by this time was the Marais short of publicity. The Association pour la Sauvegarde et Mise en Valeur du Paris Historique (ASMVPH) was formed in 1961 and in 1962 the first *Festival du Marais* was held [55].

### THE DRAFT CONSERVATION PLAN (PPSMV) FOR THE MARAIS

The Marais SS was designated on 1st April 1965 and the first plan produced between 1965 and 1967 by the architects L. Arretche, B. Vitry, M. Marot and M. Minost [56]. The basic philosophy of the plan was to cut away nineteenth-century accretions and return the Marais to its eighteenth-century state as represented on the 1739 Turgot plan of Paris [57]. It made specific recommendations for demolitions, for restoring buildings of different construction types, provided guidelines for suitable wall and roof finishes in particular areas, suggested ways of concealing the clutter of external gas, electricity and water pipes and paid attention to the design of shop fronts, street lights and signs.

The conservation plan itself is in twelve parts each covering one *région* at a scale of 1:500. Each of the twelve areas is characterized by the presence of a notable monument, a particular *site* or some strong historical association to provide clear identification. For example, area 1 is 'ancien Temple', area 4 'Archives de France', area 5 'région Carnavalet' and number 9 is 'Place Royale-Hôtel de Sully'. The plan follows the standard conventions laid down for conservation plans and portrays listed buildings, buildings which should be listed, accompanying buildings which must be preserved to maintain the character of the area, buildings of little architectural value but to be kept, probable and certain demolitions, and the sites of new buildings, open space and car parks. It is very much an architectural rather than a planning document and therein lie many of its defects [58].

Surveys carried out in connection with the plan revealed that at the time of designation, there was a resident population of some 82,000 people at densities of up to 1483 per hectare in the Jardins St. Paul block, which is close to the all time French record of the Ile St. François at Le Havre (Paris average about 580 hectare) [59]. Open space, discounting streets had been reduced to just 1.7 per cent of the surface area [60]. However, a reduction of some fourteen per cent in the population between 1962 and 1968 was recorded by the 1968 census and this trend has continued according to the 1975 census when central Paris as a whole was found to have lost eleven per cent in the years 1968–75 [61]. Not only are some of the highest densities found in the Marais but also some of the worst living conditions of the city. In some blocks, seventy-four per cent of dwellings have no private lavatory,

FIGURE 12.11. Traffic congestion is a difficult problem to solve in narrow streets like the rue Payenne.

thirty-six per cent no individual water supply, and ten per cent no electricity. A key element of the 1967 plan was to reduce the living density to eradicate cases of nine people living in two rooms with no lavatory or water [62]. To achieve this meant moving out and rehousing some 20,000 people, although 'natural' processes are helping this to a considerable extent [63].

The economic basis of the Marais in 1965 was some 7000 small businesses employing about 40,000 people. Jewellery, optical work, leather goods and ready-made clothes predominated. Wholesale trades were also important but faced difficulties over access and parking. Perhaps the most obvious of all the commercial activities at ground floor level was small-shop retailing, particularly food shops serving the cosmopolitan residents of the area. The plan envisaged a regrouping of space- and transport-demanding activities into the areas of least architectural importance and easiest access in the north-west (rue Réamur) and south-east (Boulevard Beaumarchais) of the conservation area. The draft plan considered that it was not practicable to shut off traffic from the whole area if the artisan way of life was to stand a chance of continuing. In fact the traffic proposals were very much a compromise of small-scale improvements to ease junction crossings, and eliminating parking along the most congested streets. Fundamental to the plan was the assumption that through traffic would pass around the conservation area [64].

## IMPLEMENTATION OF THE DRAFT PLAN

There are four ways in which the Marais plan has been implemented. These are first, by the declaration of an operational sector; secondly, restorations by the State of its own properties; thirdly, restoration carried out by the City of Paris; and finally, private initiatives. The *secteur operationnel* number 1 is at the forefront of publicity, effort and finance and is discussed separately. The other methods are briefly discussed in this section.

Many large mansions in the Marais are owned by the State or the City and have been, or are being, restored for public use. The State-owned Hôtels Soubise and Rohan are the home of the Archives Nationales, the Hôtel Sully is the seat of the Commission Nationale des Secteurs Sauvegardés and the Hôtel de Jaucourt of the Archives de France. The City owns and maintains the Hôtels Carnavalet and Le Peletier-de-Saint-Fargeau (Carnavalet museum), Hôtel Lamoignon (library), Hôtel d'Aumont (Commission du Vieux Paris) and Hôtels Guénégaud, Salé and Libéral Bruant (museums). It is also responsible for cleaning churches (under an order of 26th March 1852 revived by Malraux on 11th April 1959), maintaining buildings in the Place des Vosges, and is currently working on the Hôtel d'Avaux (for ICOMOS) and Hôtel de Coulanges (Maison d'Europe) [65].

The City of Paris is also financing a comprehensive restoration programme by the Régie Immobilière de la Ville de Paris (RIVP) and its architect Félix Gatier in the old *bourg* St. Paul (*îlot* Jardins St. Paul, the eastern part of the old St. Gervais *îlot insalubre* no. 16). The street pattern of this area dates from the thirteenth century, most of the buildings from the seventeenth and eighteenth centuries and the whole block was scheduled for comprehensive redevelopment when classed as *insalubre* in 1923 [66]. It covers 8830 m² and by the time work is completed, the total floor space of 32,600 m² in 1965 will be reduced to 12,000 m² resulting in a reduction in the number of dwellings from 730 to 400 [67]. The interior of the block will become a garden [68]. The operation is divided into five phases and the first three stages of 112 dwellings are just about complete. Rents of the properties are to be fixed at 8.75 per cent of the resale value after restoration to enable the indigenous population to be rehoused *in situ*. Whether this will occur in the present climate of property price inflation remains to be seen.

Private owners have carried out restorations on a number of mansions, for example, the Hôtel de Marle now houses a Swedish cultural centre and others being restored by their owners are the Hôtels Colbert de Villacerf, Bondeville and a number of houses in the Place des Vosges. But perhaps visually most striking are the more than 4000 operations of scraping and cleaning of façades and the 2500 refurbishings of shops and ground floor premises that have been done under the direction of the Agence des Bâtiments de France du Marais. This sort of activity is not without its critics. Some of the scraped buildings are so stark and white and contrast so much

FIGURE 12.12. Stark, cleaned and restored façades in the rue des Jardins St. Paul.

with their neighbours that the feeling of *ensemble* has quite gone. The stone-cleaners and façade-scrapers have been too enthusiastic with their paint stripper and sand blasters. The ASMVPH is quite clear where it stands over such work, 'carelessness of the departments responsible for the enforcement of the law on safeguarded areas has led to very poor restoration, which, as far as the architectural heritage is concerned, is just as harmful as to pull the buildings down or fail to maintain them' [69]. The compelling logic of such statements is perhaps hard to discover, but it is a view which recurs in the context of the first *secteur operationnel* discussed in the following section.

### RÉGION CARNAVALET: THE FIRST OPERATIONAL SECTOR

At designation of the conservation area, the Prefect of Paris instructed the Société Auxiliaire de Restauration du Patrimoine Immobilier d'Intérêt National (SARPI—an organization sponsored by the government) to foster restoration work in conservation areas, to constitute a SEM; the Société Civile d'Etudes pour la Restauration du Marais (SERMA), to carry out preliminary studies over an area of nine hectares centred on the Place de Thorigny [70]. This area was selected as a potential *secteur operationnel* as it contained examples of almost every type of problem likely to be encountered in the Marais. SERMA's study suggested that a first SO of three and a half hectares be delimited. This was later reduced for financial reasons to three hectares and known as the Région Carnavalet (see figure 12.13). On 16th

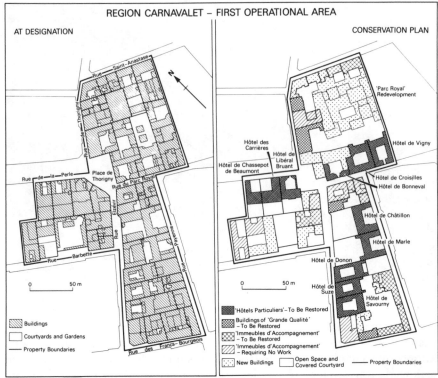

FIGURE 12.13. Région Carnavalet, the first *secteur operationnel*.

FIGURE 12.14. Hôtel Vigny (left), awaiting restoration, and Hôtel Duret de Chevry (right), restored before designation of the SS, in the Région Carnavalet.

May 1967, the City of Paris handed over implementation of the work to the Société d'Economie Mixte pour la Restauration du Marais (SO.RE.MA.). Fifty-one per cent of SO.RE.MA.'s capital is held by the City of Paris and the remainder provided by SARPI (eighteen per cent), banks (twenty-seven per cent), and insurance companies (four per cent) [71].

In some ways the Région Carnavalet is not particularly representative of the Marais as a whole. There is an extreme concentration of *hotels particuliers*; SO.RE.MA. identified eleven major historic buildings in the three hectares. The ASMVPH with their rather different and very academic scheme of classification count sixteen although they would discount, for example, 16 rue Elzévir, SO.RE.MA.'s own headquarters, because it was built in the nineteenth century, though quite in keeping with the surroundings. This area also contained some important public gardens; open space accounted in fact for thirty-three per cent of the surface area [72]. In other ways, however, it shared many of the problems common to other parts of the *secteur sauvegardé*, notably the fragmented pattern of landownership and the presence of accretionary structures in the courtyards of the *hôtels* and in the centres of the street blocks, buildings in a poor state of repair, and congestion caused by on-street parking (see figure 12.13) [73].

The results of SO.RE.MA.'s studies are summarized in table 12.1. The conservation operation was divided into three phases of a five-year programme. Buildings scheduled for demolition were first acquired either by agreement or compulsory purchase and rehousing of dispossessed families arranged, 186 dwellings and sixty-seven business premises were involved totalling 24,700 m² of floor space or forty-two per cent of the total floor area of the SO. Private owners agreed to organize fifteen per cent of these demolitions themselves while the rest was done by SO.RE.MA. at a cost of 35.5m francs. In the restoration phase, each proprietor was notified by the Prefect of work which SO.RE.MA. considered necessary (see table 12.1). Proprietors then decided whether to restore themselves or to hand over their property to SO.RE.MA. Seventy-five per cent of work on *hôtels particuliers* was carried out by owners but SO.RE.MA's share of work on the other categories was ninety per cent, costing to date 25m francs. Restoration and the third phase, the construction of new buildings, are still in progress. New buildings in the Région Carnavalet are mostly flats for sale or rent outside of the 1948 rent controls, underground car parks and offices. The original idea was for sites to be sold to developers who would work within the architectural directives of the SO but this has been one of the notable failures of the whole operation. Developers have not been attracted to work the difficult plot interior sites to strictly-defined formulae of height, mass, finish and plot ratios. SO.RE.MA. has undertaken all the construction work itself at a cost to date of 73m francs, approaching half the total expenditure of 166m francs [74]. Income from sales is expected to be 150m francs leaving a deficit of about 16m francs to be covered by government grants. But at prices of up to

TABLE 12.1. SO.RE.MA. and the Région Carnavalet (Data: SO.RE.MA.).

|  | At designation m² | At completion m² |
|---|---|---|
| Total surface area excluding roads | 26,000 | 26,500 |
| Built area | 20,000 | 11,500 |
| Open space | 6,000 | 14,500 |
| Built area as a percentage of total | 77% | 44% |
| *Buildings* |  |  |
| To be demolished | 24,700 |  |
| *Hôtels particuliers* to restore | 9,600 |  |
| Buildings of high architectural quality to restore | 6,900 |  |
| Accompanying buildings needing restoration | 8,900 |  |
| Accompanying buildings needing only internal works | 8,900 |  |
| Total restorations | 34,300 | 34,300 |
| New buildings to be constructed |  | 17,000 |
| Total floor space | 59,000 | 51,300 |
| *Land use* |  |  |
| Number of dwellings | 536 | 432 |
| Floor area of dwellings, m² | 26,500 | 32,000 |
| Number of economic activities | 148 | about 70 |
| Floor area of economic activities, m² | 32,500 | 19,300 |
| Number of parking spaces | 70 | 527 |

10,000 francs/m² for flats in the luxury Parc Royal development, sales are slower than expected. This caused some temporary financial embarrassment when the first loan repayments fell due in May 1977.

The most difficult and the most sensitive of the problems faced by SO.RE.MA. over the past ten years is rehousing displaced occupiers, a difficulty which is compounded by a general resistance to moving out of the central city environment. A survey in 1976 of residents in the southern Marais confirmed that attachments to the local area are very strong, work and home are located close to each other, there are strong family ties and a fear of friendlessness outside the Marais. These are all perceived, if not real problems [75].

Five hundred and thirty-six dwellings were affected by the conservation programme, all of which at the time of designation came within the

FIGURE 12.15. Some estimates suggest that daily life in the Marais will be disrupted by street works like these in the rue du Parc Royal for upwards of fifty years as essential public utilities are routed underground.

FIGURE 12.16. Major constructional works by SO.RE.MA. in progress in 1977. On the left a new block of retirement flats; in the background, restoration of the Hôtel Salé; on the right, the site of the exclusive Parc Royal housing development.

FIGURE 12.17. By the end of 1978 much of this work was completed and careful planting helps to blend the modern block of the Résidence de la Perle and the Salé museum.

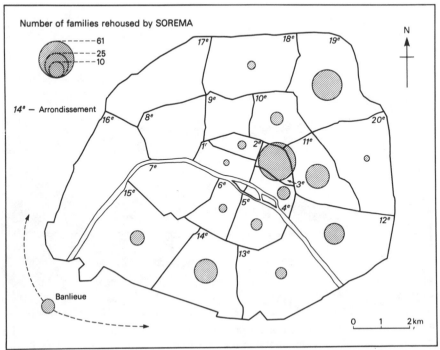

FIGURE 12.18. Number of families rehoused by the SO.RE.MA. by *arrondissements*.

*Habitations à Loyer Moderé* norms, 120 of 'average' standard (category IIC) and 416 sub-standard (mostly because of lack of WC—category IIIA). Part of the rehousing programme was organized directly by the HLM organization of the City of Paris. They rehoused 155 families in HLMs, forty-six per cent in the 19th *arrondissement,* twenty-two per cent in the 14th, fourteen per cent in the 15th, six per cent in the 12th and nine per cent in the *banlieue* (mainly at Maisons-Alfort, L'Haye les Roses and Villejuif). The remaining 350 families were the direct responsibility of SO.RE.MA. Of these, fifty-six did not require rehousing but were given a removal allowance, twenty-five left between the date of survey in 1964 and the beginning of work in 1967, and fifty were co-proprietors who took an agreed (sixty-eight per cent) or arbitrated (thirty-two per cent) cash allowance for the value of their property. Figure 12.18 shows the distribution of families rehoused; fifty-six per cent were rehoused either within the SS or in neighbouring *arrondissements.*

It is inconceivable that restoration work of this type, equally disruptive in social terms as urban renewal, could be carried out without considerable social displacement. The problem is that for the overwhelming majority, the displacement is going to be permanent. Of the 432 dwellings planned for the area, only 101 will be in HLM category IIC (previously 120 plus 416 in IIIA), ninety-one will be to IIB standard while the rest will be sold (probably 187), or rented on six-year leases (probably fifty-three) on the open market. A recurrent theme in interviews with residents is the question of rents. Everyone has his own story of rent inflation to tell, of 200 francs for three months becoming 1500 francs for one month, of flats in *hôtels particuliers* compulsorily purchased in the late 1960s for 1000 francs/m² while in 1976 it was possible to pay 8000 francs/m² for a chic Marais flat. Some of these stories are quite probably apocryphal, but the perceived effect of conservation is quite clear.

SO.RE.MA.'s declared object is to try to retain artisan activities and population, but gentrification is occurring. Few artisans are returning to the Région Carnavalet and it is unlikely that the planned pattern of activities summarized in table 12.2 will be achieved. For example, it had been hoped to install three craft workshops in a purpose-built building in the rue Barbette but their proprietors declined to pay the rent asked and moved to outer Paris. Their place has been taken by an advertising agency. Changes in the Région Carnavalet can be neatly summed up in two pairs of percentages. Industry and warehousing before conservation occupied eighty-four per cent of the commercial floor space and afterwards will occupy at best thirty-two per cent; comparable figures for offices and cultural activities are twelve per cent and 59.5 per cent respectively.

Similar changes are occurring as a result of private piecemeal improvements in the blocks adjoining the SO to the west, in the rue Aubriot, rue des Guillemites and rue Ste. Croix de la Bretonnerie area. There has been some work here by public agencies like the Sorbonne in the rue St. Croix

FIGURE 12.19. Purpose-built workshops in the rue Barbette.

TABLE 12.2. Economic activity in the Région Carnavalet (data SO.RE.MA.).

| Type | Floor space at designation | | Floor space at completion | |
|---|---|---|---|---|
| | m² | % | m² | % |
| Retail | 1,200 | 4 | 1,600 | 8·5 |
| Traditional industry | 5,600 | 17 | 3,000 | 16 |
| Nuisance industry | 15,000 | 46 | 800 | 4 |
| Warehousing | 5,000 | 15 | — | — |
| Ready made clothes | 2,000 | 6 | 2,400 | 12 |
| Offices | 3,700 | 11 | 6,800 | 34·5 |
| Cultural activities | 300 | 1 | 4,700 | 25 |

TABLE 12.3. Comparison of the use of refurbished/restored and unrestored buildings [76].

| Use | Unrestored | Restored and refurbished |
|---|---|---|
| Workshops | 16 | 5 |
| Café/bar/restaurant | 12 | 8 |
| Foodshops | 5 | 1 |
| Boutiques and luxury shops | 3 | 11 |
| Offices | 2 | 9 |
| Warehouses | 2 | 1 |

restoring property for an institute of Catalan studies, and by an HLM company in rue du Moussy building a block of thirty-one apartments and a crèche, but the majority has been done by individuals, has included very little demolition or structural work but has been mainly the scraping, cleaning and refurbishing of façades. The results of a survey of ground floor commercial uses of forty-three unrestored and thirty-eight refurbished/restored buildings west of rue Elzévir, are summarized in table 12.3 and provide some quantitative support for the idea that the Marais is acquiring a certain prestige and is undergoing a fundamental change in character.

### THE MARAIS PLAN REVISED IN 1976

At the end of 1975, the 1967 conservation plan for the Marais was abandoned and between February and May 1976 it was completely revised [77]. A number of factors precipitated this drastic course of action. The first of these was the increase in co-ownership and property prices over the past ten years. This had a severe impact on the programme of demolitions. No longer were the authorities dealing with a single proprietor, the value of whose total property was very likely to be increased by the demolition of part of it, but rather with a host of co-owners many of whom would see the whole of their property disappear. Hardly any demolition work has occurred outside the areas where the SEMs have been working. In these circumstances 'spontaneous' restorations by individual owners are producing 'luxury slums' as clandestine works, very difficult to prevent, are carried out under the cover of simple façade cleaning permits [78] (figure 12.20).

Property speculation is in many ways a process independent of restoration procedures but is exacerbated once tangible evidence of the rising prestige of an area is clear for all to see. People who will buy, 'No matter what, no matter where, at no matter what price' are, according to the consultant architect M. Minost, the most potent economic cause of the abandonment of the 1967 proposals [79]. Also, the physical impossibility of rehousing displaced families in an area which is already overpopulated is no longer in accord with present policy to avoid socially-disruptive public works.

The plan was revised in the light of these facts while still trying as far as possible to adhere to the general principles which guided the first version. The new plan continues the preservation proposals but has a radically different attitude to demolitions and new building. The category of 'definite demolitions' is retained only where absolutely necessary, first, to enhance the immediate surroundings of a major monument and secondly, where absolutely essential to improve living and working conditions. In this latter category, for example, are buildings which have an outlook from living rooms of less than 2.5 m. New buildings only figure on the revised plan in a limited number of clearly defined circumstances, for instance, to house essential services and for ground floor workshops [80].

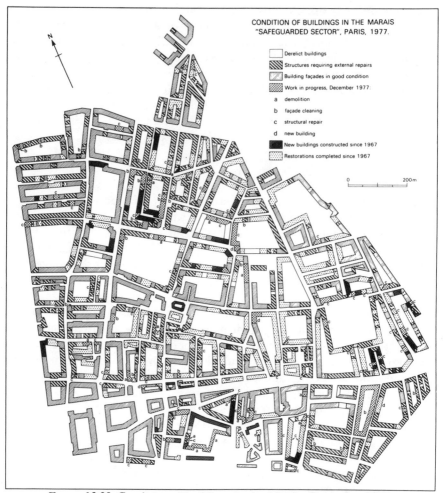

CONDITION OF BUILDINGS IN THE MARAIS
"SAFEGUARDED SECTOR", PARIS, 1977.

☐ Derelict buildings

▨ Structures requiring external repairs

▨ Building façades in good condition

▨ Work in progress, December 1977:

a   demolition

b   façade cleaning

c   structural repair

d   new building

■ New buildings constructed since 1967

▨ Restorations completed since 1967

0            200 m

FIGURE 12.20. Condition of buildings in the Marais, December 1977.

The greatest differences between the 1967 and 1976 plans are to be found in parts of the SS less generously endowed with major monuments than say the Carnavalet area. One such block is *îlot* 9/33 in the north-west of the conservation area (figure 12.21). This was a middle-class area in the eighteenth century, it became much subdivided in the nineteenth when the building density increased, and further storeys were added to buildings which have since received very little maintenance. At the time of the 1962 census it had a population of just over 1200/hectare. One typical parcel of the *îlot* was surveyed in connection with the 1976 revision. Like most of its neighbours it is a narrow strip, averaging 12 m wide, crossing the *îlot* from north to south and opening at 15 rue au Maire and 34 rue des Gravilliers. All the buildings are in a bad state of repair and many have been served with dangerous

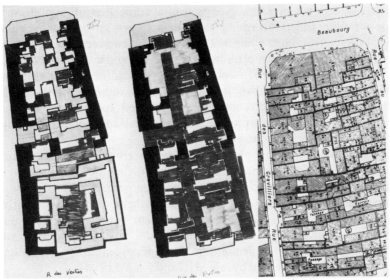

FIGURE 12.21. Îlot 9/33 in the north-west of the Marais.

building notices by the Prefecture of Police. The total ground area is 905 m², 785 m² is built on leaving just 147 m² open and most of this is taken up by an alley, the Passage Barrois. The coefficient of density is about eighty-three per cent and many buildings have outlooks of less than 3.5 m. The ten *corps du bâtiment,* mostly of six to seven storeys, contain seventy-three apartments, twenty-five commercial premises and sixty-one cellars, stores, etc., and these are divided amongst sixty co-proprietors. The actual number of occupiers is close on 200, producing a population density of about 2000/hectare, greater than that of the *îlot* as a whole.

The 1967 plan scheduled *îlot* 9/33 to receive heavier, transport-oriented industry displaced from elsewhere in the Marais. Interesting buildings fronting on to the rue des Gravilliers and the rue au Maire were to be kept but the entire interior of the block was to be demolished and replaced by a system of factories and workers' housing. This ambitious project, more in the vein of urban renewal than restoration and illustrating nicely the positive intervention side of the Malraux Act, has now been abandoned and replaced by a scheme involving only the minimum of clearances. In this respect the programme is more in accord with current thinking and proposed legislation in France which will substantially amend the Malraux Act.

## A FUTURE FOR THE PAST IN FRANCE

Some beautiful restorations have certainly been effected in *secteurs sauvegardés* but there has been no general renaissance of the historic fabric of

French cities. Some pressure groups would argue that all the clearances, façade-scraping and refurbishing have in fact been retrogressive activities. Some of these criticisms will be met by three new laws recently passed by the government to reform town planning, architecture and the finance of housing [81]. These will affect urban conservation procedures in two main ways. Firstly, they will make the land-use plan a more powerful tool for implementing conservation outside the privileged conservation areas and secondly, they amend some provisions of the Malraux Act, particularly the regulations affecting the conservation plan.

The new law on urban planning brings together and consolidates all pre-existing controls on demolitions. This one single procedure will make the policing of demolitions much easier. Demolition permits will be required in all areas delimited on a land-use plan as of aesthetic or historic importance. It also provides greatly increased protection to monuments listed on the supplementary inventory. Henceforth it will not be necessary to classify a monument to prevent its demolition. Receipts from fines levied against contraventions will be shared by ANAHE and CNMHS.

The circumstances in which a demolition permit might be granted or refused are now quite explicitly stated. The refusal of a building permit on aesthetic grounds is not as firmly based in law although the 'New Law on Architecture' should help in this respect by regulating the profession, requiring close supervision of work and setting up regional architectural councils [82]. A further innovation is that general regulations governing the density can be relaxed and building allowed at higher densities for aesthetic reasons providing that certain standards of amenity can be achieved. This should help to maintain the intimate character of historic areas and preserve existing building alignments.

Experience gained during fifteen years of work in conservation areas has emphasized the importance of, and the difficulty of obtaining, selective demolitions to improve health and appearance. Henceforth a land-use plan will be able to delimit areas in which the granting of a construction permit can be made conditional on the demolition of all or part of the existing structures [83]. This new attitude to the land-use plan is encouraging, particularly as this instrument provides a means for dovetailing conservation measures with wider planning strategies via the structure plan.

Some of the amendments to the Malraux Act introduced by the new town planning law are purely technical, resulting from the fact that it predated the 1967 Act instituting the land-use plan. But there are some more substantive changes involving the PPSMV (conservation plan) which will make this a less rigid document, more able to accommodate the reality that life does not stop in historic quarters once a conservation area has been designated, but that dynamic urban processes are always producing change [84]. The adjective 'permanent' is to be dropped and they are now called *Plans de Sauvegarde et de Mise en Valeur* (PSMV). Profound modifications will not be permitted but small changes, almost inevitable with such detailed planning documents, can be approved. There are also clauses in the law which will make the compulsory purchase of property in co-ownership easier. These measures will apply not only to *secteurs operationnels* but to whole *secteurs sauvegardés* making it easier for local associations of co-owners to cooperate in restoration projects. And the future of the past does seem to lie in the hands of those who own it, no matter how tiny a part or complex is their legal claim to it. It is neither financially possible nor socially desirable to extend the SO approach over anything more than a limited area. Attitudes of local residents towards wholesale evictions in the name of architectural perfectionism are certainly hardening. There has been violence on the streets when heavy-handed, over-zealous bailiffs moved into the rue St. Paul on 29th August 1977. Since then the Intercomité du Marais has been coordinating the various protest groups and reaffirming that many buildings in the safeguarded sector are structurally quite sound and really require only a minimum of work to bring them up to a habitable standard [85]. The role of operational sectors is now seen by all sides to be one of example; an incentive for owners to associate and to restore for themselves, taking advantage of the particular rights pertaining to syndicates in French common law [86].

In the last analysis, it does not matter how well the law is framed, however responsive are the institutions, however watchful are the implementing authorities or how careful are architects to avoid excessive pastiche and unsympathetic restorations [87]. Ultimately, success depends on the

FIGURE 12.22. Advertisements like this emphasizing the *chic, de luxe* character of the restored Marais now appear frequently in art magazines.

availability of finance [88]. When free market forces prevail, social change in historic areas seems inevitable as prestige and prices rise. There is as yet no evidence of a shortage of takers of restored city centre flats from the French middle classes with their still highly urban residential preferences even if the price of some new luxury apartments has risen beyond what people will pay at the moment. It is difficult to agree with Annick Vignier of the Ministry of Cultural Affairs who suggests that it is a *myth* that safeguarded sectors are 'areas of exclusive restorations, expensive, luxurious and weighed down with cultural provisions' [89]. These phrases in fact characterize the restored parts of the Marais rather well. But if efforts to enhance the fabric of the past in France have not yet achieved André Malraux's expectations and are not the shining example that was hoped, the future of the past in the light of recent policy changes may be more secure.

NOTES

1. A collection of papers dealing with the general philosophy of conservation in a French context is published in *Urbanisme,* 147/8, 1975. See also Hruska, E. (1967) Réflexions sur la fonction contemporaine des noyaux historiques des villes. *Urbanisme,* 101, pp. 28–41 and Brichet, R. (1968) Orientations nouvelles de la protection des édifices et ensembles anciens. *La Construction Moderne,* 1, pp. 62–72.

2. For example, Bourely, C. (1975) Le métier d'architecte des Bâtiments de France. *Les Monuments Historiques de la France,* 21 (5), pp. 1–5; Melissinos, A. (1976) Une méthode d'approche pour la protection du patrimoine architectural urbain. *Les Monuments Historiques de la France,* 22 (6), pp. 25–8; Paquet, J.-P. (1975) Théorie de la restauration. *Les Monuments Historiques de la France,* 21 (1), pp. 2–8; Baquet, A. (1974) Le cadre de vie et la conservation des centres anciens. *Urbanisme,* 136, pp. 54–7.

3. For a brief appreciation of Malraux's work see Kain, R. J. P. (1977) André Malraux: an apreciation of his contribution to conservation planning. *Town and Country Planning,* 45, pp. 177–8.

4. Bailly, G. H. and Desbat, J. P. (1973) *Les Ensembles Historiques dans la Reconquête Urbaine.* Paris: La Documentation Française; Brichet, R. (1972) La protection juridique des villes anciennes. *Monumentum,* 8, pp. 115–38; Haines, G. H. (1974) Conservation in Europe. *Housing and Planning Review,* 30, pp. 2–5; Rodwell, D. (1975) Conservation legislation, in Cantacuzino, S. (ed.), *Architectural Conservation in Europe.* London: Architectural Press, pp. 131–8; Rodwell, D. (1975) Conservation legislation: A European survey. *European Heritage,* 5, pp. 32–7; Sutcliffe, A. (1970) *The Autumn of Central Paris: the Defeat of Town Planning 1850–1970.* London: Edward Arnold, pp. 179–212; Léon, P. (1951) *La Vie des Monuments Français.* Paris: pp. 107–252; Travis, A. S. (1977) The evolution of town planning in France from 1900 to 1919 ... CURS working paper no. 47, University of Birmingham.

5. Ambassade de France (n.d.) *Preservation of Historical Monuments and Archaeological Sites In France.* London: Ambassade de France.

6. Dussaule, P. (1974) *La Loi et le Service des Monuments Historiques,* 2 vols. Paris: La Documentation Française, p. 106.

7. *Gazette des Beaux Arts,* 1283, 1975, supplement, pp. 1–2.

8. The laws relating to conservation were collected and published in 1973 in number 1345 of the *Journal Officiel de la République Française* under the title 'Protection du patrimoine historique et esthétique de la France'. Supplements are issued to update it as necessary.

9. Stungo, A. (1972) The Malraux Act 1962–72. *Journal of the Royal Town Planning Institute,* **58,** pp. 357–62; Kain, R. J. P. (1975) Urban conservation in France. *Town and Country Planning,* **43,** pp. 428–32; Kennett, W. (1972) *Preservation.* London: Temple Smith, pp. 55–65; Sorlin, F. (1968) The French system for conservation and revitalisation in historic centres, in Ward, P. (ed.), *Conservation and Development in Historic Towns and Cities.* Newcastle upon Tyne: Oriel Press, pp. 221–34; Sorlin, F. (1972) Paris, in Matthew, Sir R. *et al.* (eds.), *The Conservation of Georgian Edinburgh.* Edinburgh: Edinburgh University Press, pp. 84–96; Sorlin, F. (1975) Europe the comprehensive effort, in UNESCO, *The Conservation of Cities.* London and Paris: Unesco and Croom Helm, pp. 66–80; Stungo, A. (1972) Conservation Planning in France: an Appraisal of the Malraux Act 1962–72. Unpublished Diploma in Town Planning thesis, University College, London.

10. Sorlin, F. (1965) Salvaguardia dei centri storici urbani in Francia. *Urbanistica,* **42/43,** pp. 70–3.

11. Houlet, J. (1975) Méchanisme des interventions publiques. *Urbanisme,* **147/148,** pp. 128–29.

12. Developers are frequently allowed to contravene elements of a POS, usually to build at a higher density than the prevailing COS for the area by agreeing to finance the servicing of the site. In theory these costs should be covered by a local amenities tax (Taxe locale d'équipment—TLE) levied on the builder, but in practice many communes are unable or unwilling to finance infrastructure improvements from such taxes and ask developers for financial involvement over and above the TLE in exchange for *dérogations* or the exercise of their discretionary powers. See Racine, E. and Creutz, Y. (1975) Planning and housing: France, a developer's view. *The Planner,* **61,** pp. 83–5.

13. The present pattern of loans and grants is in a state of flux awaiting the new urban codes and housing act. The basic pattern which has applied is as follows: for owner-occupiers, loans over twenty years at six per cent for thirteen years and nine per cent for the remainder. For property on lease to tenants, thirty-year loans at 4.75 per cent for fifteen years, six per cent for the next five and nine per cent thereafter. These to cover up to two-thirds of the cost with a ceiling of 800 francs per square metre and to 150 m² per apartment (190 m² if family is more than six). The Ministry of Equipment provides grants for service infrastructure and the Ministry of Cultural Affairs disburses grants to cover the extra cost of working to the aesthetic standards imposed by the PPSMVs compared with 'normal' standards of repair and maintenance. The idea of proprietors grouping together to undertake improvement works stems from nineteenth-century legislation enabling rural syndicates to carry out *remembrement* and other agricultural improvements. In essence a majority of owners in a commune were permitted to impose their will on the minority (cf. English enclosures). The *loi d'orientation foncière* of 1967 adapted these measures to make them more amenable for urban works.

14. Paira, R. (1975) La Fédération des Sociétés d'Economie Mixte de Construction, d'Aménagement et de Rénovation. *Urbanisme*, **147/148**, pp. 152–3.
15. Bourguignon, F. (1971) Les secteurs sauvegardés: premier bilan des réalisations, premiers enseignements. *Administration*, **72**, pp. 52–3.
16. Vidal de Lauson, E. (1972) *Recherche Bibliographique sur la Restauration et la mise en valeur des Quartiers Anciens.* Paris: Commissariat Général du Plan (1971) *La Protection du Patrimoine Cultural, Rapports des Commissions du 6ᵉ Plan, 1971–1975.* Paris: La Documentation Française.
17. Anon (1974) Nouveau code pratique de l'urbanisme. *Urbanisme*, **140/141**, pp. 25–235.
18. For further details see, Canaux, J. (1974) France, in Whittick, A. (ed.), *Encyclopaedia of Urban Planning.* New York: McGraw-Hill, pp. 405–30, which also lists extensive references for further reading; Rapoport, A. (1966–67) Some aspects of urban renewal in France. *Town Planning Review*, **37**, pp. 217–27; Godard, F., Castells, M. *et al.* (1973) *La Rénovation Urbaine à Paris.* Paris: Mouton; Boury, P. (1970) *La Rénovation Urbaine dans l'Aménagement du Territoire: ses Origines, ses Objectifs, sa Technique, ses Résultats, ses Perspectives.* Paris: Editions Europoint; Beaujeu-Garnier, J. and Bastié, J. (1967) *Atlas de Paris et de la Région Parisienne.* Paris: Berger Levrault.
19. Stungo, A. (1972) Conservation Planning in France: an Appraisal of the Malraux Act 1962–72. Unpublished thesis, University College, London.
20. *Idem.*, pp. 10–12.
21. Givaudan, A. (1975) Architecture et plans d'occupation des sols. *Urbanisme*, **147/148**, pp. 130–1.
22. But see note 12, *infra*, and Loyer, F. (1975) Dix ans de rénovation. *Revue de l'Art*, **29**, pp. 57–82.
23. *Idem.*
24. Article 3 of the Act of 4th August 1962, *Journal Officiel de la République Française*, 7 August 1962.
25. A 'majority' is defined as four-fifths of proprietors representing at least four-fifths of the ground area.
26. Bourguignon, F. (1971) La restauration des quartiers anciens. *Les Cahiers Français*, **149**, p. 14.
27. Bourguignon, F. (1971) Les secteurs sauvegardés: premier bilan des réalisations, premiers enseignements. *Administration*, **72**, p. 52.
28. *Idem.*, pp. 51–3; Soucy, C. (1975) De la mise aux normes des logements à la réhabilitation des quartiers anciens. *Urbanisme*, **147/148**, pp. 102–7; Duclaud-Williams, R. H. (1978) *The Politics of Housing in Britain and France.* London: Heinemann.
29. Bastié, J. (1964) *La Croissance de la Banlieu Parisienne.* Paris: Presses Universitaires.
30. Preschez, P. (1976) Planification urbaine en centre ancien. *Les Monuments Historiques de la France*, **22** (6), pp. 2–13.
31. Data from C.N.S.S.
32. Arrou-Vignod, C. (1975) Dix ans de restaurations en secteurs sauvegardés. *Urbanisme*, **147/148**, pp. 132–3.
33. See Stungo, A. (1972) Conservation Planning in France: an Appraisal of the Malraux Act 1962–72. Unpublished thesis. University College, London, p. 142.

34. Bourguignon, F. (1971) Les secteurs sauvegardés: premier bilan des réalisations, premier enseignements. *Administration,* **72,** p. 44; for further comments see Stungo, A. (1972) The Malraux Act 1962–72. *Journal of the Royal Town Planning Institute,* **58,** p. 361; Bailly, G. H. and Desbat, J. P. (1973) *Les Ensembles Historiques dans la Renconquête Urbaine.* Paris: La Documentation Française, pp. 58–64; de Andia, B. (1976) *La Sauvegarde Des Villes D'Art.* Paris: EREP.

35. Franck, C. (1975) L'envers du décor, ou comment faire d'une vieille pierre deux coups. *Architecture d'Aujourd'hui,* **180,** pp. 4–8.

36. The key article on this topic is, Soucy, C. (1974) Restauration immobilière et changement sociale. *Les Monuments Historiques de la France,* **20** (4), pp. 15–22.

37. Vignier, A. (1974) La loi de 1962 et son application. *Les Monuments Historiques de la France,* **20** (4), pp. 4–6.

38. Soucy, C. (1976) Les coeurs d'îlots, évolution d'une pratique. *Les Monuments Historiques de la France,* **22** (6), pp. 33–6.

39. Soucy, C. (1974) Restauration immobilière et changement sociale. *Les Monuments Historiques de la France,* **20** (4), p. 17.

40. Declaration of M. Michel Guy, Secretary of State for Cultural Affairs, October, 1974; Vignier, A. (1974) La loi de 1962 et son application. *Les Monuments Historiques de la France,* **20** (4), p. 6; Lavedan, P. (1975) *L'Histoire de l'Urbanisme à Paris.* Paris: Hachette, p. 536.

41. A classic study of the social consequences of urban renewal is Coing, H. (1966) *Rénovation Urbaine et Changement Social.* Paris: Editions Ouvrières.

42. Chatelain, P. (1967) Quartiers historiques et centre ville: l'exemple du quartier du Marais, in Heinemeijer, W. F. *et al.* (eds.), *Urban Core and Inner City.* Leiden: E. J. Brill, pp. 340–55; Association pour la Sauvegarde et la Mise en Valeur du Paris Historique (1976) *Avant-projet d'un inventaire architectural et immobilier des troisième et quatrième arrondissements de Paris.* Paris: APSMVPH.

43. Stungo, A. (1972) Conservation Planning in France: an Appraisal of the Malraux Act 1962–72. Unpublished thesis, University College, London, pp. 115–16; Plan Permanent de Sauvegarde et de Protection du Marais, 12 sheets, 85 mm × 115 mm (1967); Laurentin, A. (1974) *L'Image du Centre: Le Marais à Paris.* Paris: Centre de Sociologie Urbaine; Arretche, L., Vitry, B., Marot, M. and Minost, M. (1970) Le secteur sauvegardé du Marais: histoire. *Les Monuments Historiques de la France,* **16** (2), p. 71.

44. Sutcliffe, A. (1970) *The Autumn of Central Paris: the Defeat of Town Planning 1850–1970.* London: Edward Arnold, pp. 2–5; Arretche, L. *et al., ibid.,* pp. 59–96; Lavedan, P. (1975) *L'Histoire de l'Urbanisme à Paris.* Paris: Hachette, pp. 229–40.

45. Froidevaux, Y.-M. (1976) La Place des Vosges. *Les Monuments Historiques de la France,* **22** (5), pp. 60–4; Lavedan, P. (1959) *Histoire De L'Urbanisme, Renaissance et Temps Modernes.* Paris: Laurens, pp. 277–84; Lavedan, P. (1960) *Les Villes Françaises.* Paris: Fréal; Christ, Y., Silvestre de Sacy, J., and Siguret, P. (1964) *Le Marais.* Paris: Editions des Deux-Mondes; Lavedan, P. and Goubet, S. (1970) *Pour Connaître les Monuments de France.* Paris.

46. Sutcliffe, A. (1970) *The Autumn of Central Paris: the Defeat of Town Planning 1850–1970.* London: Edward Arnold, p. 115; and (1974) Deux capitales sous le poids de l'histoire. *Architecture d'Aujourd'hui,* **176,** pp. 2–7.

47. Babelon, J.-P. (1975) Dix ans d'aménagement à Paris, 1965–1975. *Revue de l'Art,* **29,** pp. 9–56.

48. Arretche, L. *et al.* (1970) Le secteur sauvegardé du Marais: histoire. *Les Monuments Historiques de la France,* **16** (2), p. 62.

49. Sutcliffe, A. (1970) *The Autumn of Central Paris: the Defeat of Town Planning 1850–1970.* London: Edward Arnold, The battle for preservation, 1850–1914, and, The victory for preservation, pp. 179–212, 295–320; Arretche, L. *et al.* (1970) *ibid.,* pp. 59–65.

50. Arretche, L. *et al.* (1970) *ibid.,* p. 65.

51. Sutcliffe, A. (1970) *The Autumn of Central Paris: the Defeat of Town Planning 1850–1970.* London: Edward Arnold, pp. 300–3.

52. Laprade, A., Charpentier, C. *et al.* (1974) A ne pas démolir. *Connaissance des Arts,* **144,** pp. 32–7; Laprade, A. Vieux techniques et quartiers modernes. *Co-opération Technique,* **46/48,** pp. 57–60.

53. Sutcliffe, A. (1970) *The Autumn of Central Paris: the Defeat of Town Planning 1850–1970.* London: Edward Arnold, p. 308.

54. *Idem.,* pp. 312–13.

55. Association pour la Sauvegarde et la Mise en Valeur du Paris Historique (1968) *Sauvegarde et mise en valeur du Paris historique.* Paris: APSMVPH.

56. Minost, M. (1970) Propos sur le Marais. *Les Monuments Historiques de la France,* **16** (2), pp. 51–3.

57. One of the most accessible reproductions is in Sorlin, F. (1972) Paris, in Matthew, Sir R. *et al.* (eds.), *The Conservation of Georgian Edinburgh.* Edinburgh: Edinburgh University Press, pp. 84–96.

58. Stungo, A. (1972) Conservation Planning in France: an Appraisal of the Malraux Act 1962–72. Unpublished thesis, University College London, pp. 170–1; Galliot, E. and Hitier, G. (1975) Vie et mort du Marias, ou nos villes ont-elles encore une âme? *Urbanisme,* **147/148,** pp. 36–7.

59. Chatelain, P. (1967) Quartiers historiques et centre ville: l'exemple du quartier du Marais, in Heinemeier, W. F. *et al.* (eds.), *Urban Core and Inner City.* Leiden: E. J. Brill, pp. 344–6; Arretche, L. *et al.* (1970) Le secteur sauvegardé du Marais: histoire. *Les Monuments Historiques de la France,* **16** (2), pp. 68–71.

60. Lavedan, P. (1975) *L'Histoire de l'Urbanisme à Paris.* Paris: Hatchette, p. 552.

61. Stungo, A. (1972) Conservation Planning in France: an Appraisal of the Malraux Act 1962–72. Unpublished thesis, University College London, p. 128; *Le Monde,* 5 January 1977, p. 9; Anon (1976) La ville de Paris. *Local Finance,* 5, pp. 40–51.

62. Arretche, L. *et al.* (1970) Le secteur sauvegardé du Marais: histoire. *Les Monuments Historiques de la France,* **16** (2), p. 69.

63. Arretche, L., Marot, M., Vitry, B. and Minost, M. (1968) Rénovation urbaine: Le Marais. *Architecture d'Aujourd'hui,* **138,** pp. 86–7.

64. Stungo, A. (1972) Conservation Planning in France: an Appraisal of the Malraux Act 1962–72. Unpublished thesis, University College London, pp. 128, 170.

65. Lavedan, P. (1975) *L'Histoire de l'Urbanisme à Paris.* Paris: Hatchette, and information from C.N.S.S.

66. Minost, M. (1976) Paris, Secteur Sauvegardé du Marais, Opération des Jardins Saint-Paul. *Les Monuments Historiques de la France,* **22** (6), pp. 54–5.

67. Minost, M. (1974) A Paris experiment in traffic segregation. *European Heritage,*

2, pp. 42–3; Soucy, C. (1975) De la mise aux normes des logements à la réhabilitation des quartiers anciens. *Urbanisme,* **147/148,** pp. 102–7.

68. Minost, M. (1976) Les jardins du quartier du Marais. *Les Monuments Historiques de la France,* **22** (5), pp. 38–41.

69. Association pour la Sauvegarde et la Mise en Valeur du Paris Historique (1968) *Sauvegarde et mise en valeur du Paris historique.* Paris: APSMVPH, p. 5.

70. Le bilan de la SARPI in Civitas Nostra (1975) *Dix Ans de Restaurations.* Fribourg: Civitas Nostra, p. 52.

71. Data from SO.RE.MA., 1976.

72. Association pour la Sauvegarde et la Mise en Valeur du Paris Historique (1968) *Sauvegarde et mise en valeur du Paris historique.* Paris: APSMVPH.

73. Authenon, M. and N. (1968) Le Marais: étude de rénovation du premier secteur operationnel. *Architecture d'Aujourd'hui,* **138,** pp. 88–9.

74. Minost, M. (1976) Les jardins du quartier du Marais. *Les Monuments Historiques de la France,* **22** (5), p. 48.

75. I would like to thank a group of final year geography students of the University of Exeter who assisted me with this and other surveys in the Marais, and in particular Anne Maniece and Anne Russell.

76. Chi-squared test shows that differences are significant at 1 per cent level of probability.

77. Minost, M. (1976) Le Marais, un urbanisme libéral. *Les Monuments Historiques de la France,* **22** (6), p. 40.

78. Soucy, C. (1976) Les coeurs d'îlots, évolution d'une pratique. *Les Monuments Historiques de la France,* **22** (6), p. 34.

79. Minost, M. (1976) Le Marais, un urbanisme libéral. *Les Monuments Historiques de la France,* **22** (6), p. 40.

80. *Idem.,* p. 41.

81. La loi sur l'architecture, No. 77-2, 3 January 1977; Fourcade, J.-P. (Minister of Equipment) (1976) La réforme de l'aide au logement. *Le Monde,* 24 December, pp. 1, 24; La loi portant réforme de l'urbanisme, adopted by the Senate 13 December 1976.

82. Anon (1976) La loi sur l'architecture. *Architecture,* **401,** pp. 68–72.

83. Preschez, P. (1976) Planification urbaine en centre ancien. *Les Monuments Historiques de la France,* **22** (6), pp. 2–13.

84. Vignier, A. (1974) La loi de 1962 et son application. *Les Monuments Historiques de la France,* **20** (4), p. 5.

85. *Le Monde,* 6 September 1977; 2 February 1978.

86. Arrou-Vignod, C. (1975) Dix ans de restaurations en secteurs sauvegardés. *Urbanisme,* **147/148,** p. 133; circular from Alain Bacquet, Directeur de l'Architecture, Ministry of Cultural Affairs to regional offices of the Bâtiments de France, 31 January 1972.

87. Huet, B. (1975) Un avenir pour notre passé? *Architecture d'Aujourd'hui,* **180,** pp. 68–74.

88. *VIIᵉ Plan de Dévelopment Economique et Social (1976–1980),* programme 22, p. 143; this also answers some of the pleas to widen the scope of protection. See, Foucart, B. (1977) Le XIXᵉ siècle, monument historique. *Architecture,* **401,** pp. 16–19.

89. Vignier, A. (1976) Vers une mise en valeur globale des centre anciens. *Les Monuments Historiques de la France,* **22** (6), pp. 70–3.

# 13

# Conservation of the architectural heritage of Greece: means, methods and policies

## ALEXANDER PAPAGEORGIOU-VENETAS

This paper describes the present state of caring for monuments in Greece and the progress towards the integrated conservation of the country's architectural heritage. It is perhaps worth noting at the outset that although the data presented here are freely available, they have never been assembled and published before, either in Greece or abroad. This lack of published information is surprising, but can be partly explained by the fact that Greek archaeologists consider architectural heritage a 'family affair' not to be made public. This paper takes the contrary view, that the publication and dissemination of a critical analysis of Greek conservation policy can do nothing but good.

### THE NATURE OF THE ARCHITECTURAL HERITAGE AND THE EXTENT OF PROTECTIVE LEGISLATION

The great wealth of Greece's architectural heritage is justly famous and is, of course, characterized by an impressive diversity of historical origins and morphology. Apart from the archaeological remains of a number of major civilizations which flourished over some four millennia (Aegean, Minoan, Mycenaean, Classical, Hellenistic, Roman, Byzantine and Frankish) there is a 'living' architectural heritage in post-Byzantine and vernacular historic towns, Byzantine and post-Byzantine religious architecture, religious and

FIGURE 13.1. The partly restored Cavea of the theatre at Epidaurus.

civil architecture of foreign origin (Ottoman, Venetian and Frankish) and nineteenth-century neo-classical buildings.

Protective legislation is highly developed and has a long tradition; the first law on antiquities dates back to 1834, barely five years after the country became independent. The present shortcomings in the protective system lie more in operational and administrative imperfections and in a relative lack of technical resources and qualified staff than in legislative omissions. It should be noted, however, that the system of protective legislation is distinctly *passive and restrictive* and is not founded on principles of interdisciplinary cooperation and positive measures characteristic of the 'European' doctrine of 'integrated conservation'. In Greece, historic towns and groups of buildings are protected through legislation for the protection of historic sites. The concept of the 'conservation area' has not yet been introduced. It is also characteristic that the council ultimately responsible for protecting the

FIGURE 13.2. A street in the Old Town of Athens (the Plaka district).

architectural heritage has an overwhelming majority of archaeologists and is called the Archaeological Council (instead of Council for Historic Monuments or Council for the Cultural Heritage) thus reflecting the absolute priority accorded to the archaeological heritage in Greece.

Imperfections in the legislative system were recognized more than ten years ago by conservation specialists, and on the occasion of European Architectural Heritage Year a positive step was taken by research workers of the *Elliniki Etairia* (the Greek equivalent of the British National Trust) to bring legislation for the protection and rehabilitation of the architectural heritage up to date. A draft law accompanied by an introductory report on the national cultural heritage was prepared by Nikolaus Papadodimas and Avgi Marcopoulou [1]. It is still hoped that careful consideration of this draft law will stimulate the government to update current legislation. The main legislation in force to protect the architectural heritage are listed in table 13.1.

TABLE 13.1. Legislation to protect the architectural heritage in Greece.

---

*Greek Constitution of 1975*

---

Article 17 (1) introduces duties arising from the right of property.

Article 24 (1) requires the state to protect the 'natural' and 'cultural' environment.

Article 24 (6) places monuments and historic areas and structures under State protection.

Article 25 (4) defines the State's right to require of Greek citizens their duty of 'social and national solidarity'.

---

*Organization of responsible services*

---

| | |
|---|---|
| Degree No. 634/1960 | Sets up an Antiquities and Restoration Department in the Ministry of Culture and Science. |
| Legislative Degree No. 4177/1961 | Amends legislation governing the Antiquities and Restoration Department and the Archaeology and Expropriations Fund. |
| Legislative Decree No. 4280/1962 | Relates to the scientific staff of the Antiquities and Restoration Department. |
| Decree No. 687/1963 | On the regional branches of the Antiquities and Restoration Department. |
| Ministerial Order No. 31050/30.6.1963 | Institutes an Antiquities Conservation Centre under the Ministry of Culture and Science. |
| Decree No. 505/1975 | Defines the composition of the Archaeological Council of the Directorate General of Antiquities and Restoration. |

---

*Implementation of architectural heritage protection*

---

| | |
|---|---|
| Decree of 30.12.1927 | On methods for carrying out archaeological excavations. |
| Consolidating Act No. 5351/1932 | On antiquities. |
| Act No. 476/1943 | On the Athens Archaeological Society. |
| Act No. 1469/1950 | On the protection of special buildings and works of art subsequent to 1830. |

---

The legislative provisions noted in table 13.1 protect antiquities (i.e. isolated vestiges of historic or artistic buildings of the prehistoric, Classical,

Hellenistic, Roman, Byzantine and Frankish periods), historic monuments dating back to before 1830 (the year of Greek independence), historic monuments subsequent to 1830, excavation sites (i.e. designated archaeological areas and all their remains), natural sites and buildings situated within their perimeters, historic sites, and also, by implication, groups of buildings and historic districts, and historic towns and villages.

The number of objects currently protected can be obtained from the cumulative list of classifications effected by the Antiquities Service which contains approximately 4000 items. As there is not yet a complete national inventory in Greece, the number of objects in all categories meriting protection can only be assessed roughly, using as a basis an initial inventory of isolated monuments produced by the Department of Architectural History at Salonika University and from the Ministry of the Interior's 1973–74 survey of areas of national historic or artistic interest.

FIGURE 13.3. Columns and restored Cella of the Temple of Alphaia on the island of Aigina (6th–5th centuries B.C.).

TABLE 13.2. Categories of immovable cultural assets protected by current legislation and number of items currently protected and likely to be protected in the future.

| Category | Number of items currently protected | Number of items likely to be protected (including those protected currently) |
|---|---|---|
| Antiquities and historic monuments pre- and post-1830 | 3700 | 7000 |
| Archaeological excavation sites | 100 | ? |
| Natural and historic sites | 90 | Not listed |
| Groups of buildings and historic districts | 60 } | 2000 |
| Historic towns and villages | 50 } | |

Table 13.2 presents a list of categories of protected immovable cultural assets, together with the number of items currently protected and the number likely to be protected in the future. The Salonika University survey recognizes four categories of importance and places 325 isolated monuments in the top category (international importance).

## THE SYSTEM OF PROTECTIVE INVENTORIES

Up to now, one of the major shortcomings in the organization of protection of the architectural heritage in Greece has been the absence of a national inventory. The only national inventory system is a card-index classifying ministerial orders relating to the listing of an immovable asset. Needless to say, this index has little scientific or operational value. In addition, a number of *ephories* (offices of regional superintendents of antiquities) and foreign archaeological institutes possess independent archaeological inventories and photographic collections for particular areas or excavation sites. This serious deficiency was noted by the country's scientific circles many years ago and there is now every hope that it will be filled in the near future by the establishment of a National Inventory Directorate under the Ministry of Culture and Science.

TABLE 13.3. Recent inventories of monuments in Greece.

---

A.  As part of the master plan for the Greater Athens area a study identifying all the monuments in the region (Attica, Megaris, Salamis and Aigina) has been completed by a team led by the eminent architect and archaeologist John Travlos. A complete card-index of 2000 monuments and archaeological sites of all historical periods has been compiled, and these have been plotted on a 1:20,000 map of the Athens area (twenty sheets). His masterly *Lexikon zur Topographie des Antiken Athens* is in fact a complete inventory of ancient monuments in Athens [2].

B.  The work of the Department of Architectural History of Salonika University under the leadership of Professor Charalambos Bouras includes a scientific inventory of 7000 monuments of all historic periods, based mainly on an analysis of available bibliographical data.

C.  In 1973, on the initiative of the Ministry of the Interior, ten teams of architects carried out investigations in the country's ten regions with a view to identifying areas of historical or artistic interest. All 11,615 towns and villages of Greece (of which 5331 have under 200 inhabitants!) were examined and a complete card-index compiled for each of them. Two thousand were judged to be of historical or artistic interest and for these, cards conforming to the Council of Europe IECH prototypes were established and the areas classified into three categories according to the same directives. This unique, systematic work provides highly valuable basic information but has not so far been of any practical significance in view of the absence of any legislation for the creation of urban conservation areas.

D.  On the initiative of Doxiadis' Athens Ekistics Centre, a thorough study of the structures of ancient cities on Hellenic territory was carried out between 1968 and 1974. Its twenty-three volumes, covering twenty-one Greek provinces, constitute a major survey (although incomplete in that not all provinces are represented) of the possible distribution of ancient towns known from archaeological field research and literary evidence.

E.  On the initiative of the Association of Greek Architects an inventory of monuments of all historic periods on the island of Euboea, totalling 2000 has been drawn up.

F.  The Benaki Museum in Athens has recently compiled a fairly comprehensive photographic collection of the city's Byzantine, post-Byzantine and 'modern' monuments.

---

On the other hand, moves have been made in recent years to draw up sectoral inventories. The most important of these are listed in table 13.3. Although all this inventory work is very valuable for familiarizing architects and archaeologists with the architectural heritage, it cannot take the place of a national operational inventory.

## A Policy of Integrated Conservation

Legislation governing town and regional planning in Greece is fairly comprehensive, although quite recent. For decades, the only instruments for implementing town planning policy were general building regulations valid for the whole country and containing highly detailed morphological definitions for buildings (hence the relative sterility of Greek postwar architecture and its oppressive uniformity). There were also urban alignment plans which set down building lines and intensities of use, but did not specify type of use. The following pieces of recent legislation have at long last introduced a modern strategy for town and regional planning: Legislative Decree No. 8/1973 on general building regulations (a complete recasting of the earlier regulations), Legislative Decree No. 1262/1972 on the procedure for drawing up, applying and implementing master plans for urban areas, and Act No. 360/1976 on regional planning and environmental protection.

The provisions of this legislation relating to protection of the architectural heritage are of critical importance. Articles 79 and 80 of the new general building regulations provide the possibility of establishing protected groups of buildings or urban areas by a decree issued on the initiative of the Minister of Public Works. These suspend all building within the areas concerned pending the drawing up of an urban conservation plan and/or special building regulations. It gives the Ministry the right to control the appearance of new buildings (whether or not situated in protected areas) and provides for strict control of volumes, forms, colours, advertisements, functions, and traffic. The decree on master plans also specifies that proposals on environmental protection should be major elements of these documents. The Regional Planning and Environmental Protection Act defines the precise scope of environmental protection as covering not only the conservation of nature and its ecosystems but also the man-made environment and its historic structures. The Act further specifies the actual content of regional development plans which must make provision for, *inter alia,* the general nature of restrictions desirable for protecting the environment.

Independently of this legislation, which though most comprehensive is too recent to have yet borne fruit, about one hundred development studies have been prepared over the last fifteen years. These studies have helped arouse awareness of the problems of development planning and protection of the man-made environment and have provided valuable experience for the architects, planners and economists who worked on them. Almost all of these are good, scholarly studies which makes it all the more regrettable that, because of legislative shortcomings and administrative failures, their findings have had no chance of being applied up to now. Table 13.4 analyses the content and provenance of these plans. Studies devoted exclusively to urban conservation exist for the town of Kastoria in Macedonia, the old town of Rethymnon in Crete, the old 'Plaka' district in Athens, and the old town of

TABLE 13.4. An analysis of recent studies on planning and urban conservation.

| | | |
|---|---|---|
| A. | *By context* | |
| | Development plans | 15 |
| | Master plans for urban areas | 33 |
| | Plans combining the two preceding categories | (12) |
| | Tourist development plans | 19 |
| | Conservation plans: devoted wholly to conservation | 4 |
| | Conservation plans: as part of other studies | (12) |
| | Basic theoretical studies (standards, etc.) | 2 |
| | Master plan for the Athens area and special subsidiary studies | 11 |
| | Identification of towns of historical interest | 1 |
| | | |
| B. | *By initiating authority* | |
| | Ministry for Co-ordination (regional planning directorate) | 51 |
| | Ministry of the Interior: | |
| | (a) central | 9 |
| | (b) in the 'departments' | 5 |
| | (c) locally | 8 |
| | Ministry of Public Works (housing department) | 18 |
| | National Tourist Organization | 5 |
| | Greek Technical Chamber | 1 |

Chanea in Crete. Studies with a section on urban conservation include Mykonos-Delos-Reneia, the Delphi region (conservation of the towns of Arachova, Delphi, Chryso, Galaxidi and Amfissa), Corfu, Zante, Patmos, the Mani region, Skyros and Chios. Only twenty of the total of ninety-seven studies were prepared by public services or university teams, the remainder are the work of some forty private study agencies.

## A GROWING AWARENESS OF THE VALUE OF CONSERVATION

In addition to recent legislation and studies of a number of historic Greek towns, a new element in favour of efforts at integrated conservation has been added in the last few years: this is a growing awareness among urban populations of the value of historic architecture, over and above archaeological remains. Country-dwellers continue, unfortunately, to con-sider any change as 'progress' and are very suspicious of any measure to safeguard the 'old'. Over the past few years the press has given considerable support to a campaign to draw public attention to the value of the nation's

TABLE 13.5. Voluntary associations for the study and preservation of the architectural heritage in Greece.

| Name | Date of foundation | Members | Headquarters |
|---|---|---|---|
| *Archaeoligiki etairia* (Archaeological society) | 1837 | 220 | Athens |
| *Istoriki kai ethnolokigi etairia tis Ellados* (Historical and Ethnological Society of Greece) | 1882 | 61 | Athens |
| *Etairia Byzantinon spoudon* (Society for Byzantine studies) | 1919 | | Athens |
| *Institouton Byzantinon Meleton Venetias* (Venice Institute for Byzantine Studies) | 1949 | | Venice |
| *Laographiki etairia Zakynthou* (Zante Society for Folk Studies) | 1966 | | Zante |
| *Istoriki Kai archaeologiki etairia ditikis Kritis* (Historical and Archaeological Society of Western Crete) | 1968 | 228 | Chanea |
| *Laographikon kai Ethnologikon mouseion Makedonias* (Ethnological and Folk Museum of Macedonia) | 1970 | | Salonika |
| *Elliniki Etairia* (Hellenic Society) | 1971 | 1500 | Athens |
| *Kosmiteia topiou kai poleon* (Committee for Towns and Sites) | | | Athens |

'living' architectural heritage and the dangers which threaten it. As well as specialist professional bodies such as the Committee on Monuments and Sites of the Association of Greek Architects, the Greek National Committee for ICOMOS and the National Committee for European Architectural Heritage Year, a large number of voluntary associations have also been active in providing publicity. Table 13.5 lists the main organizations.

Despite all the publicity the doctrine of integrated conservation is only just beginning to be applied in Greece. There seem to be three main reasons for

FIGURE 13.4. The Byzantine fortified monastery of St. John (eleventh century) and the upper town of Patmos, the island of the Apocalypsis.

this state of affairs. First, the exclusive interest shown for so long in antiquities to the detriment of 'living' monuments; secondly, the relative shortage of resources, above all of qualified staff; and thirdly, the absence of operational coordination between the various State bodies involved and the total exclusion of local authorities from the decision-making process and from the application of conservation strategy.

In Greece, the interest of research workers (both Greek and foreign) during the nineteenth century was concentrated solely on archaeological excavations of ancient sites, and it was not until the beginning of the twentieth century that scholars such as Dhiel, Sotiriou and later Orlandos, brought about a renewed interest in Byzantine antiquities. On the other hand, the 'living' architectural heritage of the last three centuries (comprising the few remaining post-Byzantine towns, vernacular village architecture and the neo-classical urban architecture of the nineteenth century) only began to arouse interest among a few specialized research workers (architects and students of folk traditions) during the 1930s, and became a more conscious concern of the State and public opinion only after 1950. This state of affairs is clearly reflected in the wholly disproportionate distribution of manpower and resources to the services responsible for antiquities and 'living' monuments respectively. As will be demonstrated later, the resources allocated to 'living' monuments represent under ten per cent of the public funds made available for conservation work and archaeological research, while the scientific staff of the Ministry of Culture responsible for the conservation of 'living' monuments represents only two per cent of the department's total scientific staff!

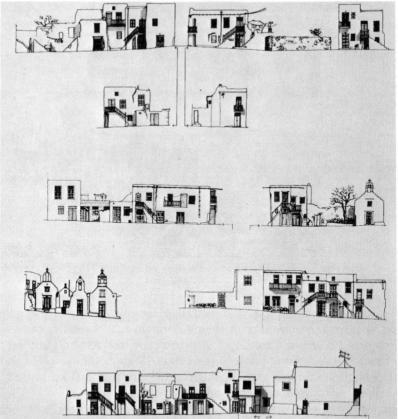

FIGURE 13.5. Drawings of houses and churches on the island of Mykonos.

Three central government bodies have responsibility for various aspects of conservation but there is little coordination between them. The Ministry of Culture is responsible for antiquities of all periods, for sites, and for restrictions on operations within the perimeters of classified sites. The Ministry of Public Works is responsible for preparing studies and regulations on the conservation of groups of buildings, and can also classify historic urban areas independently of the Ministry of Culture. Lastly, the National Tourist Organization works independently in paying for studies and the implementation of conservation plans for historic sites and groups of buildings. The only State agencies for conservation at regional level are the twenty-seven *ephories* (inspectorates). Local authorities and resident populations are rarely consulted and play absolutely no part in conservation decision-making.

The relatively short-term improvements likely to be made to the conservation system described above centre on the forthcoming establishment of Inspectorates of Monuments of Modern Times (in addition to those already existing for ancient and medieval monuments) under the Ministry of Culture and on the coordination, through legislation, of the classifying procedures of the Ministries of Culture and Public Works.

## SOCIAL ASPECTS OF CONSERVATION IN GREECE

Historic centres in Greece fall into three main groups on the social dimension. The first group (mainly, in mountain areas) is suffering severely from depopulation, hastened by abandonment and progressive decay as population leaves places where access is difficult to move to large towns or to emigrate abroad. A second group (island and coastal towns and villages) is flourishing economically due to the impact of the tourist trade, although its quality of life and the consistency of the urban fabric are gravely threatened by the resultant social and physical changes. Lastly, a third group is made up of a few medium-sized and small provincial towns which are stagnating demographically and economically (e.g. Nauplia, Hermoupolis, Corfu) but which have succeeded in more or less preserving their traditional morphology and rhythm of life. Outside these three categories there are some special cases. Some historic villages and small towns (particularly on islands such as Skyros, Patmos, Lindos, Hydra etc.) have urban patterns carefully preserved by the efforts of well-to-do summer visitors (Greek and foreign) who buy houses and convert them into second homes. Their social composition is, however, clearly altered by this trend. In the case of the picturesque old town of Athens (the so-called 'Plaka' district on the northern slopes of the Acropolis) decades of uncertainty as to its future (conservation of the nineteenth-century district or demolition to make way for widespread excavations around the Acropolis) has led to its becoming the focus of night-life with abominations of pseudo-vernacular, pastiche architecture.

The dangers to the survival of the traditional architectural and social structure of Greece's historic urban centres are totally different from those threatening town centres in Western Europe. While the main danger to the latter resides in congestion of medieval centres and the proliferation of tertiary functions in nineteenth-century residential districts, historic centres in Greece are threatened mainly by the two extremes of depopulation and deformation by the tourist trade. In Greece there is no legislation (in force or projected) to control abrupt social changes in historic urban areas or to check land or property speculation in the historic districts of towns, and the population has no role in the drawing up of conservation schemes. The Greek people have a somewhat ambivalent attitude towards conservation efforts; they are more and more convinced of the rightness of such efforts, but seem unprepared to meet the heavy financial burden imposed on private property by a restrictive conservation policy.

As most historic urban areas in Greece are villages of vernacular

FIGURE 13.6. A typical settlement of Aegean vernacular architecture.

architecture or small provincial towns with neo-classical architecture and static populations and economies, the dangers to their townscape do not arise primarily from motor traffic or other similar nuisances. The main danger is the inhabitants' desire for spurious 'innovation'; they are inclined to superficial imitation of contemporary forms of architecture without having either the appropriate knowledge or materials, and the results are visually deplorable. This trend—which can be explained in terms of social psychology by a desire for 'renewal' at any price, 'renewal' being regarded as an attribute of social status—can in the initial phase be fought only by special restrictive town planning regulations prescribing architectural volumes and forms with a view to eventually arriving, through persuasion and information, at their free acceptance by local people. It should also be noted at this point that a large number of island villages with fine vernacular architecture, particularly in the Aegean Sea (settlements with 500 to 5000 inhabitants) have been able, despite a considerable influx of tourists and the islanders' traditional 'openness' to the world, to preserve the characteristic townscape and pre-industrial tempo of life which constitute their charm. This cannot be explained simply by the existence of restrictive legislation for their protection, but is due rather to the existence of special climatic, geographical and social conditions which govern the life of these relatively isolated small communities.

## New Functions for Old Buildings

In Greece the search for new functions for old buildings is confined to public buildings and to some few private houses which are converted to new uses. Churches are (for doctrinal reasons) never converted to other uses; the maximum change which may be tolerated being the discontinuance of worship and their conversion to museums (for example the Byzantine churches at Mystra and the eleventh-century conventual church at Daphni).

Many medieval fortresses could be converted discreetly into tourist hotels and inns (following the example of the Spanish *Paradores*) though regrettably this has not yet been done. On the other hand, some modern hotels, with architecture varying in its sympathy and degree of integration with the surroundings, have been built within medieval fortifications (for example at Acronauplia and Arta).

Other important conversions, though rather limited in number, can be noted. Among these are the Hellenistic portico of Attalos in the classical agora of Athens, restored by the American School of Classical Studies of Athens and converted into an archaeological museum and the headquarters of the archaeological offices and workshops of the Agora; the small 'Bourzi' maritime fortress at Nauplia, dating back to the Venetian period, converted long ago to a luxury hotel; the palace of the Venetian Governors of Nauplia, converted into the town's archaeological museum; the residence of the Duchess of Piacenza in Athens, a graceful nineteenth-century building of neo-renaissance style, now the Byzantine museum; the former Athens municipal hospital, a large mid-nineteenth-century neo-classical building converted recently into a municipal cultural centre; the former Chamber of Deputies in Athens, also of neo-classical style, converted into a national historical museum; and the private neo-classical residence of the Michaleas family in the old town of Athens, converted in 1973–74 into a museum housing the important Cannelopoulos collection given recently to the State.

## Budgetary and Financial Resources

In Greece, the following State authorities contribute to the cost of conserving the architectural heritage: the Directorate General of Antiquities and Restoration in the Ministry of Culture and Science, the Archaeology and Expropriations Fund, and the National Tourist Organization. Furthermore, loans guaranteed by the State are granted by the mortgage bank on the recommendation of the Tourist Organization for the improvement of housing and the provision of tourist amenities in houses situated in villages with vernacular architecture. Lastly, archaeological institutes (one Greek institute—the Archaeological Society—and nine foreign ones representing France, the United States, the United Kingdom, Italy, the Federal Republic of Germany, Sweden, Switzerland, Belgium and Austria) contribute considerable funds to some twenty major excavations in Greece and towards the cost of publishing their findings. The number of these excavations and the scientific staff of the institutes concerned—about 150 research archaeologists and fellows—suggest that the accumulated total of the funds contributed by the institutes is comparable with the corresponding funds provided by the Antiquities Department of the Ministry of Culture. As the details of these institutes' budgets are in varying degrees confidential and not available for this paper, they do not appear in tables 13.6 and 13.7.

TABLE 13.6. Public and private funds devoted to conservation of the architectural and artistic heritage and to archaeological research [3].

| A. *Operational expenditure* | | *Millions of drachmas* | *Millions of U.S. dollars* |
|---|---|---|---|
| *Ministry of Culture and Science* | | | |
| Forty-five excavations | | 34 | 0.960 |
| Restoration of monuments of all historical periods | | 93 | 2.580 |
| Exhibition of excavated objects | | 20 | 0.555 |
| Restoration of works of art | | 18 | 0.500 |
| Safeguarding of historic houses and towns | | 35 | 0.980 |
| Safeguarding of sites | | 24 | 0.665 |
| | Total | 224 | 6.240 |
| *Archaeology and Expropriations Fund* | | | |
| Expropriation of land and buildings for archaeological excavations | | 68 | 1.880 |
| Publications and copies of art works | | 10 | 0.280 |
| | Total | 78 | 2.160 |
| *National Tourist Organization* | | | |
| Rehabilitation of sites, monuments and historic towns | | 34 | 0.960 |
| Pilot project of rehabilitation of groups of houses in the centres of five historic villages | | 50 | 1.390 |
| | Total | 84 | 2.350 |
| *Loans guaranteed by the state* for the provision of rooms for tourists in traditional villages | | 70 | 1.950 |
| *Private expenditure,* mean annual investment in house restoration | | 400 | 11.050 |
| Total of public and private operational expenditure | | 856 | 23.750 (A) |

| B. *Administrative expenditure* | *Millions of drachmas* | *Millions of U.S. dollars* |
|---|---|---|
| Ministry of Culture | 120 | 3.320 |
| Archaeology and Expropriations Fund | 30 | 0.835 |
| National Tourist Organization | 6 | 0.165 |
| Total administrative expenditure | 156 | 4.320  (B) |
| Total operation and administrative expenditure on conservation in Greece (A) plus (B) | 1012 | 28.070 |
| Regular State budget for 1976 | 170,000 | 4720 |
| Public investment budget 1976 | 36,000 | 1000 |
| Total State budget in 1976 | 206,000 | 5720 |

No official statistics are available on private investment in conservation. However, as this contribution must be regarded as critical to success, I have made a number of extrapolations from reliable data relating to the town of Hydra to the ten or so historic centres where extensive restorations have been undertaken by private individuals (the small towns of Lindos, Patmos, Phira, Mykonos, Monemvasia, Galaxidi, Hydra, Spetzai, Makrinitza, Corfu).

During the past ten years, approximately 200 houses (of five to ten rooms) have been bought and restored by Greek and foreign private individuals in Hydra. The cost of this restoration can be estimated at approximately 400 million drachmas ($11.05m) on the basis of an average cost per house of two million drachmas ($55,000). If this sum is multiplied by ten (some ten towns being concerned) and then divided by ten (to define the sum for private annual investment), we come back to about $11m for the private sector's probable total annual contribution towards conservation.

Table 13.6 analyses public and private funds allocated to the conservation of the architectural and artistic heritage and to archaeological research. Study of these data shows that in 1976 total expenditure on the architectural heritage amounted to $28.07m, of which only 15.5 per cent (or $4.32m) represented administrative expenditure, while the remaining 84.5 per cent (or $23.75m) was operational expenditure. Of this, 38 per cent (or $10.75m) was provided by the public sector and 39.5 per cent (or $11.05m) by the private sector, while seven per cent (or $1.95m) took the form of State-guaranteed loans to individuals. Moreover, the total expenditure of $28.07m represented 0.49 per cent of the State's regular and investment budgets ($5720m), whereas the State's administrative and operational expenditure on conservation was only 0.26 per cent of the same total.

Another interesting aspect of conservation in Greece is the amount of

TABLE 13.7. Investment in new housing and restoration of traditional houses (values in millions of U.S. dollars).

| | All housing units (public and private) | | Housing units, with State aid | | State activity as percentage of total: | |
|---|---|---|---|---|---|---|
| | | | | | In | In |
| | Number (1) | Value (2) | Number (3) | Value (4) | number (3)/(1) | value (4)/(2) |
| Annual average of new dwellings, 1960–72 | 138,208 | 425 | 5949 | 11.80 | 4.3 | 2.7 |
| Average value per new dwelling | | 0.0031 | | 0.00198 | | |
| Annual average of restored dwellings, 1960–72 | 900 | 13 | 700 | 1.95 | 78 | 14.9 |
| Average value per restored dwelling | | 0.0144 | | 0.00280 | | |

resources devoted to it compared with public and private funds invested annually in housing construction. The comparative data in table 13.7 show that the average number of restored dwellings represents a minimal proportion of 0.7 per cent (900 dwellings out of a total of 138,208), whereas the relative expenditure represents three per cent ($13m out of $425m on new housing). However, if one considers the figures for public expenditure alone, the percentages are much higher in view of the minimal share of State investment in new housing in Greece (4.3 per cent in quantity and 2.7 per cent in value of all building). The number of dwellings restored with State aid represents 11.8 per cent of new housing built by the State (700 dwellings out of 5949), whereas the relative expenditure represents 16.6 per cent ($1.95m out of $11.80m). Furthermore, the State's share in the work of rehabilitating traditional houses represents 78 per cent of the total number of housing units restored and 14.9 per cent of the total cost. This reveals a far higher cost for private restoration ($55,000 per house) compared with the modest budget for the restoration of houses under the public programme ($2800 per house).

There are only two participants in conservation work in Greece—the State and private enterprises—but unfortunately their activities are not coordinated. Local authorities and voluntary associations have no funds for conservation operations. The State's activities are paid for by direct investment and grants to departmental funds, and by guarantees for loans to individuals by mortgage banks. Private operations are funded by personal capital investment and mortgage bank loans. No tax relief or direct State grant is available to individual owners of historic houses who are prepared to invest private capital in conservation work. If their property is classified, owners are, therefore, compelled to pay for the work themselves. This is a heavy financial burden. Furthermore, they are unable to 'develop' their property by new building. They are placed under these obligations and restrictions without any compensation in the form of tax relief or grants.

Finally, the Church plays a considerable part in conserving religious architecture. All Byzantine and post-Byzantine church and monastery buildings—with the exception of some churches preserved as 'museum pieces'—are the property of the Church of Greece or the various dioceses, and are as a rule maintained by the ecclesiastical authorities out of their own funds (apart from State grants for restoring a limited number of such

FIGURE 13.7. A small Byzantine church on the island of Euboea.

buildings by the Restoration Department). The Official Statistics Service can put no figure on these parallel investments by the Church which, while representing a substantial contribution towards the overall conservation effort, nevertheless entail the danger of poor or inappropriate restoration work on the many 'minor' religious monuments in which the Restoration Department has no say.

## ADMINISTRATIVE PROBLEMS

Of the three State authorities responsible for conservation policy in Greece, i.e. the Ministry of Culture, the Ministry of Housing and the National Tourist Organization, only the first-named has specialist services for the purpose. These are the Directorate General of Antiquities and Restoration, with central and regional offices and the Archaeology and Expropriations Fund. These services, whose administrative structure and staffing are shown in table 13.8, are responsible for the administration and conservation of cultural assets; for archaeological research; for archaeological collections and museums; for the administration of regular and special resources; and jointly with the other authorities mentioned above, for the protection of historic sites, groups of buildings and towns. In Greece, the archaeological service has a long and successful tradition and provides a Civil Service career endowed with great prestige. The staff's scientific qualifications are very high; for the post of *ephorus* (Regional Superintendent of Antiquities) a doctorate is required. But the number of staff is quite inadequate for the tremendous and many-sided tasks involved. Out of a potential pool of at least 1500 qualified archaeologists, the State service employs only 200 (only half of whom are career employees, the rest working under contract). Their work load clearly exceeds their competence, entailing as it does the architectural and town planning supervision of classified towns and groups of buildings. The Ministry of Housing carries out a parallel classification of historic towns on its own, but has no operational staff for the protection of this important category of classified assets. In the circumstances, it is inevitable that only part of the substantial task of archaeological research (some major excavations and numerous 'occasional' digs) is carried out by the antiquities service and that a considerable part of such research is conducted by the Athens Archaeological Society (Greek) and by the nine recognized foreign archaeological institutes in Athens. As far as research into conservation techniques and their application (laboratory and field work) are concerned, the Restoration Department, with its extremely small scientific staff (see table 13.8) and the help of scientists and technicians working under contract, endeavours to cope not only with conservation and restoration work but also with the architectural and technical studies of a considerable number of the country's museums, libraries and archives.

TABLE 13.8. Administrative authorities responsible for conservation (data relate to 1973).

---

*Ministry of Culture and Science*

Minister, assisted by an archaeological council comprising senior Ministry officials, professors of archaeology, art and architectural history and specialists appointed by the Minister.

*Directorate General of Antiquities and Restoration*

A. *Directorate of Antiquities* (scientific staff: 95 career archaeologists, 100 archaeologists under contract)

Central Office:
Archaeological sites and excavations sector
Museums sector (only archaeological collections)
Expropriations sector

Regional Offices:
21 superintendents of archaeology
5 superintendents of Byzantine antiquities
1 superintendent of post-1830 monuments
1 superintendent of private collections

Special services:
National Archaeological Museum, Athens (collection of sculptures, bronzes, ceramics and prehistoric art)
Byzantine Museum, Athens
Athens epigraphic collection
Athens numismatic collection
60 regional archaeological museums
The Antiquities Conservation Centre (workshops for marble, works in metal, ceramics, icons, mosaics, mural painting, physico-chemical research) (scientific and technical staff: 35)
Two museum conservation workshops, the Athens National and Byzantine Museums (technical staff: about 20)

B. *Directorate of Restoration* (scientific and technical staff)
Central service: 20 architects, topographers and civil and mechanical engineers, 10 draftsmen
Regional services in the superintendents' offices: 15 architects, 10 supervisors, 150 architectural restoration technicians

Central service:
Studies sector
Implementation sector

Regional services:
Attached to the various superintendents' offices under the responsibility of the *ephoroi*

C. *Archaeology and Expropriations Fund* (scientific staff, i.e. archaeologists and engineers: 10)
Archaeological receipts sector
Archaeological publications sector
Staff sector
Accounts sector

In 1973, an Antiquities Conservation Centre was set up as the first attempt at a national level to coordinate the work of all aspects of restoration, particularly laboratory work. Although the centre has made great progress in recruiting staff, it has not yet been able to obtain really satisfactory premises from which to operate.

In the author's view it is necessary to take a number of urgent steps to remedy the shortage of qualified staff and reform the unwieldy administrative structure of conservation. The Ministry of Culture requires at least 200 additional staff (i.e. double the number of existing archaeologists) in order to enable Greek archaeological science not only to administer the cultural assets entrusted to it, but also to study them in a satisfactory way. The number of attendants at museums and excavations needs to be doubled. The average of four attendants for each unit is quite inadequate if one considers that the National Museum of Athens on its own employs over seventy attendants and that a large number of archaeological sites have only one or two. A central inventory directorate is required with adequate staff and suitable premises to carry out the essential task of processing the data of existing partial inventories and compiling a national scientific and operational inventory. Regional superintendents' offices should be established to care for the post-1830 monuments. About twenty architects and town planners specializing in integrated conservation should be employed and given immediate responsibility as superintendents. A speedy development of the newly-created Antiquities Conservation Centre ought to be promoted and provided with the necessary staff and resources. An advisory archaeologist and/or architect of the antiquities service attached to each diocese is required to supervise restoration of religious architecture carried out by the Church. Finally, legislation is required to enable the Ministry of Culture and Science to act as conservation coordinator with a view to avoiding duplication and overlapping of powers (for example classification by the Ministry of Culture and the Ministry of Housing, independently of one another).

TECHNICAL PROBLEMS: MATERIALS AND STAFF

The problem of the supply of traditional materials desirable for conservation work hardly arises in Greece. Where the restoration of ancient monuments is concerned, stone (marble of various kinds, porous stone, etc.) can be provided from the same quarries as in ancient times or from modern quarries nearby. The materials needed for the restoration of Byzantine monuments and vernacular architecture (local stone, burnt brick, pine or chestnut wood, Byzantine tiles) are simple and easily found. The same is true for nineteenth-century neo-classical architecture. Although there is no shortage of materials in their raw state, some problems arise over the production of certain traditional architectural elements; special orders have to be given for wrought iron gates and railings, for banisters and decorative components in marble or ceramic, or for old Byzantine tiles (with flat elements—*stroteres* and curved ones—*kalypteres*). But the difficulty is primarily one of cost as few specialist contractors still possess the technical 'know-how'.

As far as scientific staff (architects and town planners specializing in integrated conservation) are concerned, the situation in Greece is as follows: out of 4000 practising Greek architects, twenty or so have taken specialist courses at institutes abroad, while some forty became specialists by practical experience. Only five out of forty qualified town planners in Greece have specialized in conservation planning. These figures show that the notorious imbalance which exists in all European countries between professional staff concerned with new building and those dealing with integrated conservation is even more acute in Greece. However, the severest shortage is of outlets for professional training in Greece. Apart from some rudimentary tuition on conservation and protection problems given to students by the Departments of Architectural History of the Architecture Faculties at Athens and Salonika, there is no possibility of obtaining professional training in Greece today. The same applies to the training of specialist craftsmen. They must pick up their trade on the job by learning from the experience of others.

### Recent Developments

Some significant developments have occurred in recent years and ought to be noted. As a result of persistent initiatives by Constantine Tripanis, Professor Emeritus of classical literature at Oxford University and former Minister of Culture, two very important decisions have been implemented since 1977. First, a new administrative structure for the Ministry of Culture has been introduced by law. This allows not only a more efficient distribution of tasks but will bring the total staff from about 400 today to about 1200 in ten years time and double the number of museum attendants. As a first step in this direction, the Ministry has recently launched a competition to attract fifty young architects and archaeologists. Secondly, in 1975 a National Scientific Committee for the Preservation of the Monuments of the Acropolis of Athens was set up by the Minister. For the first time in Greece, matters of conservation are handled not just by archaeologists, but by an inter-disciplinary team including structural and chemical engineers, architectural historians and conservation specialists. In January 1977 an international campaign to save these monuments was launched in Athens by the Secretary General of UNESCO. This joint action programme has not been acted upon because of a strong feeling of national pride by the Greek government which decided recently to pick up the whole cost of the fifteen-year programme (estimated to be $20m). A Greek team under the coordinating guidance of John Travlos and Charalambos Bouras has begun to construct exact measured drawings of the Erechteion and has started an inventory of the numerous architectural relics scattered on the plateau. It is organizing an *in situ* display of these and preparing to undertake the dismantling of the Corae Prostasis (Karyatides).

During 1979 the Ministry of Housing laid down special building regulations for 400 historic towns and villages (out of a total of 2000). This can be considered a first step towards the introduction of a policy of integrated conservation at a city planning level in Greece.

The most recent event of importance is the organization of an exhibition on Aegean Art at the Louvre in Paris and at the Metropolitan Museum in New York. This is the first time in the history of the modern Greek State that a major display of Greek art has been organized abroad. It has been enabled by recent legislation although public opinion in the country is polarized strongly either for or against the so-called 'exportation' of antiquities. This illustrates a new and important fact in everyday life in Greece and has to do with a renaissance of identification with the nation's cultural heritage. If this is not diverted into absurdly over-nationalistic channels, it could be decisive for the preservation and integration of the Greek architectural heritage.

NOTES

1. Papadodimas, Nikolaus and Marcopoulou, Avgi (1975) *Prostasia Mnimion kai Synolon* (Preservation of Monuments and Groups of Buildings). Athens: Elliniki Etairia.
2. Travlos, John (1971) *Lexikon zur Topographie des Antiken Athens.* Tubingen: Wasmuth.
3. Expenditure of the Ministry of Culture and Science from regular and public investments budget data for 1976; Archaeology and Expropriations Fund data for 1975; National Tourist Organization from the public investment budget of 1976; Loans for the provision of 'guest' rooms in traditional villages made on the recommendations of the Tourist Organization and calculated at a rate of 20,000 drachmas per bed × 3500 beds; private expenditure is the approximate mean annual private investment in the restoration of private houses in historic towns and villages. Drachma/U.S. dollar ratio as in 1975, i.e. 36.4 drachma = $1.00.

# 14

# Townscape images:
# a study in meaning

## COLIN MORRIS

*The one charm of the past is that it is the past.* Oscar Wilde [1]

There have been very few analyses of the nature of man's appreciation of buildings from different periods of history [2]. In this paper an attempt is made to examine the meaning of people's images of the five principal period styles in the temporal spectrum of English townscapes. In a secondary sense, this research constitutes an objective justification for the conservation of old buildings. The results of analysis suggest that man's images of townscape may be coloured by an imbalance between a sophisticated sense of orientation to old buildings, and a less developed ability to come to terms with modern townscapes. The implication of this psychological investigation is, therefore, that the destruction of old buildings should be prevented wherever possible, and that contemporary architecture should in future be based on traditional concepts of scale and design.

### ATTITUDES TO TOWNSCAPE

The great amount of literature which has been published about conservation and townscape should not be allowed to obscure the fact that very little is known with any surety about people's conscious or subconscious commitment to buildings from the past, or to those being constructed today. Conservationists and students of urban aesthetics have tended to concentrate on various aspects of the three dimensions of urban space, such as the physical condition of building fabric or the visual significance of the shapes created by the layout of streets in a town. They have altogether omitted to examine the contribution made by the age of a building to the environmental well-being which is derived from it. Since the formation of the Society for the Protection of Ancient Buildings in 1877, which may be taken to mark the beginnings of conservation in Britain as we understand it today, there has been a gradual shift in emphasis away from individual buildings to areas, and the threshold of architectural and historic significance has crept slowly forward in time. In the last few years a start has even been made on listing those buildings from the period 1914 to 1939 which are considered to be outstanding [3]. Consequently, with more than 260,000 buildings listed and over 4500 conservation areas designated, there is now legislative protection for a greater range and number of buildings of 'special architectural or historic interest' than ever before [4]. Yet despite these comprehensive powers, old buildings are being destroyed at an alarming rate.

Much of the blame for this is levelled at legislators and planners who are responsible for maintaining Britain's heritage, and who appear to have failed to keep architects and the pressures of money and traffic in check. There are indeed many flaws in the way the legislation is organized. For example, the listed building procedures are framed in such a way that it is more difficult to refuse a demolition than to grant consent. At planning enquiries, too, the planner's role is often to justify preservation rather than to prevent demolition. The minute allocation of public expenditure is another serious problem, since many private owners who are required to bear the financial burden of maintaining their properties, simply cannot afford to do so. However, the primary malaise afflicting the conservation movement is that its whole weight is perhaps misguidedly concentrated on fabric instead of people. Conservationists have urged the restoration of countless old buildings without realizing that their appeals to the public would probably be more effective were they to attempt to explain why an old building is valuable, and why its loss from the built environment would be a retrograde step. In particular, they should stress that concern should not be about bricks and mortar, tangible and important though they are, but that aura of the past which they instinctively know derives from them. It is this, after all, which is potentially such a significant source of contentment for man. They have failed to do this, however, and as a result their arguments have had less impact on society as a whole than they might have otherwise had.

In recent urban aesthetics literature, too, the psychological importance of old buildings has generally been understated. Such works as those of Kevin Lynch and Thomas Sharp in the 1960s prepared the way for an understanding of man's ability to interpret townscape as an unfolding kinetic experience [5]. Yet neither work really emphasizes the role of old buildings in creating that variety and richness of character without which serial vision would be a highly elusive concept. The relationship between time and aesthetics has been more strongly implied in the new and rapidly expanding discipline of architectural psychology. Research in this field suggests that many people prefer complex visual environments to simple ones; consequently, they tend to dislike contemporary designs because of their deliberate and monotonous emphasis on simplicity of line and texture [6]. P. F. Smith contends that modern architecture fails to generate contentment because it epitomizes the importance which Western society places on logic and rationality. He argues that it appeases only the intellect, and denies the emotions the stimulation once richly provided by townscape, and today found only in traditional urban ensembles. Smith's conclusion is that if cities are to be a source of well-being they should possess both new stimuli and familiar reassurances, since without a dialectic rhythm between the intellect and the emotions 'environment drops psychologically stone dead' [7].

The primary objective of this study of townscape images is neither to issue propaganda in the name of conservation, nor to develop theories of urban aesthetics still further. Rather, it is to consolidate the intuitive conclusions of both conservationists and architectural psychologists that the visual austerity of modern architecture constitutes a negative component in townscape, whereas visually richer buildings from different periods in the past possess qualities which tend to provide aesthetic pleasure and inspire feelings of general well-being. This research, therefore, examines people's images of the medieval, classical, industrial, romantic and modern period styles of English townscape, and an analysis is made of the underlying psychological meaning of these images.

## METHODOLOGY

At an early stage in the study, it was decided to concentrate on examining the townscape images of first-year geography and social studies students at the University of Exeter, students at Exeter College of Art and Design, and planners employed by local authorities in different parts of the country. The university students were chosen to provide a foil to the artists and planners who, by virtue of their training and experience, are likely to be more perceptive of line, shape, colour and texture, and the criteria upon which historic and architectural interest are conventionally defined. Altogether, 287 people took part in the tests. There are many and varied techniques designed and used to measure visual meaning. From the wide range available, the semantic differential (hereafter SD) was chosen because it is easy to administer, yields data which are quantitative and may be analysed easily, and, most important, is multidimensional. This characteristic is crucial, since men's mental images subsume numerous impressions and dimensions of judgment. Osgood, who formulated the technique in the 1950s, realized that words possess meanings assigned to them through other words [8]. Thus, the SD was developed to explore the implications of mental associations generated by words.

Bipolar adjectives are arranged on a seven point scale and each is applied to the stimulus word, or visual concept. The subject considers the applicability of each scale to the concept and marks the appropriate space, thus:

### CATHEDRAL

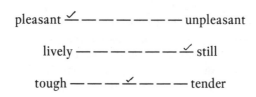

The semantic scales used in this study were generated by a content analysis of a number of texts relating to historic buildings and conservation, in order to ensure the relevance of the semantic space so defined for the description of townscapes. This produced forty-three semantic scales under the four headings of historic heritage, architectural heritage, environmental character, and aesthetic qualities. Some of the scales are composed of short phrases because it is impossible to convey every nuance of the four themes in pairs of single words. In preliminary tests, ten of the scales polarized poorly, which proved them to be ambivalent in meaning [9]. These scales were eliminated from further consideration, and the thirty-three scales used in subsequent tests and analysis are incorporated in figure 14.3 below.

Colour slides were chosen as the best surrogate for presenting the five period styles. The direct experience of environment possesses the advantage of engaging all the senses at the same time, but no town or city contains a comprehensive temporal range of buildings, and it would obviously have been impossible to have transported one group of people around the country, interesting though this might have been. Moreover, there is the problem inherent in any free exploration that it is very difficult to determine which characteristics of environment are actually experienced by each respondent [10]. In particular, the buildings in any one area are often from so many periods that the time-message of the scene is confused and difficult to define.

More than three hundred slides were taken during a series of visits to twelve towns and cities in England considered to be potentially rich in good examples of the five period styles. Streets and façades of both renovated and rather dilapidated secular medieval buildings in stone, and wood and plaster were photographed in Canterbury, Chester, Chichester, Petersfield, Stratford, Winchester and York, while Bath, Brighton, Chichester and Birmingham furnished examples of classical townscapes. The hundred or so classical scenes range from pure Renaissance eighteenth-century crescents and circles in Bath to the more elaborate and anglicized decor of Regency Brighton, Chichester town houses, and imposing nineteenth-century

Greco-Roman public buildings. Birmingham, Chester, Exeter and Sheerness provided examples of old industrial factories, and of terraced houses which vary from small enclaves transformed by recent renovation to scenes of the utmost dereliction. In countless towns and cities the entire legacy of nineteenth-century artisan housing seems to have disappeared almost without trace. The romantic revival in English architecture and town planning, marked by a return to pitched roofs, revealed gables and soaring steeples in an open setting, is represented by the green vistas of Bournville, and the harder brick, stone and slate edifices which abound in parts of York, Chester and central Birmingham. Of England's many postwar cities, Birmingham yields perhaps the clearest pictures of both imaginative and less-inspired modern designs, some for high- and some for low-rise offices and homes, but virtually all in the predominant contemporary accents of concrete, glass and chrome.

Many slides were deliberately taken as alternative views of the same buildings and scenes, and after the least successful of these had been discarded, fifty-four slides were left and these formed the basis of the tests involving the university students. Their perception of similarities between the slides, as demonstrated by a cluster analysis, led to the rejection of a further twenty-four slides which duplicated particular styles of building [11]. The remaining set of thirty slides was made up of equal numbers of medieval, classical, industrial, romantic and modern slides in order to maintain a balance between each of the period styles.

During the preliminary stages of choosing the slides, tests were carried out to establish the possible effect of some photographic inconsistencies on people's perceptions of townscape. Surprisingly, there has been little research into this important area of environmental psychology [12]. Five Exeter scenes from the set of thirty slides were rephotographed: one in darker shadow, another from a different angle and seen through denser foliage, a third without a prominent tree in the foreground, a fourth showing parked cars, and a fifth picturing fewer people, in a gloomier setting than in the original slide. The five pairs of slides were mixed with others and shown to a small group of university students, and their responses to each pair were compared using a series of Student's $t$ tests [13]. In the matrix of thirty-three semantic scale evaluations of each pair of slides, only four of the 165 $t$ values indicate a significant difference in evaluation at the 95 per cent probability level. The fact that there is no significant difference in the remaining 97 per cent of the evaluations suggests that photographic inconsistencies have but minimal influence on perception and preference. This conclusion is important, because this study of townscape images is based on people's impressions of slides. The dearth of reliable information on this subject remains a problem. In view of the popularity of photographic stimuli in environmental psychology this is undoubtedly an issue which deserves much deeper investigation [14].

## The Analysis of Townscape Images

The responses of the students, artists and planners to the thirty slides, using the thirty-three semantic scales, provides data for an analysis of townscape images. The reactions of each group were examined separately, but the simplified discussion in this paper is based on the analysis of a fourth composite data set of seventy-two respondents, made up of equal numbers of people from each group. A discussion of the results of a factor analysis provides an introduction to a more detailed examination of people's responses to a selection of the slides.

### THE DIMENSIONS OF MEANING

The technique of factor analysis is one which simplifies and organizes large amounts of multivariate data. Early development of the technique occurred within psychology in order to relate various states of mind to underlying dimensions of personality. Osgood proved SD data to be amenable to factor analysis in the 1950s, and the technique has subsequently been used in many SD studies of environmental preference and evaluation [15]. In this research into townscape images, factor analysis examines the perceived relationships between the semantic scales in order to explain the underlying meaning of the images of the slides. The variation between any group of objects, in this study the thirty slides, is most simply expressed in terms of scores observed on a number of descriptive variables, the semantic scales. Factor analysis searches data for inter-relationships between variables, and sets of similar variables are gradually transformed into a smaller number of orthogonal, or uncorrelated factors. To make these factors easier to interpret, they are 'rotated' slightly, so that as many as possible of the variables have high loadings on one factor and negligible loadings on others. The factors thus summarize the total variance in data with as small a residual error as possible [16].

Varimax rotation produced four factors with an eigen value of greater than 1.0, proportionately weighted as shown in table 14.1. The level of explanation afforded by the factors is 94.615 per cent, which is exceptionally high. The

TABLE 14.1. Proportional weighting of factors.

|  | Percentage | Cumulative percentage |
|---|---|---|
| Factor I | 70.954 | 70.954 |
| Factor II | 11.850 | 82.804 |
| Factor III | 7.956 | 90.760 |
| Factor IV | 3.855 | 94.615 |

TABLE 14.2. Rotated factor matrix.

| Scales (left-hand attributes) | Factors | | | |
|---|---|---|---|---|
| | 1 | 2 | 3 | 4 |
| Old | 0.92907 | 0.29317 | −0.08167 | 0.06170 |
| Historic | 0.96477 | 0.21829 | 0.02102 | 0.06727 |
| Is historically interesting | 0.97705 | 0.11496 | 0.15842 | 0.01078 |
| Stirs your historical imagination | 0.98228 | 0.12996 | 0.10732 | −0.01482 |
| Brings history to life | 0.97615 | 0.14677 | 0.11321 | −0.01803 |
| Makes you think about history | 0.98332 | 0.12175 | 0.08159 | 0.01570 |
| Makes you aware of a link with the past | 0.96667 | 0.22404 | 0.02359 | 0.04381 |
| Has an aura of permanence | 0.83841 | 0.03542 | 0.36921 | 0.15849 |
| Is worth keeping | 0.90540 | 0.09291 | 0.39337 | −0.01593 |
| Valuable buildings | 0.92854 | 0.04002 | 0.35462 | 0.00932 |
| Interesting architecture | 0.91268 | −0.02650 | 0.36399 | −0.10031 |
| Distinguished architecture | 0.90731 | −0.15089 | 0.34952 | 0.06452 |
| Ornate | 0.70220 | −0.02393 | 0.43344 | −0.03940 |
| Buildings are in harmony with one another | 0.57779 | 0.52675 | 0.41361 | 0.31141 |
| Symmetrical | −0.06459 | 0.15102 | 0.13238 | 0.92645 |
| Horizontal | −0.07663 | 0.80989 | 0.20190 | 0.24986 |
| Built at a human scale | 0.31613 | 0.91477 | 0.19639 | −0.04240 |
| Large-scale | 0.00869 | −0.94998 | 0.07180 | 0.19747 |
| Well-preserved | 0.27617 | −0.04903 | 0.92131 | −0.08369 |
| Tidy | 0.14424 | 0.19740 | 0.89449 | 0.31487 |
| Possesses a distinctive visual identity | 0.91593 | −0.05077 | 0.34164 | −0.08255 |
| Full of character | 0.96675 | 0.10539 | 0.20852 | −0.06849 |
| Friendly | 0.60764 | 0.58212 | 0.48665 | −0.11009 |
| Private | 0.15027 | 0.84597 | 0.05439 | 0.23622 |
| Safe | 0.27844 | 0.20688 | 0.83016 | 0.20517 |
| Alive | 0.60990 | 0.29015 | 0.67313 | −0.20534 |
| Good | 0.87590 | 0.17950 | 0.42883 | −0.03382 |
| Artistic | 0.85329 | 0.00386 | 0.48563 | −0.04530 |
| Beautiful | 0.81917 | 0.21002 | 0.50495 | −0.02816 |
| Pleasant | 0.79357 | 0.27916 | 0.52270 | −0.02439 |
| Attractive | 0.82030 | 0.23376 | 0.50392 | −0.08430 |
| Charming | 0.80809 | 0.32047 | 0.45266 | −0.11816 |
| Like | 0.87306 | 0.20355 | 0.41393 | −0.06219 |

meaning of the factors can be deduced from the rotated factor matrix (table 14.2) and the matrix of factor scores (table 14.3). The loadings in the former

TABLE 14.3. Matrix of factor scores.

| Slides* | Factor scores | | | |
|---|---|---|---|---|
| | 1 | 2 | 3 | 4 |
| *Medieval townscapes* | | | | |
| (The Shambles, York) | −1.33917 | −0.61562 | −0.31194 | 1.89660 |
| | −1.20530 | 0.37234 | −1.01851 | 1.45615 |
| | −0.97683 | −0.97782 | −0.85368 | −0.56569 |
| | −0.74873 | −1.08462 | 1.64105 | 0.01463 |
| | −0.80063 | −0.63875 | −1.23823 | 0.09215 |
| (Bootham Bar, York) | −1.68908 | 1.01206 | 0.18743 | −0.09522 |
| *Classical townscapes* | | | | |
| | −0.76406 | −0.06631 | −1.21995 | −1.57623 |
| | 0.03033 | 0.09545 | 0.14862 | −1.47712 |
| (Lansdown Crescent, Bath) | −0.66521 | 0.18668 | −0.53134 | −1.62239 |
| (East Pallant, Chichester) | −0.29654 | −0.74036 | −0.83600 | 0.46681 |
| | −0.80790 | 0.50847 | 0.35131 | −1.70383 |
| | 0.38801 | −0.08811 | −0.92837 | −1.22051 |
| *Medieval townscapes* | | | | |
| | −0.69263 | 0.79227 | 1.75405 | 0.26293 |
| | 0.35925 | −1.12713 | 1.38867 | 0.39899 |
| | 0.78853 | −1.28560 | 0.38678 | −0.51943 |
| (Clifton Street, Exeter) | 0.39321 | −1.00846 | −0.15754 | 0.65908 |
| | 0.71797 | −1.16991 | 0.45531 | −0.17467 |
| (Albion Street, Chester) | −0.14269 | −1.04736 | 2.87474 | −0.40244 |
| *Romantic townscapes* | | | | |
| (Selly Manor, | −0.78690 | −0.79889 | −0.96028 | 1.68134 |
| Bournville) | 0.77321 | −0.76479 | 0.65202 | −0.17994 |
| (Grosvenor Park Road, | −0.96859 | 0.13362 | 0.47884 | 1.01230 |
| Chester) | 1.39558 | −0.93535 | −0.70121 | −0.56594 |
| | −0.21740 | 0.44113 | 0.17177 | −0.20249 |
| | −0.80183 | 1.50668 | −0.17896 | −0.66538 |
| *Modern townscapes* | | | | |
| | 1.03114 | 2.24541 | −0.08892 | −0.54487 |
| | 1.32523 | 0.58976 | −0.69465 | 0.95987 |
| (Central Library, | 1.18020 | 1.28201 | −1.10602 | 1.02032 |
| Birmingham) | 1.16171 | 1.71554 | 0.91269 | 1.56159 |
| (Aston High Park, | 1.50081 | 0.61877 | 0.30273 | 0.53040 |
| Birmingham) | 1.85835 | −1.15109 | −0.88020 | −0.49691 |

* Only the ten slides whose image traces are described in this paper are named.

represent the contribution made by the scales to the character of the factors, and interpretation is greatly facilitated in this analysis by the fact that each scale loads highly on only one factor. The second matrix tabulates the contribution of each factor to the image of each slide, and these scores are often useful for resolving ambiguities in the rotated factor matrix.

Factor I is by far the most important factor, explaining 70.954 per cent of the variance in the data. The rotated factor matrix (table 14.2) demonstrates a direct association between all ten of the scales which contrast past with present, and a miscellany of those which describe architectural quality, environmental character and aesthetic judgment. The majority of these scales are heavily weighted, but the especially high loadings of the historic heritage scales suggest that the perception of differences between the past and the present may lie at the heart of the meaning of the factor. The factor suggests that people's perception of the age of a building may be an important determinant of their observations concerning its architectural merit, or its character and aesthetic qualities. To support this premise, the matrix of factor scores (table 14.3) reveals an interesting gradation from the high negative, or predominantly favourable factor scores of the six medieval slides, to the high positive, or generally unfavourable factor scores of the modern slides. It would be absurd to argue from this that old buildings are perceived as fundamentally good and new buildings as bad, since there are several breaks in the continuum of factor scores which challenge such a simplistic argument. Moreover, it need hardly be said that the analysis is based on people's responses to only thirty slides, which obviously cannot be taken to reflect every kind of English townscape. In particular, it could be argued that the set of slides is deficient in examples of unattractive old buildings or interesting modern architecture. Nevertheless, the evidence of the two matrices is sufficiently straightforward to indicate that a sensitivity to the age of buildings should be interpreted as a fairly central dimension in people's images of townscape.

Factor II accounts for 11.850 per cent of the variance in the data, and indicates a distinctive relationship between several of the scales which describe aspects of architectural scale and environmental character. The heavy loading on *large-scale—small-scale* in the rotated factor matrix (table 14.2) suggests that physical scale is the key to interpreting the factor. *Small-scale* correlates with *horizontal, private, friendly, harmony* and *human,* while *large-scale* correlates with *vertical, public, unfriendly* and, by implication, *'disharmony'* and *'inhuman'.* The pattern of these loadings implies that an element of human compatibility with townscape is determined by its size, and the degree of 'verticality' of buildings in it. The high positive, or particularly adverse factor scores of slides of high-rise buildings in the matrix of factor scores (table 14.3) emphasize the disorienting effect of townscapes which are predominantly vertical in line. The fact that the number of slides with high positive scores marginally exceeds those with high negative, or favourable scores suggests that while people react quite strongly against high-rise structures, it may be that they subconsciously take smaller, horizontal buildings for granted.

Factor III isolates 7.956 per cent of the variance, and demonstrates a direct association between *well-preserved–poorly-preserved, tidy–untidy* and *safe–dangerous* (table 14.2). These loadings suggest that a tidy and well-preserved façade may often seem synonymous with physical security, while a drab and perhaps tumbledown building can evoke fear of hazard. The extremely high positive, condemnatory factor score for the slide of Albion Street, Chester (table 14.3), which depicts decaying industrial terraced housing, suggests that many people may take more notice of scenes of obvious dilapidation than of scenes of careful restoration. Thus, structurally-sound and attractively-decorated buildings may represent a perceived norm. The factor implies that a building may seem to be in need of renovation because it is untidy or unsafe, even though it may not be recognizably historic, but the relative weighting of factors I and III suggests that awareness of the physical condition of buildings is much less important than perception of their age.

Factor IV accounts for only 3.855 per cent of the variance in the data and the loadings in the rotated factor matrix (table 14.2) are dominated by a high score for *symmetrical–asymmetrical,* which indicates a peripheral and perhaps subconscious awareness of contrasts in architectural proportion and balance. The inverse relationship between this scale and the aesthetics scales suggests that, as a general rule, some people may prefer buildings to be asymmetrical rather than too regular. The high negative factor scores (table 14.3) for all but one of the six classical slides imply that buildings in this broadly symmetrical style are recognized as a distinctive architectural genre.

Naturally, there are problems in the use of factor analysis, as there are with any multivariate statistical technique. It has been claimed, for instance, that the varimax rotation in the final stage of computation produces a loss of orthogonality, and that the interpretation of factors is essentially a subjective process [17]. These criticisms may be justified in some cases, but they are successfully challenged in this research by the consistent results of the separate factor analysis of the three groups, which have been aggregated in the simplified discussion here [18]. It would perhaps be wisest to regard factor analysis as a very powerful descriptive device which, it has been claimed, is likely to remain an attractive tool of analysis because it seldom produces right answers [19]. In a field as intangible as environmental psychology this is perhaps advantageous. Thus, although the results of this analysis should not be taken too literally, the four dimensions of meaning do provide an extremely useful descriptive framework for understanding people's images of the slides.

IMAGES EVOKED BY THE SLIDES

The reactions of the students, artists and planners to each slide were evaluated in terms of image traces, which are an invaluable descriptive tool in research involving the SD. The thirty-three mean scale values for each slide are traced diagrammatically to represent the image of the slide visually. The outline frame within which the trace is drawn expresses the range of the image from the left-hand to the right-hand extremes of the scales, so the character of each image may be easily judged by eye. It has not been possible to include image traces of all thirty slides in this paper, and the discussion is, therefore, based on just ten of the slides which evoked characteristic images of the period styles. These slides are reproduced, in black and white, in the figures below. The aggregated traces used here can be taken as a fairly accurate guide to the responses of the three groups. The relationship between them can be estimated by a device which measures the goodness of fit between traces; goodness of fit is defined as a difference between means for two groups of subjects of less than 1.0 on a given scale [20]. The percentage goodness of fit between the three groups and the composite data set is consistently greater than 90 per cent, which suggests that the students, artists and planners share very similar townscape images. The most noticeable divergence is caused by the greater appreciation shown by the planners for classical and, to a lesser extent industrial townscapes, while the artists appear to be slightly more vehement in their condemnation of contemporary architecture. The descriptions which follow conform to the customary adverbial range of SD scales from 'slightly' (the $\pm 1$ interval in the seven point scale), to 'quite' ($\pm 2$) and 'extremely' ($\pm 3$), which the subjects were instructed to observe.

The image traces of medieval townscape incorporate most of the positive attributes of the semantic scales. None of the other period styles are so consistently described as historically interesting, or are as well-liked and appreciated for their architectural character. The fact that these townscapes are the oldest in the set of slides is presumably the reason for this favourable view. However, the rather subdued response of most people to a slide of a dilapidated half-timbered house in Stratford suggests that good restoration plays an important role in colouring people's liking for these townscapes.

The image trace of The Shambles, York (figures 14.1 and 14.3) epitomizes people's responses to the other medieval slides. This view, of one of the few substantially complete medieval streets in Britain, is readily identified as extremely old and historic, and is said to be exceptionally rich in historical associations. The medieval slides do not evoke an aura of permanence so readily, but they are all thought to be extremely valuable and well worth keeping. The buildings in each slide are recognized as predominantly vertical in line and as in asymmetrical harmony with one another. Architecturally, they are considered to be interesting rather than especially distinguished or ornate. The medieval slides are all described as attractive and extremely rich in visual character, but The Shambles appears to be the most pleasant and well-liked of the six scenes.

FIGURE 14.1. The Shambles, York.

FIGURE 14.2. Bootham Bar, York.

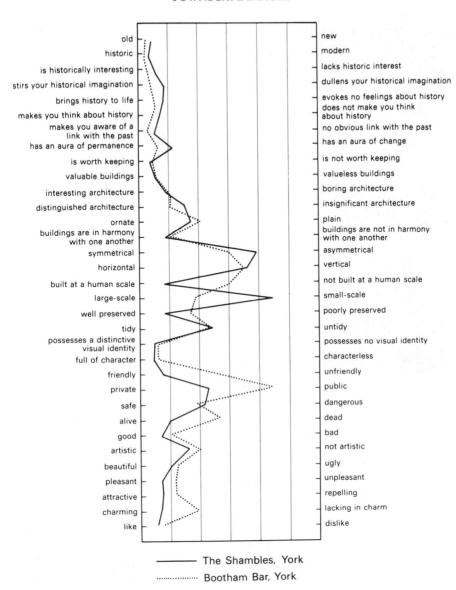

FIGURE 14.3. Image trace for medieval slides.

FIGURE 14.4. Lansdown Crescent, Bath.

FIGURE 14.5. East Pallant, Chichester.

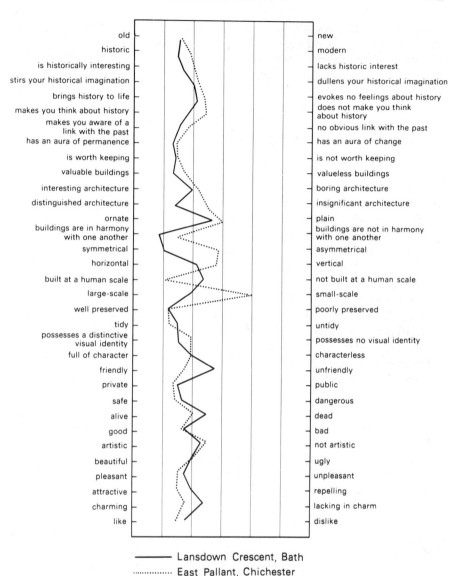

| | | |
|---|---|---|
| old | | new |
| historic | | modern |
| is historically interesting | | lacks historic interest |
| stirs your historical imagination | | dullens your historical imagination |
| brings history to life | | evokes no feelings about history |
| makes you think about history | | does not make you think about history |
| makes you aware of a link with the past | | no obvious link with the past |
| has an aura of permanence | | has an aura of change |
| is worth keeping | | is not worth keeping |
| valuable buildings | | valueless buildings |
| interesting architecture | | boring architecture |
| distinguished architecture | | insignificant architecture |
| ornate | | plain |
| buildings are in harmony with one another | | buildings are not in harmony with one another |
| symmetrical | | asymmetrical |
| horizontal | | vertical |
| built at a human scale | | not built at a human scale |
| large-scale | | small-scale |
| well preserved | | poorly preserved |
| tidy | | untidy |
| possesses a distinctive visual identity | | possesses no visual identity |
| full of character | | characterless |
| friendly | | unfriendly |
| private | | public |
| safe | | dangerous |
| alive | | dead |
| good | | bad |
| artistic | | not artistic |
| beautiful | | ugly |
| pleasant | | unpleasant |
| attractive | | repelling |
| charming | | lacking in charm |
| like | | dislike |

———— Lansdown Crescent, Bath
·············· East Pallant, Chichester

FIGURE 14.6. Image trace for classical slides.

Bootham Bar, York (figures 14.2 and 14.3) is described as less attractive than the other medieval slides. It is seen to be quite large in scale, but it is thought neither as vertical nor as inhuman as bigger buildings in other period styles. The most striking perceived attribute of the Bar is its exceptional ability to evoke the past. In particular, it seems to represent a marked degree of permanence amidst the changing townscapes of today. Massive stone walls therefore appear to be more easily identified as an unaltering reminder of the Middle Ages than more conventionally attractive houses and shopping scenes seem to be.

The six image traces of classical townscape tend to contradict the accepted view that British building in the eighteenth and early nineteenth centuries was the peak of our architectural achievement. It is not surprising that medieval buildings are thought to possess a richer patina of age, but it is very interesting that the carefully designed crescents and terraces of Bath and elsewhere are described as architecturally and aesthetically less valuable than haphazard assemblages of medieval buildings. The greater sensitivity of the planners to classical townscapes suggests that only a trained eye fully appreciates the subtleties of the British Renaissance.

The slides of early classical townscapes, of which Lansdown Crescent, Bath (figures 14.4 and 14.6) is perceived to be a fairly typical example, seem to possess very similar patterns of historical association. Most are assimilated as quite old and historic and as worth keeping. The classical scenes are described as having the power to suggest a link with the past and often seem able to symbolize permanence, but they tend to stimulate the historical imagination rather less. These formally unified townscapes are not considered to be as horizontal in line as academic arguments would suggest, but many are appreciated for their extremely harmonious and symmetrical appearance. The architecture itself is described as quite distinguished in style without being ornate. The rather different town houses in the East Pallant, Chichester (figures 14.5 and 14.6) seem to be characterized by much weaker symmetry, but the line of the street is defined as broadly horizontal. The general impression of this architecturally less-unified row of houses is of a smaller and more intimate scale than that found in Bath. Aesthetically, it is thought to be one of the most satisfying of the classical townscape slides.

The residential styles of Bath and Chichester are preferred to more monumental nineteenth century building styles. A slide of the Greco-Roman façade of Birmingham Town Hall, for instance, is described as considerably less attractive and weaker in historical associations. The architecture is recognized as being both more ornate and less interesting, and the building does not seem as intimate in scale as the eighteenth century buildings. The negative response to a slide of contemporary 'Georgian' pastiche housing implies that few people are particularly attracted to modern neo-classicism, although the analysis shows these buildings to be preferred to many other new dwelling styles.

The image traces of many of the industrial slides are comparatively neutral, which suggests that the three groups of people are rather disinterested in nineteenth-century industrial architecture. Large and imposing factories are perceived to possess some character, and seem to have the capacity to symbolize something of the greatness of Britain's industrial supremacy during the last century, but humbler workshops and rows of terraced houses from the same period of economic growth appear to project history only weakly, if at all. Many people seem to find industrial buildings visually boring, and aesthetically rather dull.

Most terraced houses are described as small and human in scale and this seems to be their most valuable perceived attribute. It is noticeable, however, that many people seem to be scarcely aware of the architectural subtleties which distinguish one terrace from another. Clifton Street, Exeter (figures 14.7 and 14.9), for example, is part of a rejuvenated area, but its image trace is extremely similar to that of a nearby street which has not been modernized. The houses in Clifton Street are not actually described as being in a better state of repair, but they are considered to be fairly attractive, and architecturally less uninteresting than those nearby. The perceived effect of the renovation seems chiefly to be that it gives the houses greater character and more intimacy.

Albion Street, Chester (figures 14.8 and 14.9), on the other hand, is easily recognized as having fallen into a state of irreversible decay, and its image trace diverges considerably from those of the other slides of terraced housing. The buildings are considered to be not much more boring or characterless than those in Clifton Street, and they are thought no less worth keeping. However, Albion Street is described as by far the most unattractive and unfriendly of the slides of terraced houses, presumably because of its extremely dilapidated condition. These crumbling houses are recognized as similar to those in the other industrial slides in that they evoke a slight link with the past, but they are apparently more easily termed old than historic. This is an interesting distinction; the analysis of the image traces reveals that many of the medieval and classical slides are, conversely, more easily recognized as historic than as old.

It is very difficult to generalize about romantic images, because they are characterized by a great variety of styles which have occurred during the century or so of the romantic revival. The comparatively adverse reactions to romantic townscapes of the early twentieth century, such as ubiquitous half-timbered semi-detached houses and gardens, suggests that the genuinely romantic in townscape is thought of as possessing a deeper patina of age. Of the nineteenth-century styles, medieval reconstructions and careful attempts at pastiche, such as Selly Manor, Bournville (figures 14.10 and 14.12) seem able to provoke a clearer and more distinctive image of the spirit of Pugin and Ruskin than elaborately-designed buildings in stone and patterned brick [21]. Selly Manor is thought to be quite old and is described

FIGURE 14.7. Clifton Street, Exeter.

FIGURE 14.8. Albion Street, Chester.

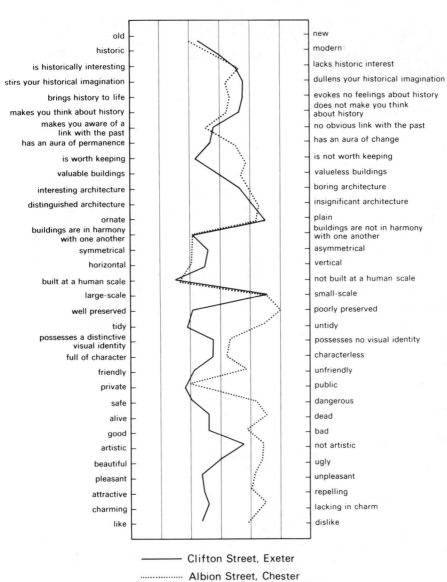

——— Clifton Street, Exeter

·············· Albion Street, Chester

FIGURE 14.9. Image trace for industrial slides.

FIGURE 14.10. Selly Manor, Bournville.

FIGURE 14.11. Grosvenor Park Road, Chester.

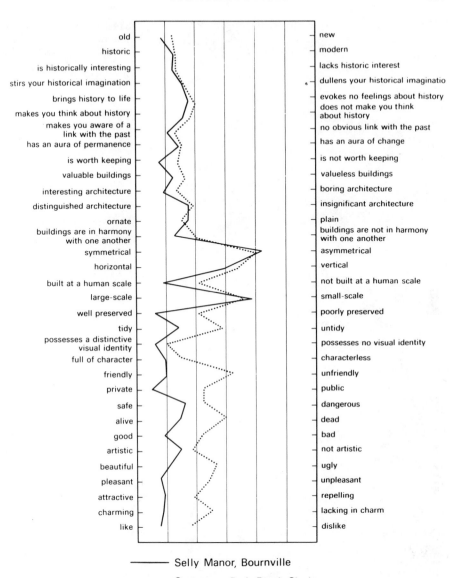

| old | new |
| historic | modern |
| is historically interesting | lacks historic interest |
| stirs your historical imagination | dullens your historical imagination |
| brings history to life | evokes no feelings about history |
| makes you think about history | does not make you think about history |
| makes you aware of a link with the past | no obvious link with the past |
| has an aura of permanence | has an aura of change |
| is worth keeping | is not worth keeping |
| valuable buildings | valueless buildings |
| interesting architecture | boring architecture |
| distinguished architecture | insignificant architecture |
| ornate | plain |
| buildings are in harmony with one another | buildings are not in harmony with one another |
| symmetrical | asymmetrical |
| horizontal | vertical |
| built at a human scale | not built at a human scale |
| large-scale | small-scale |
| well preserved | poorly preserved |
| tidy | untidy |
| possesses a distinctive visual identity | possesses no visual identity |
| full of character | characterless |
| friendly | unfriendly |
| private | public |
| safe | dangerous |
| alive | dead |
| good | bad |
| artistic | not artistic |
| beautiful | ugly |
| pleasant | unpleasant |
| attractive | repelling |
| charming | lacking in charm |
| like | dislike |

——————— Selly Manor, Bournville

·············· Grosvenor Park Road, Chester

FIGURE 14.12. Image trace for romantic slides.

FIGURE 14.13. Central Library, Birmingham.

FIGURE 14.14. Aston High Park, Birmingham.

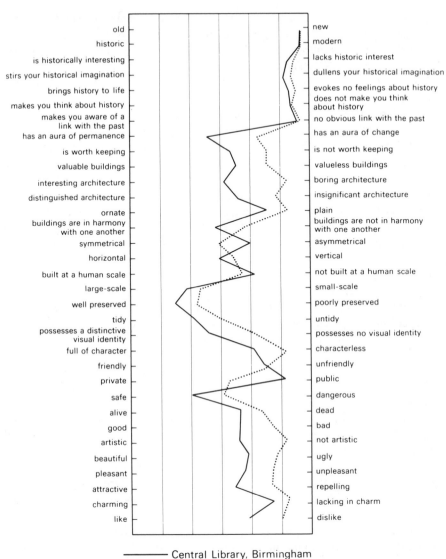

| old | new |
| historic | modern |
| is historically interesting | lacks historic interest |
| stirs your historical imagination | dullens your historical imagination |
| brings history to life | evokes no feelings about history |
| makes you think about history | does not make you think about history |
| makes you aware of a link with the past | no obvious link with the past |
| has an aura of permanence | has an aura of change |
| is worth keeping | is not worth keeping |
| valuable buildings | valueless buildings |
| interesting architecture | boring architecture |
| distinguished architecture | insignificant architecture |
| ornate | plain |
| buildings are in harmony with one another | buildings are not in harmony with one another |
| symmetrical | asymmetrical |
| horizontal | vertical |
| built at a human scale | not built at a human scale |
| large-scale | small-scale |
| well preserved | poorly preserved |
| tidy | untidy |
| possesses a distinctive visual identity | possesses no visual identity |
| full of character | characterless |
| friendly | unfriendly |
| private | public |
| safe | dangerous |
| alive | dead |
| good | bad |
| artistic | not artistic |
| beautiful | ugly |
| pleasant | unpleasant |
| attractive | repelling |
| charming | lacking in charm |
| like | dislike |

———— Central Library, Birmingham

·················· Aston High Park, Birmingham

FIGURE 14.15. Image trace for modern slides.

as fairly rich in historical associations. The house is seen to be small in scale, and architecturally rather asymmetrical, and the variety of shapes and textures incorporated into the design of the building are said to be extremely interesting, but less distinguished or ornate in appearance. The overall impression of the house appears, nevertheless, to be one of great character and charm.

The less well-liked slide of Grosvenor Park Road, Chester (figures 14.11 and 14.12) illustrates a harder style of romantic townscape, the slides of which may be said to have been described as asymmetrical variations on a vertical theme. The intricately varied shapes in stone, slate and ironwork in Grosvenor Park Road are seen to be combined in harmony, and the architecture is considered to be among the most ornate to be found in the slides of hard romantic townscape. The building is recognized as human in scale and as possessing some character, but it seems slightly unfriendly. The overall aesthetic response to the slide appears rather tentative, although the ensemble is described as quite artistic, and is preferred to larger and more elaborate examples of romantic townscape. A slide of Chester Town Hall, for example, seems more vertical and much less intimate in scale. This civic monument is considered to be charmless, and much less interesting than the smaller building in Grosvenor Park Road.

The images of medieval and modern townscapes appear to be almost directly polarized. The contemporary textures and designs illustrated in the six modern slides are consistently described as visually barren, and often as extremely devoid of character, while such elements of contemporary urban scenery as high-rise buildings and ring roads are thought to be discordant. The analysis suggests that low-rise buildings can generally be more successfully integrated into traditional townscapes, but reactions even to these tend to be adverse.

The slide of the Central Library, Birmingham (figures 14.13 and 14.15) is notable chiefly for the fact that it is considered to be architecturally much less boring than the other modern slides. The shapes and textures in the scene are said to be related in asymmetrical harmony, and the design, though described as quite plain and extremely modern, is thought to be neither as insignificant nor as lacking in visual identity as those of most contemporary buildings. Nevertheless, the Library is considered rather large and quite unfriendly, and aesthetic reaction to it tends to be negative.

The vista of high-rise residential development in Aston High Park, Birmingham (figures 14.14 and 14.15) is more strongly disliked, in common with most of the other slides of modern townscapes. The buildings are defined as large in scale and vertical, are said to possess very little positive character, and are described as extremely boring visually. The elements of the scene are felt to be out of harmony with one another, and the overall effect is perceived as not only unfriendly, but also slightly dangerous. A slide of Queensway, one of Birmingham's central ring roads, evokes an even more negative image. The predominant line of the very large shapes in concrete, steel and tarmac is described as extremely vertical, and the scene is condemned as characterless and inhuman.

## CONCLUSIONS AND IMPLICATIONS

This brief analysis of image traces corroborates the results of factor analysis. In particular, the evidence of the traces complements the interpretation of factor I, which implies that the age of the building may be a very important determinant of its perceived character. Thus, medieval buildings, and classical townscapes to a slightly lesser degree, seem to possess the most historic and architectural interest. The chief attribute of the industrial terraces of the nineteenth century seems to be their intimate scale, while romantic architecture possesses more character but projects the past only moderately. The slides of contemporary buildings are dismissed as discordant intrusions in traditional townscape. The conclusion to be drawn from these paths of analysis is that people's images of townscape may be said to be characterized primarily by an imbalance between a well-developed sense of orientation to historic townscapes, and a reluctance or inability to accept contemporary architecture. In accordance with the proportional weighting of the three main factors, the traces also underline the potentially harmful effect of large-scale and vertical buildings, such as those found in modern townscapes in particular, and the important role played by a building's physical condition in colouring people's response to it. Thus, one of the medieval slides seemed less attractive than many of its fellows because of its relatively dilapidated appearance, and Albion Street, Chester was shown to be the least valuable of the industrial scenes because of its advanced decay.

It remains true, however, that 'we know very little about our conscious or subconscious reactions to the quality of our visual surroundings' [22]. The development of a comprehensive body of theory is therefore a matter of some urgency. The first step towards a more complete understanding of townscape images might be to examine the attitudes of as many sections of society as possible, in order to test further the conclusions of this study. An important objective of subsequent work should be the compilation of a complete catalogue of the meaning of all building types in the temporal continuum of townscape, using a wider range of slides from each period style. Successive research might involve gauging people's experience of such important facets of townscape as regional identity, modes and degrees of restoration, and the ubiquitous hybridization which results from the mixing of pure styles. The more detailed nature of such investigations would call for the use of in-depth interview techniques in the field which afford a deeper insight into the nature of perception and preference. Field experience of this kind could perhaps also be used to attempt to define an optimal unit of space-time which might be used as the basis for mapping the space-time of particular towns and cities. The construction of catalogues and maps would be of particular value to clinical and architectural psychologists who are engaged in evaluating the relationship between visual quality and social behaviour, and in developing theories of urban aesthetics.

It is apparent from this study that we cannot afford to ignore either the massive annual losses of old buildings which are taking place everywhere, or the visual austerity of the townscapes which arise in their place. Contemporary architecture represents the superimposition of a fundamentally new style of building on a continuum of styles which is hundreds of years old, and people plainly find it very difficult to reconcile this degree of innovation with the urban tradition of many centuries. The psychological view is that if man is to conquer and to dominate change he must reconcile his memory of the past with optimism for the future [23]. It appears that the newest urban environments do not alleviate, but rather exacerbate man's inborn uncertainty and latent fear of the future.

The great wealth of historic buildings which have been destroyed cannot of course be restored, and it would be impossible now to remove all traces of modern architecture from towns and cities throughout Britain. The devastating attitudes of the last few decades can be reversed only by man's acceptance of the radical implications of the environmental overstimulation, or too much change, which is so painfully evident in townscapes today. Man must be alerted to the dangers of what Toffler has termed environmental future shock [24]. The essential need is for a carefully coordinated policy of education which might take as a starting point the primary conclusion of this study, that most people seem to be oriented to historic buildings and find it difficult to come to terms with contemporary architecture. Wherever possible, the destruction of old buildings should be halted. People must be taught that they dare not continue carelessly to destroy the environmental collage of time which has been slowly built up over hundreds of years. The loss of this richly diverse collage endangers not only man's inner well-being but perhaps even the continuation of urban society as it has existed throughout history. Planners and politicians, architects and their clients, and members of giant development corporations must all be urged to base their plans and designs for the built environment upon more traditional concepts of scale and ensemble, and the visually interesting colours and textures of the past. If new architecture and townscape could be seen to arise out of tradition, people might be able to accept the inevitability of the future and cease to find environmental change a challenge to their well-being.

## NOTES

1. Wilde, O. (1891) The Picture of Dorian Gray, in Wilde, O. (1963) *The Works of Oscar Wilde*. London: Hamlyn, p. 434.

2. Several authors imply that old buildings may be important to man in their intuitive essays on the mediocrity of contemporary architecture. See, for example, Lozano, E. (1974) Visual needs in the urban environment. *Town Planning Review,* **45**, pp. 351–74. Lozano proposes the hypothesis that while traditional townscapes contain visual inputs which generate a satisfying sense of orientation and variety, the total simplicity of modern architecture results in oppressive feelings of monotony and disorientation. In a few studies, a tentative attempt is made at assessing the relative perceived merits of old and new townscapes, using objective techniques. See, for instance, Burke, G. (1974) Do residents care much about Reading? *Built Environment,* March, pp. 118–21. He describes a simple questionnaire survey, which suggests that an overwhelming majority of Reading's residents do not wish to see the town's Victorian and Georgian buildings destroyed to make room for a new civic centre.

3. For a comprehensive summary of the main provisions of conservation legislation, see Cambridgeshire and Isle of Ely County Council (1973) *A Guide to Historic Buildings Law,* 3rd ed. Cambridge: Cambridgeshire and Isle of Ely County Council. Current listing procedures are outlined in Department of the Environment (n.d.) *A Guide to the Legislation on the Listing of Historic Buildings.* London: Department of the Environment. The designation of conservation areas is described in Smith, D. L. (1974) *Amenity and Urban Planning.* London: Crosby Lockwood Staples, pp. 193–4.

4. These statistics were provided by the Department of the Environment in January 1979. Totals are constantly rising and it is therefore impossible to give exact figures at any time. The Department hope, however, that since local authorities have now had twelve years in which to designate conservation areas, the inventory of these at least should soon be complete. The total of 4500 includes 500 areas which are said to be outstanding.

5. See Lynch, K. (1960) *The Image of the City.* Cambridge, Mass.: MIT Press; Sharp, T. (1968) *Town and Townscape.* London: Murray.

6. See, for example, Rapoport, A. and Kantor, R. (1967) Complexity and ambiguity. *Journal of the American Institute of Planners,* **33** (4), pp. 210–21. In particular, note the references to other studies given in footnote 17, p. 220.

7. Smith, P. F. (1977) *The Syntax of Cities.* London: Hutchinson, p. 96. See also Smith, P. F. (1974) Familiarity breeds contentment. *The Planner,* **60** (9), pp. 901–4.

8. For a thorough survey of the semantic differential, see Osgood, C. E., Suci, G. J. and Tannenbaum, P. H. (1957) *The Measurement of Meaning.* Urbana: University of Illinois Press; and Heise, D. R. (1970) The semantic differential and attitude measurement, in Summers, G. F. (ed.), *Attitude Measurement.* Chicago: Rand McNally, pp. 235–53.

9. See Heise, D. R. (1965) Semantic differential profiles for 1,000 most frequent English words. *Psychological Monographs,* **79** (8), pp. 1–31. Heise's polarity coefficient expresses a scale's polarization, or distance from neutrality, in semantic space. The higher the measure, the more evocative is the scale; conversely, the lower it is, the more ambivalent is the meaning of the scale. For a fuller discussion of the elimination of the ten scales, see Morris, C. J. (1978) Townscape Images: a Study in Meaning and Classification. Unpublished Ph.D. thesis, University of Exeter, pp. 72–80.

10. See, for instance, Lowenthal, D. and Riel, M. (1972) *Publications in Environmental Perception. 1. Environmental Assessment: A Case Study of New York City.* New York: American Geographical Society, p. 2. 'To walk through an area ... does not yield responses that are necessarily "typical", let alone comprehensive; one might react quite differently to the same localities were one standing still, riding a bicycle, or sitting in a moving car'.

11. Cluster analysis is a technique of numerical classification which searches for groupings in data, and simplifies the description of large sets of multivariate data. In the centroid clustering technique used in this study, the slides are classified into groups of similar slides, and the process of grouping is repeated to form a dendogram, or linkage tree. For a recent overview of the technique, see Everitt, B. (1974) *Cluster Analysis—An SSRC Review of Current Research.* London: Heinemann.

12. See, for example, Peterson, G. L. (1967) A model of preference: quantitative analysis of the perception of the visual appearance of residential neighbourhoods. *Journal of Regional Science,* 7 (1), pp. 19–23. In this study, Peterson uses a number of slides of suburban housing, which also picture moving and stationary cars. Factor analysis produced a factor recognized to be about 'quality of photography', but Peterson makes no attempt to determine the precise influence of the cars, or of any other variables, on people's perception of the photographs.

13. The value of Student's *t* test in gauging the statistical significance of differences between sets of data, is discussed in Gregory, S. (1963) *Statistical Methods and the Geographer.* London: Longman, pp. 137–42.

14. These tests are described in greater detail in Morris, C. J. (1978) Townscape Images: a Study in Classification and Meaning. Unpublished Ph.D. thesis, University of Exeter, pp. 389–402.

15. See Osgood, C. E. *et al.* (1957) *The Measurement of Meaning.* Urbana: University of Illinois Press, p. 25. For an example of the use of factor analysis in SD studies in environmental perception, see Lowenthal, D. and Riel, M. (1972) *Publications in Environmental Perception. 6. Structures of Environmental Associations.* New York: American Geographical Society.

16. For a short, but comprehensive account of the theory and application of factor analysis, see Goddard, J. and Kirby, A. (1976) *An Introduction to Factor Analysis.* Norwich: Geo-Books, University of East Anglia.

17. See, for instance, Chojnicki, Z. and Czyz, T. (1976) Some problems in the application of factor analysis in geography. *Geographical Analysis,* 8, pp. 416–27.

18. For a fuller discussion of the factor analyses of the three groups, see Morris, C. J. (1978) Townscape Images: a Study in Classification and Meaning. Unpublished Ph.D. thesis, University of Exeter, pp. 153–72.

19. Goddard, J. and Kirby, A. (1976) *An Introduction to Factor Analysis.* Norwich: Geo-Books, p. 36.

20. For an example of the use of image traces, and of the value of goodness of fit, in research into environmental attitudes, see Zube, E. H. (1973) Scenic Resources and the Landscape Continuum: Identification and Measurement. Unpublished Ph.D. thesis, Clark University, Worcester, Massachusetts.

21. The fabric of Selly Manor is in part medieval, and comes from a house which was dismantled and reassembled in Bournville. Nevertheless, the house and

grounds are typical of the romantic movement in town planning at the end of the nineteenth century.

22. Worskett, R. (1969) *The Character of Towns: An Approach to Conservation.* London: Architectural Press, p. 12.

23. For an introduction to the psychology of time, see Fraisse, P. (1964) *The Psychology of Time.* London: Eyre and Spottiswoode.

24. See Toffler, A. (1970) *Future Shock.* London: The Bodley Head. Toffler's theme is that there are discoverable limits to the amount of change which the human organisms can absorb. By endlessly accelerating change without first determining the limits of his resistance to it, man, Toffler asserts, is submitting himself to demands which he simply cannot tolerate.

# Index